UNION ORGANIZING

UNION ORGANIZING

Management and Labor Conflict

William E. Fulmer

PRAEGER SPECIAL STUDIES • PRAEGER SCIENTIFIC

Library of Congress Cataloging in Publication Data

Fulmer, William E.
    Union organizing.

    1. Trade-unions--United States--Organizing. I. Title.
HD6490.172U64   1982   331.89'12   82-16172 ·
ISBN 0-03-062603-X

Published in 1982 by Praeger Publishers
CBS Educational and Professional Publishing
A Division of CBS, Inc.
521 Fifth Avenue, New York, New York 10175 U.S.A.
© 1982 by Praeger Publishers

456789 052 9876543

Printed in the United States of America

PREFACE

The current level of union organizing is at an all-time high. During the 1970s the American labor movement filed an average of 11,182 petitions each year with the National Labor Relations Board asking for an election to establish their right to represent employees. This level represented an 11.5 percent increase over the 1960s and a 45.9 percent increase over the 1950s.

In spite of the historical increases in union organizing activity, in recent years the number of petitions seems to be leveling off. In addition, the number of decertification efforts has dramatically increased, and unions are losing an increasing percentage of both decertification and certification elections. Consequently, it has become fashionable to question the long-term survival of the American labor movement. Union officials, however, often predict a resurgence of unions. Regardless of which prophecy is right, the 1980s is likely to be a period of increased organizing effort, as labor seeks to recoup membership losses of the past few years.

This book seeks to explore the subject of organizing in an analytical and unbiased manner. The specific objectives are: first, to inform the relative novice about the details of the organizing process and thereby alleviate some of the fears and uncertainties that often plague those new to the field of labor relations; and second, to help the more experienced practitioners, whether labor or management, to understand better the intricacies of the organizing process and thereby better prepare for future campaigns.

A unique characteristic of this book is the use of three detailed cases to tell the story of union organizing. Chapters 3, 5, and 6 describe in considerable detail three very different organizing campaigns. Chapter 3 allows for a relatively objective interpretation of the problems in one company that made a union look attractive to its employees. Chapter 5, which is written from a management perspective, allows for analysis of an effective management campaign and Chapter 6, written from a union perspective, allows for analysis of an effective union campaign. Each of these three chapters is supplemented with comments to highlight some of the lessons to be learned from these campaigns. The remaining chapters cover such topics as the legal framework for organizing, the process and procedures of organizing, the use and abuse of consultants and unfair labor practices in campaigns, and the increasingly common practice of decertification. An appendix that answers 50 commonly asked questions about organizing appears at the end of this book.

For the individual or organization wishing to use additional organizing cases to supplement the materials in this book, the following cases should be considered:

> The First National Bank of Salt Lake City (A)-9-474-139
> Gotham Construction Company-9-458-003
> Vapco Company (A)-9-676-030
> Vapco Company (B)-9-676-031
> Acromag, Incorporated-1-377-092

These cases can be ordered from the Intercollegiate Case Clearing House, Graduate School of Business, Harvard University, Boston, MA 02163 (617-495-6117).

I am grateful to the following organizations for permission to use copyrighted material: Intercollegiate Case Clearing House (Andre Cookie Company A, B, and C; The International Brotherhood of Electrical Workers A, B, and C; and Table Ware Plastics, Inc., A and B); Harvard Business Review ("Step by Step Through a Union Campaign," July-August 1981 and "When Employees Want to Oust Their Union," March-April 1978); California Management Review (Decertification - A Threat to Collective Bargaining?" Summer 1981); Business Horizon ("Resisting Unionization," January-February 1981); and Richard D. Irwin, Inc., (Problems in Labor Relations, 1980).

Several people have contributed to this book. Adelle Lewis, Pat Criswell, and Lisa Patrick assisted with the typing of the manuscript. Two graduate students assisted in the development of materials included in this book: Tamara Gilman (Chapter 6) and Charles Ganus (Appendix). Annette Lusk and Lee Suddath provided editorial assistance. I also would like to acknowledge the assistance of the business schools of Harvard University and the University of Alabama in my long-term research in the area of union organizing. Finally, I would like to express my appreciation to the union, management, and government officials, whose cooperation made this book possible.

CONTENTS

UNION ORGANIZING

1

THE SIGNIFICANCE OF UNION ORGANIZING

Each year since 1960, more than 9,000 work places have been involved in a serious union organizing effort. Since 1935 more than 30 million workers have voted in some 500,000 elections as part of individual organizing efforts.[1] For many of these managers and some of the employee representatives involved, it may be their first and only involvement in such a campaign. For many it is a frightening experience full of unknowns. Not only are the rules of the campaign unknown, but the consequences of breaking the rules are usually unknown. It is the purpose of this book to present the subject of union organizing in as objective a light as possible and with sufficient detail that all participants, whether labor or management, can benefit from the presentation.

THE FREQUENCY OF ORGANIZING CAMPAIGNS

Organizing campaigns occur frequently in the American economy. As can be seen in Table 1.1 in 1980 9,828 petitions for representation were filed. No doubt countless other efforts to organize work places were undertaken that did not result in a sufficient showing of employee interest to merit the formal filing of a petition with the National Labor Relations Board (NLRB), or involved work places that were outside the jurisdiction of the NLRB.

Partially because of the declining percentage of union victories, U.S. unions represent a decreasing percentage of the work force. In 1978, union members as a proportion of the non-agricultural work force had dropped to its lowest

TABLE 1.1

Number of Certification Petitions Filed, Elections and
Union Victories, 1950-1980

Year	Number of Petitions	Number of Elections	Percent of Union Victories
1950	8,206	5,619	74.5
1951	9,460	6,432	74.0
1952	9,571	6,765	72.9
1953	8,241	6,050	71.9
1954	7,028	4,663	65.6
1955	6,160	4,215	67.6
1956	7,121	4,946	65.3
1957	6,774	4,729	62.2
1958	6,284	4,337	60.8
1959	7,959	5,428	62.8
1960	8,795	6,380	58.6
1961	9,177	6,354	56.1
1962	9,704	7,355	58.5
1963	9,562	6,871	59.0
1964	10,018	6,940	58.5
1965	10,255	7,176	61.8
1966	10,820	7,637	62.3
1967	11,193	7,496	60.7
1968	10,449	7,241	58.7
1969	10,308	7,319	56.0
1970	10,332	7,426	56.8
1971	10,904	7,543	55.1
1972	11,666	8,066	55.6
1973	11,897	8,526	52.8
1974	11,891	7,994	51.7
1975	11,037	7,729	50.4
1976	11,846	7,736	50.5
1977	11,578	8,308	48.8
1978	10,338	7,168	48.9
1979	10,333	7,026	47.9
1980	9,828	7,021	49.0

Source: NLRB Annual Reports.

TABLE 1.2

Membership in National Unions and Employee Associations
in United States, 1930-1978

| Year | Union Membership | | Union and Employee Association Membership | |
	Membership (000)	Percent of Employees in Nonagricultural Establishments	Membership (000)	Percent of Employees in Nonagricultural Establishments
1930	3,401	11.6		
1935	3,584	13.2		
1940	8,717	26.9		
1945	14,322	35.5		
1950	14,267	31.5		
1952	15,892	32.5		
1954	17,022	34.7		
1956	17,490	33.4		
1958	17,029	33.2		
1960	17,049	31.5		
1962	16,586	29.9		
1964	16,841	28.9		
1966	17,940	28.1		
1968	18,916	27.9	20,721	30.5
1970	19,381	27.3	21,248	30.0
1972	19,435	26.4	21,657	29.4
1974	20,199	25.8	22,809	29.1
1976	19,634	24.5	22,662	28.3
1978	20,246	24.0	22,880	27.1

Source: Bureau of Labor Statistics.

point in 40 years (Table 1.2). Furthermore, the total number of union members seems to have stabilized at approximately 20 million.

It would be inaccurate to suggest that this leveling in union membership is solely the result of a decreasing percentage of union victories in certification elections. Table 1.3 shows that unionized employees tend to be concentrated in industries such as construction, transportation, mining, transportation equipment, metals, and the federal government—industries that have been hit hard by the recessions of the late 1970s and early 1980s. Furthermore, unionization as a percentage of the work force is highest in the Middle Atlantic and Midwest states and lowest in the South (Table 1.4). With the movement of jobs from the Frostbelt to the Sunbelt, it is not surprising that union membership is experiencing little growth.

THE IMPORTANCE OF ORGANIZING CAMPAIGNS

Organizing campaigns usually occur only once in a union-management relationship, yet the importance of organizing to both unions and managers is far greater than the frequency might indicate. For unions its importance is obvious. Without some form of organizing, there is no labor movement. It is through organizing that unions obtain their financial resources and people and, ultimately, their power. In the words of one AFL-CIO official, "organizing is the most important part of the labor movement. Nothing happens until organizing takes place."[2]

Many managers indicate the degree of their concern over union organizing by the expenditure of relatively large sums of money to avoid union organizing successes. The major costs to management during an organizing campaign are likely to be: lost sales and overall productivity reductions during the campaign; the cost of management time in conducting a campaign; the legal fees to attorneys or consultants; and lost employee time. It is not uncommon to find companies spending thousands of dollars, sometimes in an unsuccessful effort, to avoid unionization. In 1975 it was estimated that organizing campaigns cost management between $100 and $125 per employee.[3] In that same period, some American unions were spending 20 percent of their general fund for organizing. With the inflation rates of recent years, these costs no doubt have escalated dramatically. Because of these costs, it is imperative that both labor and management make the most efficient use of the resources they commit to organizing campaigns.

For personnel managers and first-line managers, their job fundamentally changes once a union is formed. In a 1977 report of a survey of 1,400 personnel executives,

TABLE 1.3

Degree of Union Organization by Industry

75 Percent and Over

Transportation
Construction
Mining

50 to 74 Percent

Transportation equipment	Primary metals
Apparel	Tobacco manufacturers
Federal government	Paper
Manufacturing	

25 to 49 Percent

Telephone and telegraph	Petroleum refining
Food and kindred products	Fabricated metals
Stone, clay & glass products	Electrical machinery
Lumber	Rubber
Machinery, except electrical	Leather
Electric, gas utilities	Furniture
Government	Local government
State government	

Less than 25 Percent

Printing, publishing	Chemicals
Nonmanufacturing	Textile mill products
Instruments	Services
Finance	Agriculture & Fishing
Trade	

Source: Bureau of Labor Statistics.

TABLE 1.4

Distribution of Membership of National Unions by State and as a Proportion of Employees in Nonagricultural Establishments, 1976 and 1978

State	Membership (000)				Total Union Members as a Percentage of Employees in Nonagricultural Establishments			
	1976	1976 Rank	1978[a]	1978 Rank	1976 (revised)	1976 Rank	1978	1978 Rank
All States	19,874	—	20,459	—	24.9	—	23.6	—
Alabama[b]	229	23	257	23	19.0	25	19.2	25
Alaska	50	43	43	46	29.1	13	26.2	13
Arizona[b]	117	32	122	30	15.4	35	13.8	37
Arkansas[b]	102	34	109	33	15.5	34	15.0	33
California	2,148	2	2,184	2	26.3	14	23.7	17
Colorado	175	27	172	27	17.4	31	15.2	32
Connecticut	309	17	296	18	24.9	18	21.9	22
Delaware	49	44	52	43	20.7	24	21.0	23
Florida[b]	365	16	367	16	13.1	44	11.7	46
Georgia[b]	261	20	271	20	14.2	38	13.6	38
Hawaii	129	29	120	31	36.9	3	32.1	6
Idaho	41	46	47	45	14.1	39	14.3	36
Illinois	1,451	4	1,497	4	31.8	8	31.5	7

State								
Indiana	621	8	643	8	30.7	11	29.3	10
Iowab	192	26	212	26	18.5	27	19.2	26
Kansasb	125	31	117	32	15.0	37	12.8	42
Kentucky	275	19	274	19	24.7	19	22.4	21
Louisianab	213	25	227	24	16.2	32	16.0	30
Maine	67	40	74	39	17.9	29	18.3	27
Maryland–D.C.	440	14	458	14	21.2	23	21.0	24
Massachusetts	570	10	611	9	24.6	21	24.5	14
Michigan	1,165	6	1,223	6	35.7	5	34.6	3
Minnesota	385	15	411	15	25.3	15	24.4	15
Mississippib	87	35	103	35	12.0	47	12.7	44
Missouri	572	9	578	10	31.8	7	30.0	8
Montana	60	42	67	41	23.9	22	24.1	16
Nebraskab	87	35	92	36	15.2	36	15.3	31
Nevadab	69	38	80	37	24.7	20	22.9	20
New Hampshire	43	45	48	44	13.7	30	13.2	40
New Jersey	697	7	683	7	25.3	16	23.0	19
New Mexico	73	37	54	42	18.7	26	12.1	45
New York	2,515	1	2,753	1	37.1	2	39.2	1
North Carolinab	141	28	147	28	6.8	49	6.5	50
North Dakotab	26	48	34	47	12.1	45	14.6	35
Ohio	1,289	5	1,294	5	31.5	9	29.5	9
Oklahoma	126	30	138	29	13.5	42	13.4	39
Oregon	221	24	232	23	25.2	17	23.1	18
Pennsylvania	1,642	3	1,595	3	36.4	4	34.2	4
Rhode Island	114	33	108	34	31.1	10	27.1	12
South Carolinab	68	39	76	38	6.6	50	6.7	49

TABLE 1.4 continued

State	Membership (000)				Total Union Members as a Percentage of Employees in Nonagricultural Establishments			
	1976	1976 Rank	1978[a]	1978 Rank	1976 (revised)	1976 Rank	1978	1978 Rank
South Dakota[b]	21	50	24	50	9.6	48	10.3	48
Tennessee[b]	288	18	303	17	18.3	28	17.7	28
Texas[b]	563	11	575	11	12.0	46	11.0	47
Utah[b]	62	41	68	40	13.4	43	12.9	41
Vermont	30	47	33	48	17.8	30	17.4	29
Virginia[b]	252	21	258	21	13.6	41	12.7	43
Washington	453	13	496	13	35.3	6	33.1	5
West Virginia	232	22	226	25	38.9	1	36.8	2
Wisconsin	506	12	522	12	29.3	12	27.8	11
Wyoming[b]	25	49	28	49	16.0	33	14.9	34
Membership not classifiable[c]	133	--	60	--	--	--	--	--

a Based on reports from 125 national unions and estimates for 49. Also included are local unions directly affiliated with the AFL-CIO and members in single-firm and local unaffiliated unions.

b Has right-to-work law.

c Includes local unions directly affiliated with the AFL-CIO.

Note: Because of rounding sums of individual items may not equal totals. Dashes indicate no data in category.

Source: Bureau of Labor Statistics.

labor relations was ranked first in a list of important issues to be faced in unionized firms. Where once they could deal with employees on an individual basis, in a unionized operation the personnel executive must work with and through the union. First-line supervisors will be able to take fewer unilateral actions in a unionized work force. Not only will the union challenge some and perhaps many management actions, but managers' actions also will be more closely monitored by the personnel office so as not to establish precedents that become binding on all supervisors.

Union organizing also results in changes for individual employees. No longer can employees bargain with management on an individual basis. Furthermore, they now have dues and occasionally special assessments to pay. In addition, they often feel a sense of divided loyalties--they work for one organization and are members of another. Sometimes those two organizations have disagreements that are so severe that individuals must choose sides, such as in the case of a strike. In spite of some of the potential problems associated with union membership, employees often find the union to be the most effective way to express their job-related frustrations. A recent study of retail stores found that employees who were dissatisfied with their supervisors, career futures, coworkers, and other aspects of their job were more likely to form unions to help them redress some of their concerns.[4] As Tables 1.5 and 1.6 show, many workers believe that unions not only can help them on the job, but also significantly influence public policy, thus giving the workers a strong voice in national affairs.

COVERAGE OF THE NLRB

In most union-management matters, management initiates action and unions respond. A major exception is found in the establishment on the union-management relationship. Frequently, dissatisfied employees will invite a union to undertake an organizing effort. Occasionally unions will come in unsolicited. Except in the construction industry, employers do not take the initiative in establishing a collective bargaining relationship without running the risk of violating the National Labor Relations Act.* There is,

---

*Under the Landrum-Griffin Act of 1959, in states without right-to-work laws, employers in the construction industry are allowed to take the initiative in establishing a labor-management relationship without violating government policy. This is in keeping with long-established practices in the construction industry.

TABLE 1.5

Evaluation of Union Performance
(percent)

Issue	Not good at all	Not too good	Somewhat good	Very good	Mean
Wages	4.7	19.8	42.5	32.9	3.04
Fringes	7.7	21.8	41.9	28.6	2.91
Job security	7.6	18.0	50.8	23.6	2.90
Safety/health	6.5	21.5	50.7	21.3	2.87
Say on job	15.2	34.3	41.9	8.6	2.44
Interesting job	22.5	43.1	29.5	4.9	2.17
Say in union	16.2	27.9	37.3	18.7	2.58
Say in business	25.8	37.7	30.1	6.3	2.16
Feedback from union	10.5	23.3	36.5	29.6	2.85
Handling grievances	8.7	15.7	40.9	4.7	3.02

Note: Union members were asked how good a job their unions were doing in addressing various issues. Ratings were valued on a four-point scale, with "Not good at all" worth one point and "Very good" worth four. The mean is the average value of response.

Source: Bureau of Labor Statistics, Department of Labor, Monthly Labor Review, April 1979, p. 30.

TABLE 1.6

American Workers' Beliefs about Trade Unions (percent)

Belief	Strongly Agree	Agree	Neither Agree Nor Disagree	Disagree	Strongly Disagree
Big-Labor Image Beliefs					
Influence who gets elected to public office	37.5	46.0	1.8	12.7	1.1
Influence laws passed	24.0	56.6	3.8	14.4	1.2
Are more powerful than employers	24.8	41.6	6.2	25.4	2.0
Influence how the country is run	18.1	53.4	4.8	21.7	1.9
Require members to go along with decisions	18.5	56.0	3.9	20.1	1.6
Have leaders who do what's best for themselves	22.8	44.7	6.4	24.0	2.1
Instrumental Beliefs					
Protect workers against unfair practice	20.5	63.0	3.4	11.2	2.0
Improve job security	19.2	61.0	2.8	14.5	2.5
Improve wages	18.9	67.6	3.2	8.7	1.7
Give workers their money (dues) worth	6.9	38.5	6.3	36.9	11.3

N = 1,515
Source: Bureau of Labor Statistics, Department of Labor, Monthly Labor Review, April 1979, p. 24.

however, a temptation for some employers to seek out "cooperative" unions and enter into "sweetheart" contracts.

The National Labor Relations Act, as amended, specifically calls for the determination of majority status and the appropriateness of the unit. Although unions and employers can voluntarily agree on such matters, most cases involve the use of the NLRB. Although some employees are specifically excluded from NLRB procedures (such as supervisors, agricultural workers, independent contractors, family members, domestic servants, and government employees), most U.S. employees are covered by the NLRB's jurisdiction. Therefore, if management refuses to recognize voluntarily a union and there is a question as to whether the union represents a majority of the employees in the unit or a question over the appropriateness of the unit, the matter can be settled by the NLRB. For purposes of this book, it will be assumed that all organizing efforts are covered by the National Labor Relations Board and that all campaigns are governed by the provisions of the National Labor Relations Act of 1935, as amended.

Because union survival is being threatened by various forces, Peter Drucker recently predicted that "labor relations in the next years are bound to be turbulent. It means that unions will not fight rationally, but with the desperation of a cornered animal."[5] On the other hand, Lane Kirkland, president of the AFL-CIO, argues that "the prophets of doom have badly misread both the present strength and the future prospects of trade unionism in America."[6] A recent dues increase for the building trades department of the AFL-CIO is primarily to be used to increase organizing efforts in the construction industry.[7] Whether labor is on the defensive or just gearing up for a major period of growth, the next few years are likely to be a period of increased organizing effort by the American labor movement.

NOTES

1   National Labor Relations Board, <u>Forty-Second Annual Report of the National Labor Relations Board</u> (Washington: U.S. Government Printing Office, 1977), p. 1.

2   John O'Malley, "The Science of Organization," speech to the sixty-first Trade Union Program at Harvard University, February 15, 1977.

3   Woodruff Imberman, "How Expensive is an NLRB Election?," <u>MSU Business Topics</u>, Summer 1975, p. 15.

4   W.C. Hamner and F.J. Smith, "Work Attitudes as Predictors of Unionization Activity," <u>Journal of Applied Psychology</u>, 1978, pp. 415-21.

5   Peter F. Drucker, <u>Managing in Turbulent Times</u> (New York: Harper and Row, 1980), p. 204.

6   Urban C. Lehner, "Unions Rekindle Organizing Effort with New Tactics to Lure Members," <u>Wall Street Journal</u>, July 28, 1980.

7   "Labor Letter," <u>Wall Street Journal</u>, March 16, 1982, p. 1.

2

THE LEGAL FRAMEWORK

For over 45 years it has been the official policy of the U.S. government to encourage union organizing. In 1935 Congress believed that the denial by some employers of the right of employees to organize, and the refusal by some employers to accept the procedure of collective bargaining, led to strikes and other forms of industrial strife that had the effect of obstructing commerce. In addition, Congress believed that the inequality of bargaining power between employees and employers tended to aggravate recurrent business depressions.

To deal with such problems, Congress, in the National Labor Relations Act of 1935, stated:

> It is hereby declared to be the policy of the United States to eliminate the causes of certain substantial obstructions to the free flow of commerce and to mitigate and eliminate these obstructions when they have occurred by encouraging the practice and procedure of collective bargaining and by protecting the exercise of workers of full freedom of association,

The author gratefully acknowledges permission to use parts of his chapter, "Union Organizing" Problems in Labor Relations, © 1980 by Richard D. Irwin, Inc. Used with permission of Richard D. Irwin, Inc.

> self-organization and designation of
> representatives of their own choosing,
> for the purpose of negotiating the terms
> and conditions of their employment or
> other mutual aid or protection.

To accomplish this policy, Section 7 of the act stated that employees should have the right "to self-organization, to form, join or assist labor organizations to bargain collectively through representatives of their own choosing, and to engage in other concerted activities for the purpose of collective bargaining or other mutual aid or protection."

ELECTION PROCEDURES

The National Labor Relations Act does not require employee representatives to be selected by any particular procedure. However, the act does provide that one of the methods can be a secret ballot election. The Board can conduct such an election only after a petition has been filed requesting one. A petition for certification typically is filed by an employee, a group of employees, or an individual or labor organization acting on behalf of the employees. An employer* can file only if one or more individuals or organizations have claimed recognition as the exclusive representative of the same group of employees.

In most cases the petition is filed by employees or by unions on behalf of employees. Such a petition must be supported by a substantial number of employees who wish to be represented for collective bargaining and must state that the employer refuses to recognize their representatives. The evidence that a substantial number of employees desire representation normally is in the form of signed and dated authorization cards from at least 30 percent of the employees, or a petition indicating a desire for representation that is signed and dated by 30 percent or more of the employees. The use of authorization cards is much more

---

*For purposes of the National Labor Relations Act, the term employer "includes any person acting as an agent of an employer, directly or indirectly." The term "labor organization" means "any organization of any kind, or any agency or employee representation committee or plan, in which employees participate and which exist for the purpose in whole or in part, of dealing with employers concerning grievances, labor disputes, wages, rates of pay, hours of employment, or conditions of work."

common. The request for representation, whether cards or a petition, must be filed with the nearest regional director of the National Labor Relations Board. Once a petition has been filed, the party against whom it is filed has a right to a hearing even if there are no issues to be resolved.

When the employer is notified that a petition has been filed, the name of a field examiner is communicated by the NLRB to both the employer and the union. Both parties are also notified of a hearing to be conducted on the question of representation. The examiner then contacts the parties and if a consent agreement can be affected on all issues, the hearing may be avoided. In such an agreement the parties state the time and place agreed on for the election, the choices to be included in the ballot, and a method to determine who is eligible to vote. The parties also would authorize the NLRB regional director to conduct the election. This type of election is called a "consent election."

The representation hearing may take place on the same day as an informal conference with an NLRB field examiner. The examiner sometimes changes roles and serves as a hearing officer. The presence of a court reporter who records the proceedings verbatim is the only change in the group. Frequently, however, the hearing is scheduled at a later date and may be conducted by a field examiner or a regional attorney.

The hearing is an investigatory procedure, not adversarial in nature. The hearing officer is required to obtain a complete factual record. To do so the officer can subpoena documents and people and may even observe operations and interview employees or members of management. The officer seeks to answer such questions as:

- Is there a question of representation?
- Does the employer qualify for coverage by the NLRB?
- Is the union a labor organization within the meaning of the act?
- Do any existing collective bargaining agreements or prior elections bar the petitioner from representation?
- Is the proposed unit appropriate?
- Are there questions of eligibility of certain employees?
- Is there a sufficient showing of employee interest to justify an election?

The accompanying signatures are used by the regional director to determine if there is a showing of interest. The director also determines if the petition has been filed by a suitable party, that is, is this union in compliance with various goverment regulations and thereby entitled to use the services of the NLRB? Also, is the petition timely? The Board will not conduct more than one election in a bargaining unit during any 12-month period. If there was a representation election and the union won, the union could be certified one week after the election. If there is no agreement on a contract within 12 months after certification, a new petition from another union could be honored. An employer also could petition for a new election after 12 months if there were valid grounds for believing the union no longer represented a majority. If the union had won the original election and a valid contract had been agreed to, the contract would act as a bar to subsequent petitions for its life or for three years, whichever came first. When a contract is in force, a petition must be filed between the ninetieth and sixtieth day prior to its expiration. In contracts of three years or more, the 90-day-60-day provision applies to the period prior to the third anniversary date and to each yearly anniversary thereafter. The decisions of the regional director regarding the suitability of the filing party, the adequate showing of interest, and timeliness of the petition cannot be appealed.

Since the NLRB obtains its authority from Congress by way of the National Labor Relations Act, and the power of Congress to regulate labor relations is limited by the commerce clause of the United States Constitution, the NLRB can only direct elections and certify the results in cases of the an employer whose operations affect commerce. Because of the broad interpretation of the phrase "affect commerce," the authority of the NLRB extends to all but purely local enterprises. The Board, however, has chosen to limit the exercise of its power to cases involving enterprises whose affect on commerce is substantial. Thus certain jurisdictional standards have developed that define "substantial."

The Board's standards are as follows:[1]

1. Non-retail business: direct sales of goods to consumers in other states or indirect sales through others of at least $50,000 a year, or direct purchase of goods from suppliers in other states, or direct purchases through others of at least $50,000 a year.

2. Office buildings: total annual revenue of $100,000 of which $25,000 or more is derived from organizations which meet any of the standards except the indirect outflow and indirect inflow standards established for non-retail enterprises.

3. Retail enterprises: at least $500,000 total annual volume of business.

4. Public utilities: at least $250,000 total annual volume of business, or $50,000 direct or indirect outflow or inflow.

5. Newspapers: at least $200,000 total annual volume of business.

6. Radio, telegraph, television and telephone enterprises: at least $100,000 total annual volume of business.

7. Hotels, motels, and residential apartment houses: at least $500,000 total annual volume of business.

8. Privately owned hospitals and mursing homes operated for profit: at least $250,000 total annual volume of business for hospitals; at least $100,000 for nursing homes.

9. Transportation enterprises, links and channels of interstate commerce: at least $50,000 total annual income from furnishing interstate passenger and freight transportation services; also performing services valued at $50,000 or more for businesses which meet any of the jurisdictional standards except the indirect outflow and indirect inflow standards established for non-retail enterprises.

10. Transit systems: at least $250,000 annual volume of business.

11. Taxi cab companies: at least $500,000 annual volume of business.

12. Associations: these are regarded as a single employer and the annual sales of all association members are totaled to determine whether the Board's standards apply.

13. Enterprises in the Territories and the District of Columbia: the jurisdictional standards apply in the Territories; all businesses in the District of Columbia come under NLRB jurisdiction.

14. National defense: jurisdiction is asserted over all enterprises affecting commerce when their operations have a substantial impact on national defense, whether or not the enterprises satisfy any other standard.

15. <u>Private non-profit universities and colleges</u>: at least $1,000,000 gross annual revenue from all sources (excluding contributions not available for operating expenses because of limitations imposed by the grantor).

Ordinarily, an enterprise doing the volume of business listed in the above standards will necessarily be engaged in activities that "affect" commerce. The Board must find, however, that the enterprise does in fact affect commerce.

The NLRB will request that the employer furnish a list of employees working in the unit described in the petition. Each employee should also be designated with a job classification for the pay period immediately prior to the date of notification. This list will provide the basis for an eligibility voting list to be used at the election.

The Board also will ask the employer to supply evidence of any other union claiming to represent the same employees. This may take the form of correspondence and existing or recently expired collective bargaining contracts. This information is required to assure that all interested parties can be notified in case they wish to intervene in procedures.

The most difficult issue to be resolved at many representation hearings is the matter of an appropriate bargaining unit. An appropriate unit has been defined as a group of two or more employees acting together in bargaining. A unit may extend to one or more employers, or it may include one or more work places of the same employer, or it may be a subdivision of a plantwide unit such as a unit of professional employees or skilled employees.

It is the Board's concern to group together employees who have a substantial mutual interest in wages, hours, and other conditions of employment. The Board seeks to determine whether the employees share a similar community of interest. Although the concept of "appropriate" is elusive, a number of tests are used by the Board:

- Extent and type of union organization of employees.
- Bargaining history in the industry.
- Similarity of duties, skills, interests, and working conditions of employees.
- Organizational structure of the company.
- Desire of the employees.

Both unions and managers have a substantial interest in the composition of the bargaining unit. The composition of the unit may strongly affect whether or not the union will win the election since both parties may have reliable sources of information about the intention of employees long before a secret ballot election is held. Also, the

composition of the unit may determine whether effective
bargaining can take place after an election is won by the
union. If the parties agree on the unit, it may not be
altered by the NLRB unless people are listed who are excluded from coverage by the law. In addition, professional
employees may not be included in a unit of nonprofessional
employees unless a majority of the professional employees
vote to be included. No craft unit may be held inappro-
priate on the ground that a different unit was established
by a prior Board decision. Also, plant guards, who enforce
rules for the protection of property or safety on any employer's premises, may not be included in a unit with other
employees. If labor and management do not agree on the
bargaining unit composition, an NLRB field examiner will
attempt to secure agreement through an informal meeting
with the parties.

After the hearing is closed, the transcript is turned
over to a regional attorney to draft a tentative decision
for consideration by the regional director. The hearing
officer is not permitted to make any findings of credibility
or talk to the attorney who prepares the draft decision.
The decision is ultimately issued by the director and deals
with all the questions listed above. Most frequently, the
director defines the appropriate unit and directs an
election.

A regional director's decision is subject to limited
review on appeal by either party. On infrequent occasions,
when there are no Board precedents, the regional director
may transfer the case to the Board for a decision. It is
for the Board, however, to determine whether a review be
granted. It does this only when there are no known
precedents or guidelines.

It is possible for the employer to obtain a review of
the bargaining unit by refusing to bargain with a newly
certified union. If the union files an unfair labor practice charge under Section 8 [a] (failure to bargain in good
faith), the employer can raise the issue as a defense. The
Board will grant review only where one or more of the
following reasons exist:

- There is a substantial question of law or policy
raised and there is no officially reported Board precedent.
- The regional director's decision on a substantial
factual issue is clearly in error as well as prejudicial.
- The conduct of the hearing results in a prejudicial
error.
- Compelling reasons exist for reconsideration of an
important Board rule or policy.

In rare situations, it is possible for an election to
be held without either a hearing or a showing of interest

being requested. Section 8 [b] (7) provides that when a petition is not filed within a reasonable period (not to exceed 30 days) after the commencement of recognitional or organizational picketing, the NLRB shall order an election and certify the results. Thus when an election under this section is appropriate, the election is scheduled sooner than under the ordinary procedure and is called an "expedited election."

THE ELECTION

Once an election has been directed, notices are sent to the employer and most be prominently posted to inform employees about the time and place of the election and the eligibility of the voters. The NLRB notices of election and sample ballots must be posted by the company at least 72 hours before the election in conspicuous places throughout the premises. Persons on layoff and those engaged in a legal strike receive notices of the election from the Board by mail at their homes. Election details such as time, place, and notice of election are usually left to the regional director, who generally obtains the agreement of the parties on these matters. Since 1966, once an election has been directed, the employer has been required to furnish a list of the names and addresses of all employees in the bargaining unit for the use of all parties.[2]

A voters' eligibility list is prepared by the employer and submitted to the Board after designation of the election day. Employees who can vote are those in the defined bargaining unit who are on the payroll on the date of the election and during the last pay period prior to the decision or agreement by parties to a consent election. Those who are on layoff with reasonable expectation of recall can vote; so can those who are on vacation. Voters must be present themselves in person as there is no provision for absentee ballots.

Elections usually are held within 30 days after they are directed. A different date may be set in cases where employment is seasonal and changes in operations prevent a normal workforce from being present within 30 days. The Board will postpone an election because of unfair labor practice charges, but in certain cases will proceed to the election if the charging party so requests.

On election day the Board's agent arrives at the plant to go over the eligibility list with the parties, crossing out the names of those who have quit and adding the names of those who might have been mistakenly omitted or who have joined the company after the list was prepared. The agent also examines the physical arrangements to make sure the vote will be secret. The election is not only supervised

by the Board with a Board field examiner or attorney as the
agent in charge, but the company and the union are also
permitted to have observers at the polls. Usually there is
one observer for each party. Their purpose is to identify
the persons who are eligible to vote. The observers are
not permitted to do any electioneering, and they may not be
in attendance if their presence would be interpreted as
influencing the employees to vote or not to vote.

Employees simply present themselves to vote. They
identify themselves and their identity is confirmed by the
observers. Their names are checked off the eligibility
list by both observers under the supervision of the NLRB
agent. Employees are not required to sign anything. When
a voter is challenged, that vote is set aside in a sealed
envelope for later consideration. Rarely do fewer than 90
percent of eligible voters participate.

When the voting is over, the ballots are counted by the
NLRB agent in the presence of observers who are requested
to sign an election tally form. If the challenged votes
are sufficient to affect the outcome of the election, they
must be evaluated by the regional director. Sometimes if
important questions of fact are related to the challenges,
the director will conduct a hearing on challenged votes.

The Board's agent must challenge all voters whose names
are not on the eligibility list. Either party, through
their observers, may challenge those whose eligibility status has not been agreed upon. All challenged persons are
allowed to vote unless a decision by the director specifically excludes them. Their ballots are placed by the voter
in a brown perforated envelope. Each side of the perforation is a self-contained envelope. One side contains the
name of the voter, place of work, the reason for the challenge, and the name of the challenger; the other side contains the ballot. The whole envelope is sealed by the voter
and placed in the ballot box. When the voting has been completed, all brown perforated envelopes are removed first and
the Board's agent tries to get agreement on whether the ballots within should be counted. If agreement to count them
is secured, the ballots are removed from the envelopes and
counted along with all others. If there is no agreement,
the challenged ballots are set aside and all unchallenged
ballots are counted. If the election is so close that
challenged ballots might affect the outcome, the final certification of the election must await the results of a subsequent investigation and possible hearing on the challenges. There may not at that stage be a determination
based on agreement between the parties. If it is decided at
a subsequent hearing that certain challenged votes should be
counted, the envelopes of those voters are ripped apart at
the perforation and the part containing the employee's name
is destroyed. Then the ballots are commingled and counted.

A majority of those actually participating in the election, rather than a majority of those eligible to vote, is required for certification in NLRB elections. Thus if an election results in a tie vote, a petitioning union does not win. If two or more labor organizations appear on the ballot and neither of them nor the "no union" choice receives a majority of the ballots, the Board conducts a runoff election between the two choices receiving the largest number of votes.

LABORATORY CONDITIONS

Based on a 1948 decision involving the General Shoe Corporation, the Board's function in an election proceeding is "to provide a laboratory in which an experiment may be conducted under conditions as nearly ideal as possible, to determine the uninhibited desires of the employees."[3]

Any party to an election who believes that the Board's standards are not met may, within five days after the tally of ballots has been furnished, file objections to the election with the regional director under whose jurisdiction the election was held. The director's rulings on these objections may be appealed to the Board for a decision except in the case of elections that are held by consent of the parties, in which case the regional director's rulings are final.

There are many disagreements over what type of conduct constitutes interference. In general, unfair labor practices committed after the filing of an election petition interfere with the election. Other types of conduct, not amounting to an unfair labor practice, might also sufficiently interfere with the fairness of an election to warrant setting aside the results. An election will be set aside if it was accompanied by conduct that the NLRB feels created an atmosphere of confusion or fear of reprisals, and thus interfered with the employees' freedom of choice. In any particular case the Board does not attempt to determine whether the conduct actually interfered with the employees' expression of free choice, but rather if the conduct tended to do so. The following activities are typical of those that have been considered sufficient grounds to interfere with employee free choice:

- The threat of loss of job or benefits.
- Employees being fired who discouraged or encouraged union activities.
- Campaign speeches to assembled groups of employees on company time within the 24-hour period before the election.
- Threats or the use of physical force or violence against employees.

TABLE 2.1

Types of Cases

1. Charges of Unfair Labor Practices (C Cases)

Charge Against Employer	Charge Against Labor Organization	

Charge Against Employer

Section of the Act CA

8(a)(1) To interfere with, restrain, or coerce employees in exercise of their rights under Section 7 (to join or assist a labor organization or to refrain).

8(a)(2) To dominate or interfere with the formation or administration of a labor organization or contribute financial or other support to it.

8(a)(3) By discrimination in regard to hire or tenure of employment or any term or condition of employment to encourage or discourage membership in any labor organization.

8(a)(4) To discharge or otherwise discriminate against an employee because he has given testimony under the Act.

8(a)(5) To refuse to bargain collectively with representatives of his employees.

Charge Against Labor Organization

Section of the Act CB

8(b)(1)(A) To restrain or coerce employees in exercise of their rights under Section 7 (to join or assist a labor organization or to refrain).
8(b)(1)(B) To restrain or coerce an employer in the selection of his representatives for collective bargaining or adjustment of grievances.

8(b)(2) To cause or attempt to cause an employer to discriminate against an employee.

8(b)(3) To refuse to bargain collectively with employer.

8(b)(5) To require of employees the payment of excessive or discriminatory fees for membership.

8(b)(6) To cause or attempt to cause an employer to pay or agree to pay money or other thing of value for services which are not performed or not to be performed.

Section of the Act CC

8(b)(4)(i) To engage in, or induce or encourage any individual employed by any person engaged in commerce or in an industry affecting commerce, to engage in a strike, work stoppage, or boycott, or (ii) to threaten, coerce, or restrain any person engaged in commerce or in an industry affecting commerce, where in either case an object is:

(A) To force or require any employer or self-employed person to join any labor or employer organization or to enter into any agreement prohibited by Sec. 8(e).

(B) To force or require any person to cease using, selling, handling, transporting or otherwise dealing in the products of any other producer, processor, or manufacturer, or to cease doing business with any other person, or force or require any other employer to recognize or bargain with a labor organization as the representative of his employees unless such labor organization has been so certified.

(C) To force or require any employer to recognize or bargain with a particular labor organization as the representative of his employees if another labor organization has been certified as the representative.

Section of the Act CD

(D) To force or require any employer to assign particular work to employees in a particular labor organization or in a particular trade, craft, or class rather than to employees in another trade, craft, or class, unless such employer is failing to conform to an appropriate Board order or certification.

1. Charges of Unfair Labor Practices (continued)		2. Petitions for Certification or Decertification of Representatives (R Cases)	3. Other Petitions
Charge Against Labor Organization (continued)	Charge Against Labor Organization and Employer	By or in Behalf of Employees	By or in Behalf of Employees
Section of the Act CP 8(b)(7) To picket, cause or threaten the picketing of any employer where an object is to force or require an employer to recognize or bargain with a labor organization as the representative of his employees, or to force or require the employees of an employer to select such labor organization as their collective bargaining representative, unless such labor organization is currently certified as the representative of such employees. (A) where the employer has lawfully recognized any other labor organization and a question concerning representation may not appropriately be raised under Section 9(c), (B) where within the preceding 12 months a valid election under Section 9(c) has been conducted, or (C) where picketing has been conducted without a petition under 9(c) being filed within a reasonable period of time not to exceed 30 days from the commencement of the picketing; except where the picketing is for the purpose of truthfully advising the public (including consumers) that an employer does not employ members of, or have a contract with, a labor organization, and it does not have an effect of interference with deliveries or services.	Section of the Act CE 8(e) To enter into any contract or agreement (any labor organization and any employer) whereby such employer ceases or refrains or agrees to cease or refrain from handling or dealing in any product of any other employer, or to cease doing business with any other person.	Section of the Act RC 9(c)(1)(A)(i) Alleging that a substantial number of employees wish to be represented for collective bargaining and their employer declines to recognize their representative.* Section of the Act RD 9(c)(1)(A)(ii) Alleging that a substantial number of employees assert that the certified or currently recognized bargaining representative is no longer their representative.* By an Employer Section of the Act RM 9(c)(1)(B) Alleging that one or more claims for recognition as exclusive bargaining representative have been received by the employer.* *If an 8(b)(7) charge has been filed involving the same employer, these statements in RC, RD, and RM petitions are not required.	Section of the Act UD 9(e)(1) Alleging that employees (30 percent or more of an appropriate unit) wish to rescind an existing union-security agreement. By a Labor Organization or an Employer Board Rules UC Subpart C Seeking classification of an existing bargaining unit. Board Rules AC Subpart C Seeking amendment of an outstanding certification of bargaining representative.

<u>Note:</u> Charges filed with the National Labor Relations Board are letter-coded and numbered. Unfair labor practice charges are classified "C" cases and petitions for certification or decertification of representatives as "R" cases. This table indicates the letter codes used for "C" cases on pages 24 and 25, and "R" cases on page 25 and also presents a summary of each action involved.

<u>Source:</u> NLRB, "A Layman's Guide to Basic Law under the National Labor Relations Act" (Washington, D.C.: Government Printing Office, 1971), pp. 24–25.

If the regional director believes that the objections are substantial, a new election may be held or a hearing conducted to determine the validity of objections. If no objections are filed after an election, or if objections ultimately are dismissed by the regional director or the Board, the NLRB issues a certification of the results of the election.

UNFAIR LABOR PRACTICES

Unfair labor practices are actions that inhibit or prevent employees from exercising their rights under the National Labor Relations Act. Over 90 percent of all unfair labor practice charges concern union organizing campaigns and certification procedures. Because there is such an interaction between representation and unfair labor practice cases, investigations and settlement efforts in one context frequently will be useful in the other and hearings may be consolidated because the issues in both cases are common.

As can be seen in Table 2.1, unfair labor practices of employers are identified in Section 8[a] of the National Labor Relations Act, those of labor organizations in Section 8[b], and Section 8[e] lists an unfair labor practice that can be committed only be an employer and a labor organization acting together.

There are five basic employer unfair labor practices:

- Interference, restraint, or coercion.
- Illegal assistance or domination of a labor organization.
- Discrimination in employment for union activities.
- Discrimination for participation in an NLRB proceeding.
- Refusing to bargain in good faith.

The following eight general types of unfair practices are forbidden to labor organizations:

- Restraint or coercion.
- Attempt to cause discrimination for union activities.
- Refusing to bargain in good faith.
- Secondary boycotts, sympathy strikes, or boycotts to force recognition of an uncertified union, and jurisdictional strikes.
- Charging excessive or discriminatory membership fees.
- Featherbedding.
- Recognitional and organizational picketing by noncertified unions.
- Hot cargo agreements.

Any person may file an unfair labor practice charge with the Board, whether or not they have any personal interest in the outcome. However, it should be noted that the NLRB has no authority to initiate unfair labor practice cases. When a new charge is received by the field offices, a field examiner or attorney is assigned to conduct an investigation of the facts. After completing the investigation, the examiner recommends to the regional director either the issuance of an unfair labor practice complaint or the dismissal of the charge. If the director finds that the charge has merit, efforts are initiated to affect settlement. If this effort is unsuccessful, a complaint is issued against the party being charged. Should the director decide to dismiss the charge, this generally closes the door on a case. The charging party can appeal to the Office of Appeals within the General Council's Office in Washington, D.C. Rarely is a regional director's decision reversed.

Once the regional director has issued a complaint, the person alleged to have violated the law is required to answer the complaint, admitting or denying its allegations. In the majority of cases the respondent agrees to settle the complaint without the necessity of a formal hearing. If such an agreement is not reached, a formal hearing is scheduled before an administrative law judge in the community in which the alleged unfair labor practice occurred. The hearing is a formal, adversarial proceeding, roughly comparable with a lawsuit in any civil court. After hearing all of the evidence, the administrative law judge writes a formal decision and recommendations. This document summarizes the issues, states the facts, discusses applicable provisions of the statute and precedent, and then determines that the act has or has not been violated. If the conclusion is that the respondent has violated the law, a suitable remedy will be recommended. Attempts to remedy unfair labor practices are most often accomplished through cease-and-desist orders. Occasionally an affirmative order is issued, such as for employees to be "made whole." A typical settlement in a discriminatory discharge case would be to require the employer to reinstate the employee with back pay plus interest and to post a notice in the work area.

Sometimes unfair labor practices are considered so flagrant that the administrative law judge believes a fair election is impossible. The administrative law judge may then order the company to bargain with the union without an election, provided that the union has furnished evidence that more than 50 percent of the employees wish to be members. If the union has committed such flagrant unfair labor practices, the election results, even if favorable to the union, could be set aside. The Board frequently has held such acts as assemblying employees on company property by the company or the union to express opinions respecting the election within 24 hours prior to the election, the presence of supervisors at polling places on election day, and the distribution of marked sample ballots as being serious enough for setting aside an election.

The administrative law judge's decisions are influenced by such factors as the nearness of the incident to the time of election (the nearer, the more influence it is likely to have on the employees' votes) and the history of the employer's actions regarding union organizing attempts. A judge's decision can have exceptions filed to it by either party. The appealing party simply sets forth exceptions to particular findings in the judge's decision.

Unfair labor practice charges are a common feature of organizing campaigns. Although many charges are dropped after the Board's certification, once filed, a charge can-not be dropped without approval of the regional director.

On receipt of the Board's decision, any party may appeal to the federal Court of Appeals. Parties who choose not to appeal have two choices: comply with the decision or await the Board's filing of a petition in the appropriate circuit court to enforce its order. On a few occasions, following court enforcement of a Board order, contempt proceedings may be initiated against parties who have failed to comply. Failure to comply can lead to civil and criminal fines.

NOTES

[1] The standards are summarized in NLRB, A Layman's Guide to Basic Law under the National Labor Relations Act (Washington, D.C.: U.S. Government Printing Office, 1971,) pp. 46-47.

[2] Excelsior Underwear, Inc., 156 NLRB 1236, 61 LRRM 1217 (1966).

[3] General Shoe Corporation, 77 NLRB 124, 21 LRRM 1337 (1948).

3

WHY EMPLOYEES FORM UNIONS

PERSONNEL DEPARTMENT

Approximately six months after James Bell was hired as its new personnel director, the Andre Cookie Company, located in East Chicago, Illinois, was confronted with an organization campaign by the Amalgamated Bakery Workers of America (ABWA). It was the union's third attempt in five years to organize the company's approximately 1,100 production workers. Andre was the largest of the five cookie companies in the East Chicago area, of which only one—Brown Cookie Company—was already organized.

Prior to joining Andre, Bell had been engaged in personnel work with banking and financial institutions. He was hired because of his knowledge and experience in psychological testing, which the president of Andre believed offered a solution to such company problems as turnover, absenteeism, and productivity.

The company's wage rates generally were competitive with other cookie manufacturers, but considerably below those paid by most other area employers. This factor, in combination with a tight labor market, resulted in a plant work force in which 60 percent held two jobs. Each year

Andre Cookie Manufacturing Company
Copyright © 1975 by the President and Fellows of Harvard College. This case is a revision of the (A), (B), and (C) cases prepared by William E. Fulmer. Reprinted by permission of the Harvard Business School.

the plant experienced a turnover rate of approximately 50 percent. Labor costs constituted approximately 60 percent of total manufacturing costs.

The company had a three-step grievance procedure under which workers could: present their grievances directly to their supervisor; appeal to the personnel office within 24 hours on forms available in the personnel office; appeal to an employee relations committee composed of the personnel director, the production vice-president, and the president. The procedure was virtually never used. Employees appeared reluctant to go to the personnel office.

Nevertheless, one incident that could be termed a grievance occurred shortly after Bell became personnel director. Fifty employees from department no. 22, the special-pack department, met with Bell to protest the speed of a conveyor that paced their work. The majority of the workers had been hand-cutters, but a few months earlier had been assigned to the conveyor line when hand-cutting was eliminated. Their jobs now required considerably less skill than hand-cutting and resulted also in substantially lower earnings, from a straight incentive-paid average of $6.42 per hour to an hourly base of $4.62. They had on only one day "earned" their base rate by meeting the stand-ard on the new line, and had never reached the level where incentive earnings became effective. After the "hearing" with the employees, Bell talked with the industrial engi-neer who had determined the speed of the conveyor, and the latter assured Bell that it was not too fast. Bell thought that the situation was complicated by the fact that the employees' supervisor, who did not approve of the new in-centive system, also did not have the confidence of the workers. Nothing was done in the matter.

ORGANIZATIONAL CAMPAIGN

Two previous unionization attempts had occurred at Andre in recent years. Both efforts resulted in clear de-feat for the union. In the last election the union had lost by a vote of 800 to 325. Both campaigns and elec-tions were conducted without violence or serious incident.

At the outset of the present campaign, management doubted that the union would receive any more votes this time. Bell was of the opinion that the workers actually did not want a union, but that they were using it as a threat to obtain wage increases. Management thought that the workers would not be willing to jeopardize the existing informal and familylike atmosphere for a union-management relationship. According to management, the employees enjoyed the lack of strict supervision and laxity with regard to absenteeism, tardiness, long rest periods, and

time off for personal reasons. Employees frequently
requested, and were granted, personal loans by the company.

The union's new drive was launched on April 12, with
the call to a "special meeting of the Andre employees" to
be held April 16 "for the purpose of organization." Leaflets with this notice were distributed as the workers left
the gate after each of the three shifts. On April 26, and
again in May 24, the union distributed letters containing a
stamped, self-addressed card for the employees to sign and
return, to indicate their desire for an NLRB certification
election. In July identical letters were sent to the workers of Andre and two other unorganized cookie plants
announcing a "concerted effort" to organize all cookie
workers.

In August the union distributed several fliers suggesting to Andre employees that the wages paid in the Best
Pastry Company, one of the organized local plants, were
substantially higher than those paid by Andre. Bell felt
that this implied comparison was unfair to Andre because
the wages cited by the union were from another industry
and, even so, applied only to a few employees in the union
plant.

Meanwhile, Bell recommended to management the following
wage increase: starting wages to be raised from $4.00 per
hour to $4.15--the rate already in effect in the one union-
ized cookie company (the other nonunion companies paid
$4.08 per hour); and the top wages of "service" employees
to be raised from $4.15 to $4.25 per hour. The last group
constituted indirect labor and therefore, unlike those engaged in direct production, could not earn incentive rates
and were dissatisfied with their much lower earnings. Of
these recommendations, top management approved only a $.10
increase in the hiring rate, instituted on August 19, when
about 25 people were raised to $4.10 per hour.

Bell met Vincent Anderson, the union business agent in
charge of the organizing campaign, after the latter had
made several unsuccessful attempts to meet with a company
representative. The first meeting occurred when Anderson
called on Bell to obtain some union material delivered to
Andre "by mistake." Anderson informed Bell at the same
time that the union had cards from more than 30 percent of
the employees, enough for an election. He requested a
meeting during the last week of August. Later, management
agreed, and the date was set for August 27. After the
first encounter, Bell characterized Anderson as "congenial
but probably not capable of great strategy."

At the August meeting, Anderson declared that he already represented a majority of Andre employees and urged
recognition of local no. 34 as exclusive bargaining agent.
The company refused, stating that it would not recognize
any union without certification after an NLRB election.

On September 5 George Beech, the chief examiner of the NLRB regional office, called a meeting to determine the appropriate bargaining unit for the election. The meeting was attended by K. Harold, the local union president, Anderson, Bell, and the company counsel. It was agreed to exclude the following: office and full-time plant clerical employees, salesmen, boiler-room engineers, guards, supervisors, and full-time inspectors. Anderson was belligerent at this meeting. When company counsel conjectured that the "usual campaign" would be conducted by each side, Anderson announced it would be "a fight, not a campaign." September 25 was agreed on as the voting day, although the union preferred an earlier date and the company a later one.

Bell felt that Anderson, by taking an adamant, belligerent position with respect to every issue, had tended to alienate Beech, while he and other company representatives had gained his goodwill. Bell thought Beech a "stimulating" individual and "considerate" of management's position.

On September 23 Anderson called again on Bell to examine job titles of those whom the company listed as eligible to vote. Since he was not familiar with the jobs, he was in no position to question the accuracy of the list. Bell found him friendly, almost solicitous.

During the weeks preceding the election, rumors circulated that the company was planning to mechanize many present manual jobs and to eliminate several types of products. Also, it was rumored that management had threatened to go out of business if forced to deal with a union. Management took no formal step to counteract these rumors, but urged their supervisors to discount them if queried. Management considered, but rejected, a plan to assemble groups of employees and urge them to vote against the union, because it believed that under the Taft-Hartly Act such action might be considered unfair if union solicitation were not also permitted on company premises.

Mail campaigns were conducted by the company and the union between September 6 and September 25, the election date. Most of the letters from the company were drafted by Bell and submitted in long sessions to the president, treasurer, and vice-president of production. Changes made by these individuals were so extensive that Bell frequently found it difficult to recognize the revised letters. The vice-president of production went over each letter with the supervisors before it was mailed to the homes of employees. Management generally felt that their most effective communication was the letter of September 23, correcting the union's letter of September 20, dealing with wage rates at Brown's. Bell felt the union's letter backfired since comments he heard indicated employee disgust with the inaccuracies. Brown employees also were reported to be enraged with the union for publicizing rates they were alleged to, but did not in fact, enjoy. The company's and the union's letters are presented in the Appendix to this chapter in chronological order.

ELECTION

The election took place on September 25 without incident. Of the 1,044 eligible employees, 958 voted, 475 against and 473 for the union. Ten additional votes were challenged and therefore not opened immediately. Eight persons were challenged by union observers who claimed that these persons were either full-time clerical or supervisory personnel and therefore not eligible to vote, and two were challenged by the NLRB representative because their names were omitted from the eligible voting list or incorrectly listed.

Thus the results remained in doubt. Since the challenged and as yet uncounted votes could determine the outcome, the chief examiner requested Bell to prepare and submit detailed job descriptions for each worker challenged by the union. On the basis of the job descriptions and, if necessary, after individual interviews, the NLRB would rule on whether each employee was or was not properly included in the previously determined bargaining unit. With respect to the two employees whose votes were challenged on the basis of the voting list, an examination of previous payrolls would be determining.

In a separate move, the union requested the NLRB to invalidate the September 25 election and to set another one. On October 1, the union filed its objections to conduct affecting the result of the election, alleging:

That prior to election, wage increases were granted to a substantial number of employees, including increases in department no. 64, for night-shift employees and in starting rates;

That individual employees were threatened with reprisals if they supported the union;

That the employer circulated a document purporting to be a copy of a portion of the official ballot; and

That on the day of the election, representatives of the employer telephoned certain employees and promised that if they came in to vote they would be paid all expenses.

The company denied that their actions had constituted interference in the employees' rights to self-organization or were in any way unfair.

Bell explained the difficulty that occurred in department no. 64. On July 15, because of the installation of six machines, department no. 64 was reduced from 65 to 36

employees. By August 24 mechanical problems were to be
worked out so as to permit the application of a new incentive rate under which earnings would not be influenced ad-
versely by breakdowns. Meanwhile, for the period July 15
to August 24, average pay earned prior to July 15 was to be
allowed.

Mechanical problems continued after August 24, but
wages on September 5 were based on the rate applied August
27 when mechanical difficulties made normal earning impossible. On September 6 management decided to extend to September 5 the period during which average pay was to be
guaranteed employees in this department. Consequently, on
that day the company informed the employees that they would
be reimbursed for the differential in earnings for the week
in question. The union charged that the granting of this
form of back pay was designed to influence the outcome of
the election.

Bell concluded that these events in department no. 64
were unrelated to the election. "In any event," he said,
"this arrangement and the establishment of new starting
minimum for employees occurred prior to the date [September
3] that the NLRB executed its stipulation that there would
be an election; therefore, as I understand it, these incidents may not be used to set aside the election." He knew
nothing of any increase for night-shift employees.

He dismissed the second objection "as isolated and un-
substantiated." It was alleged that a foreman had threatened one employee with the loss of overtime "if the union
got in." However, the employee refused to sign an affi-
davit to such an effect.

With respect to the "sample ballot," counsel assured
the company that the objection was not a valid one. The
union construed the partial reproduction of the ballot at
the bottom of the September 23 letter as violating a rule
enunciated by the Board, which proscribes "the reproduction
of any document purporting to be a copy of the Board's
official ballot, other than one completely unaltered in
form and content and clearly marked 'sample' on its face."
Counsel pointed out that the letter contained only a fac-
simile of the voting boxes of the official ballot and was
not actually a reproduction of the official ballot.

There was no disagreement as to the fourth objection.
On the morning of the election day, one of Bell's clerks
telephoned all eligible absent employees who could be
reached by telephone, reminded them it was election day and
that they would be reimbursed for transportation expenses
if they desired to come in and vote. Of approximately 25
employees thus reached, only three applied for reimburse-
ment. Two of these were given $.75 and $1.25, respectively, for bus fares, and one was given $7.00 for taxi fare.
The company thought it relevant that free transportation

was extended to all employees without distinction and that
employees were free to accept or reject the offer.

Although the rulings on these several issues were not
to be handed down for a month or more, management was confident it had once again defeated the union. It felt certain that of the challenged votes, no more than two would
be disallowed. Of the six remaining, the grapevine had
five of these as having cast their votes for the company
and one for the union. Of the two challenged by the NLRB,
the grapevine placed one for the company and one for the
union. Finally, the attempt to invalidate the entire
election was interpreted as an act of desperation. Consequently, in the weeks following the election, management
turned its thinking to the year ahead. Since a general
"one-year" rule on elections governed, the union was prohibited from seeking another election within the next
twelve months.

PLANNING AHEAD

Management was divided as to the approach to labor
relations that was best to follow after this campaign and
election. One group felt that the employees always had
been treated fairly and that their actions indicated they
"were not grateful." This group felt that management
should "give the employees what they deserved": closer
supervision and stricter discipline.

Included in this group was Production Vice-President
O. M. Barnes, himself formerly director of personnel. He
thought that the personnel department should move slowly in
introducing new ideas and in assuming additional authority.
He had been somewhat of a patriarch several years ago, and
was still very much respected by the older employees. He
had, however, been adamant in his opposition to union
attempts to organize in the past.

The other group felt that a "positive" employee relations program was called for. This group could be expected
to support many of the measures advocated by Bell, such as
periodic rate reviews, merit increases, revision of incentives, improved job analyses, supervisory development,
increased benefits, and a larger and more frequently
appearing house organ with a pictorial approach.

Bell's experience to date in introducing such measures
was mixed. Psychological testing for hiring and placement
had been accepted. On the other hand, a credit union he
had developed "fell flat on its face" early in September
because "no one from top management would take any responsibility for it." Later a second look appeared to favor
proceeding with the plan. Another project was also under
way. An industrial engineering firm had been employed to

revise and make more "realistic" standards and incentives. The goal was to lower standards in order to make incentives a higher percentage, perhaps 60 percent of the total wage.

Bell thought that the temporary failure of the credit union idea was the result of the low prestige the personnel department presently had in the Andre organization. The usual ratio of trained personnel staff to total employees was one to 100, but Andre had only two for a total force of 1,400. Bell had one assistant who screened, hired, and assigned employees. They were assisted by six clerical workers who processed insurance forms and made statistical studies.

The proper function of a personnel department in a non-unionized company, in Bell's opinion, was to be "somewhere between the employees and management, but apart from either." Workers needed leadership, and a personnel director could provide that leadership and hence obviate the need for a union. He could serve as the workers' spokesman and thus save them union dues.

Bell considered the present an ideal time for undertaking this unique function. With the continual threat of the union, the need was obvious. With the changes that had occurred in management recently, the moment was opportune. Having just joined the company and already having established some rapport with many employees, he saw himself as the natural person for this role. Indeed, when he took over the personnel job, many asked him, "What are you going to do for us?" Thus he believed he might be able to serve as a "messiah" for Andre employees.

Bell was "not against unions per se." However, the company had to be in a stronger profit position and more efficient before entering negotiations with a union. Furthermore, since certain management people might have difficulty in adjusting to a union, a conflict was likely to develop and everyone would be hurt.

Bell advocated a major shift in employment policy. He wanted to increase the percentage of part-time employees until only 300 of the most essential of the total production force would be full time, the remainder engaged in four-to-six-hour shifts. The jobs to be filled on short shifts required very little training. Because of better selectivity on the present short shift, 5 to 11, output had been better than on the other shifts. Part-time employees would be less concerned with fringe benefits and less inclined to support union efforts. It would therefore be possible to pay higher wage rates for part-time workers than presently was paid to full-time workers.

In October and early November the most pressing problems centered around wage policy. The other cookie companies in the area, including the one organized firm, had granted their employees wage increases in October ranging from $.10 to $.15 per hour. Some members of Andre management advocated a similar increase for their employees. Others favored waiting until the following summer, "closer to the union's elections again next year," and perhaps coinciding with the installation of the new incentives. The elimination of the Christmas bonus also was seriously considered.

CLEVELAND DEVELOPMENTS

No sooner had the company surmounted the effort at unionization and begun planning for the next year than it was confronted, in early October, with "another brush fire," this time involving its warehouse in Cleveland. Although organizational attempts were launched simultaneously in both East Chicago and Cleveland, the Cleveland situation had not, at first, been regarded as serious.

The Cleveland warehouse, operated by the Andre Sales Corporation, a wholly-owned subsidiary, employed only five nonsupervisory workers. The campaign by the Confectionery Workers Union, a rival union to ABWA, resulted in certification on September 16. After the NLRB had tallied three votes for the union and two against and had certified the union, management brought to the attention of the NLRB the claims of the four of the workers that they had not voted for the union and did not want the union. The NLRB held that there must have been a "change of heart," and that did not constitute grounds for setting aside the election.

Contract negotiations with Local no. 80 of the Confectionery Workers Union quickly broke down when it became clear that the parties were far apart on demands for a "maintenance of membership" clause, dues checkoff, and a request for a $.10 wage increase. On October 8 the union called a strike and threw a picket line around the warehouse. However, the strike did not seriously handicap the company since it was able to maintain delivery by shipping directly from the East Chicago plant. The company also had arranged with other manufacturers sympathetic with Andre's labor troubles to make a number of shipments for it.

Later Local no. 80 decided to bring pressure against Andre at East Chicago. On November 5 Bell observed from his office window several strangers as they got out of a taxi with suitcases, suggesting they were from out of town. With Anderson on the scene to welcome them, Bell suspected trouble. Within a few hours, these four men had thrown up a picket line at shipping and receiving entrances, carrying signs declaring that Local no. 80 of the Confectionery Workers Union was on strike against Andre Sales Corporation, which was labeled as "unfair." The four pickets from Local no. 80, of which one was an employee of the Cleveland warehouse, were joined by Anderson, a few other officials of Local no. 34, and two employees of Andre at East Chicago.

The Teamsters Union refused to cross the picket line. Since almost all shipping was handled by truck, both shipping and receiving were effectively blocked. Although the company was located along a rail siding and did make two rail shipments, it could not rely wholly on this means of transportation. It attempted to persuade officials of the Teamsters local union, with whom it had "certain previous contacts," to continue shipments. The local Teamsters officials indicated, however, that they could not cooperate in this instance and intimated that they were, in fact, themselves interested in the East Chigaco warehouse workers.

No attempt was made to prevent employees from entering or leaving the plant. On the second day of picketing a minority of the employees, presumably those who wished most to support unionization, did not report for work. The company preferred not to accumulate inventory, and therefore laid off a large percentage of the 1,100 production employees on Thursday, November 6, and the entire force on Friday. The plant was closed on Saturday, Sunday, and Monday (a holiday) and remained closed on Tuesday.

Confronted with the picket line that the Teamsters refused to cross, the company sought the advice of the law firm it had used on a number of occasions in the past. Andre relied on these lawyers in its current labor difficulties even though these particular lawyers had little experience in labor matters.

What about an injunction against the picket line? Counsel thought it might be possible and agreed to take the case to court. The state court disclaimed jurisdiction because, as the unon's lawyers pointed out, it involved interstate commerce and damages in excess of $3,000. To justify an injunction, the company hoped to establish the picketing as constituting a secondary boycott, something expressly outlawed by the Taft-Hartly Act.* Since the dispute was between Local no. 80 and Andre Sales Corporation and the picketing in Chicago was directed toward and injurious to a neutral party, the Andre Cookie (manufacturing) Company, company management believed it might have a case. Since both the parent and its subsidiary corporation largely used common facilities, were owned by identical interests, and in reality were separate only for financial purposes, counsel thought it would be difficult for the company to prove its case.

---

*A secondary boycott may be picketing or a strike action directed toward a neutral party not directly involved in the dispute, such as a supplier or a customer.

On Tuesday evening, November 11, realizing the futility of presenting the case to a federal court, the company president flew to Cleveland and settled with Local no. 80. The settlement included a union shop, dues checkoff, and a $.25 wage increase.

After the contract with Local no. 80 was signed and the pickets removed, management called back its forces and resumed operation.

ANALYSIS OF THE ANDRE SITUATION

The Andre Cookie Company is a good example of an organization that gave relatively little thought to the management of its people. Although management apparently defeated the union for the third time in the past five years, the union's support has continued to grow. Unless something drastic occurs in the near future, the union will succeed in convincing a majority of the work force to choose it as their bargaining representative next year.

Why are the Employees Dissatisfied with Andre Cookie?

A careful examination of Andre's practices and policies suggests several serious problem areas that can lead to employee unrest.

Wages

Although the management of Andre paid competitive wages for the cookie industry, its wages were below those for other industries in the area. As is often the case, especially in a labor-intensive industry, management was in the difficult position of having to explain to its employees why they were not "worth" what employees in neighboring plants were worth, even though they may work as hard and in less desirable conditions. Another aspect of Andre's wage policy that may have upset a significant number of workers was Andre's use of merit raises. Frequently this suggests the possibility of favoritism being shown by management. Furthermore, as the ABWA's September 20 letter reported, only 500 out of 1,200 employees received merit raises during the year of the campaign. A further possible indication that wages were a major concern to the employees was that 60 percent held two jobs.

Technological Change

Often when there are changes in the equipment to be used by workers, job security becomes a major employee concern.

This is particularly true when an employee's pay is tied to a rate of output. Shortly after James Bell came to Andre, the jobs of 50 employees in department no. 22 were changed from a hand-cutting operation to less skilled jobs on the conveyor belt. Not only did this affect their status as skilled workers, but it also reduced their pay from $6.42 per hour to $4.62, a 28 percent cut in pay. Equipment changes also occurred in department no. 64 that resulted in the elimination of 45 percent of the jobs in that department (from 65 to 36). During the weeks preceding the election, rumors circulated that the company planned to mechanize "many present manual jobs and eliminate several types of products." Management made no serious effort to counteract these rumors.

Inadequate Grievance Procedure

The company's grievance procedure was "virtually never used." Some managers may have interpreted this to mean that workers had few grievances against management. A more likely interpretation was that the procedure was viewed by the workers as useless. Not only was the procedure totally controlled by management, but in the one recent case where it was used to protest the changes in department no. 22, Bell took the word of one industrial engineer over the word of 50 employees and "nothing was done in the matter." It is not surprising that employees "appear reluctant to go to the personnel office." Bell believed that some of the employee unrest was the result of supervisors not having "the confidence of the workers," yet the supervisor was the first step in the grievance procedure.

Changes in the Incentive System

As indicated earlier, some of the unrest in department no. 22 was the result of changing the incentive rates. In addition, an industrial engineering firm had been employed to "review and make more 'realistic' standards and incentives." Although the goal was to lower standards, given the experience of department no. 22 this could not help but increase the anxiety of Andre employees about future earnings.

The Status of the Personnel Department

It is clear that the Personnel Department is not very important to Andre's top management, yet it is supposed to be the employees' representative. Even Bell acknowledges the "low prestige" of his department. By industry standards, the department was understaffed. The changes in Bell's campaign letters were "so extensive" that he fre-

quently found it "difficult to recognize the revised
letters." His proposal for a credit union for employees
"fell flat on its face" because "no one from top management
would take any responsibility for it." His recommendations
to management for various wage increases were largely
ignored. If the employees wanted a strong voice in dealing
with management, it was not the Personnel Department.

Bell

Bell was not the man to be dealing with a union organizing campaign, as his background was inadequate for the
job. To illustrate, he did not use an expert labor attorney; consequently the company wound up in the wrong court
when seeking an injunction. He did not know that it was
legal to assemble a group of employees and urge them to
vote against the union without the union being given solicitation rights on company premises. He underestimated the
union business agent. To be fair, it should be acknowledged that Bell was not hired to run a union campaign and he
did not have sufficient time to implement many of his plans.

Effective Union Campaign

By reporting rumors of planned mechanization and
threats by the company to go out of business. the union was
able to effectively raise the issue of job security in the
minds of Andre employees. In addition, the union seemed to
have been reasonably effective in raising the wage issue.
Even when deficiencies were pointed out in some of their
contracts, the union responded by admitting the problems
and pointed out that it needed to organize a majority of
the cookie plants if it was to make conditions comparable
to the bread and cake industry. In its last letter to employees, the union seemed to try to clear up some of the
confusion that employees were experiencing over the dis-
crepancies in union and management claims.

Ineffective Company Campaign

The company, in contrast to the union, seemed to add to
the confusion of employees with its last letter. Late in
the campaign it attacked the integrity of the union and its
officers by dragging up information that probably dated
from Senate hearings in the 1950s. At the very beginning
of the campaign management seemed surprised and unprepared,
in spite of two prior campaigns. Apparently the company
had done little to improve conditions for its employees
since the last election.

The Future Direction of Andre

As of November it seemed clear that the company had narrowly defeated the union. With such a close vote, another campaign could be expected next year. Therefore Andre's management had to decide what, if anything, it would do in the near future.

One group of managers wanted to punish employees for being so ungrateful as to challenge management's authority. Perhaps by tightening up on supervision and discipline, management could increase the turnover rate above the current 50 percent level and essentially replace its "ingrates." Although the areas of supervision and discipline may need to be improved, a punitive approach likely will assure the union's success next year.

A second group of managers wanted to introduce positive employee relations programs. Although this may have seemed like a reward to the "ungrateful" employees, it may have convinced employees that they could gain improved working conditions without a union. If management chose to pursue a positive approach, at least two questions needed to be answered: How many improvements should be made? When should the improvements be made?

A third option facing the company was to do nothing. Given the recent history of the company and the split within management ranks as to which direction to pursue, this was the most likely outcome, and a union victory was virtually guaranteed for next year.

Cleveland Situation

There is a tendency by some managers to quickly resolve a problem like the one in Cleveland without recognizing the implications of their solution. Although there were only five employees involved, it could and did provide an opportunity for the union to get into East Chicago by way of the back door.

Another indication that the Cleveland situation was not fully appreciated was the unwillingness of management to see the strike through. Management should not have taken the strike unless it was willing to see it through. Management's actions indicated that it was not prepared for a strike. In addition, it was quite likely that initially it could have settled for a relatively small cost. This raises the question as to whether the proper strategy in early negotiating sessions is to be hard-nosed, to prove to the employees that a union will not get them anything, or settle quickly and avoid the cost of a strike.

The president's actions in the Cleveland situation were very questionable. Although some observers believed that the president did what a president should do (that is, take over in crises), others believed that he should have stayed in Chicago. A good case can be made for the latter position. Not only did his presence indicate panic, but he was unskilled in bargaining--as results indicated. Also, it usually is desirable to avoid "summit bargaining." When an impasse is reached, a bargaining president has no place to turn. A bargainer frequently needs a way out when the bargaining gets tough, if for no other reason than to gain some perspective on the issues.

There was little doubt but that the settlement in Cleveland would affect East Chicago. The $.25 increase would almost certainly have to be extended to Chicago or guarantee a union victory next year. It also was clear that a picket line could be a very effective weapon in dealing with Andre management, since truck drivers were unwilling to cross the picket line. Furthermore, in the next Chicago campaign, it would have been inconsistent for management to argue that unions are undesirable after management had agreed to a union shop that required all Cleveland employees to join the union to keep their jobs.

The Cleveland settlement seemed to be a clear example of an organizing situation where management pursued short-range solutions that had long-range implications. Not only was the Cleveland settlement based on expediency, but the president's decision to take a strike was quickly reversed, which signaled a lack of well-thought-out objectives.

It came as no great surprise to most observers of the Andre situation that one year later the union won an overwhelming victory in its campaign to organize East Chicago. James Bell resigned soon thereafter.

APPENDIX

ANDRE COOKIE COMPANY

September 6

TO YOU, AS AN ANDRE EMPLOYEE:

On two previous occasions, the Amalgamated Bakery Workers attempted to become a part of your working lives. They sought to come between you and your Management—to speak for you, instead of permitting you the advantage of speaking for yourself. Now they seek to do so again.

Union representation is not a matter to be considered lightly for it affects your livelihood and that of your family. Please consider the following:

Local 34, Amalgamated Bakery Workers Union, representing only one, rather small, plant cannot bring competent "know-how" to Andre.

Local 34 cannot improve our products.

Local 34 cannot increase the Company's earnings, and it is only through increased earnings that we can offer you more advantages.

Every employee is important to our Company. Our jobs depend on what we can produce and sell at a profit. Increased wages and benefits depend on the progress and profits of our Company. The future prosperity of this Company depends on what we do to accomplish these objectives.

Andre, in business for 110 years, had been a leader in dealing fairly with you and the public which buys its products. The prosperous years have been shared with you. No cookie plant in East Chicago is a better, safer place in which to work. No Union had a part in this in the past —and there is no real reason why it should have in the future.

Sincerely,

O. M. Barnes
Vice President

ABWA LOCAL #34

ATTENTION ANDRE EMPLOYEES: September 10
     You recently received a letter signed by Mr. O. M. Barnes,
Vice President.
     It is our intent to save all of the letters received from the
Company, because the Union will answer each and every letter
article by article; so as you can formulate your own opinion on
whether the Company has been fair to you.
     ARTICLE ONE of the letter makes reference to the importance
of management representing you instead of an honest decent union.
How come all of a sudden management has taken an interest in you?
     The Company says you should speak for yourselves. How much
consideration could you possibly get speaking as an individual as
opposed to a Union with ELEVEN HUNDRED MEMBERS? Why do you think
management wants you to represent yourselves? The answer is
obvious. In UNITY there is STRENGTH.
     Still answering the letter, where the statement was made by
the Company that Local #34 cannot improve our products. Local
#34 does not endeavor to improve the products of any company, but
very definitely CAN AND WILL IMPROVE YOUR WORKING CONDITIONS.
     In the same letter your employer says that Local #34 cannot
improve the Company's earnings. Local #34 never claims to
improve the company's earnings; but we DEFINITELY WILL IMPROVE
THE VACATION PLAN AND THE PENSION PLAN.
     Answering the same letter where the Company says your jobs
depend on what you can produce and sell at a profit, increase of
wages depend on the progress of the Company. Our answer to that
is this. Your Company is always talking about sharing this and
sharing that with its employees. So what does the Company do?
It hires efficiency men to cut expenses here and cut expenses
there. But who gets all the savings? The Company, of course.
All you get is more work for the same money and sometimes less.
     Your Company also states that it has been in business for 110
years and has been a leader in dealing fairly with you. Recently
you had an incident in Department #64 where the Company reduced
the earning power of its employees by installing new machinery
and eliminating bonus earnings.
                         IS THAT FAIR?
               IS THE COMPANY TRYING TO HELP YOU?
     The only reason the Company changed its position in Department
#64 is simply because the Union is outside attempting to get in-
side to negotiate fair and honest wages for all its employees.
                         Fraternally yours,

                         Vincent Anderson
                         Business Agent

P.S. Remember, keep the Company's letters. The Union will
      answer each and every one of them. Read the Union's
      letters--then you make up your mind.

September 16

ANDRE COOKIE COMPANY

TO YOU, AS AN ANDRE EMPLOYEE

We believe you and your family should examine for your-selves the employee benefits of the only cookie company organized by Local #34. Here is a factual comparison of your benefits with Andre as compared with the benefits of the only cookie company organized by Local #34 for twenty years:

ANDRE	THE UNIONIZED COMPANY

PENSION PLAN

Andre has paid pensions for many years with no employee contributions. The plan is being funded by annual Company contributions of more than $400,000.	No provision in Union contract and no Company pension plan.

YEAR-END BONUSES

Last year, bonuses ranged from a minimum of $50.00 to one week's pay for those with one year's service. Andre has paid year-end bonuses in all but seven of the last 51 years.	Last year, Company paid bonuses ranging from $5.00 after 30 days' service to $50.00 after 3 years service.

GROUP INSURANCE

$10,000--most of which the Company pays for. Employee buys paid-up insurance with weekly contributions, all of which is returnable with interest upon retirement or termination.	No provision in Union contract; however, Company provides $5,000 term insurance, which has no paid-up or cash-surrender values upon termination of employment.

SICKNESS AND ACCIDENT INSURANCE

Insured plan with weekly benefits of $100 to $150 a week for 13 weeks. Employee pays 60¢ to 95¢ a week. Company pays balance.	No provision in Union contract; however, Company provides an insured plan of $40 to $60 a week for 13 weeks.

ANDRE	THE UNIONIZED COMPANY

HOSPITAL AND SURGICAL INSURANCE

$100.00-a-day Blue Cross-Blue Shield plan for both employees and pensioners, paid jointly by employee and Company.	No provision in Union contract; however, Company provides an insured plan which pays up to $60.00 a day.

PROFIT-SHARING PLAN

Plan adopted in 1949 qualified under Internal Revenue regulations, paid when profits permit.	No profit sharing.

SHIFT PREMIUM

10¢ an hour.	No provision in Union contract.

OVERTIME PREMIUM

After 40 hours' work per week.	After 40 hours' work per week or 8 hours' work per day.

MEDICAL SERVICE

Three nurses covering all shifts, plus a doctor, in daily attendance.	Nurse in daily attendance. Doctor available one morning a week; otherwise, on call.

REFIEF PERIODS

15 minutes in morning. 10 minutes in afternoon.	10 minutes in morning. 10 minutes in afternoon.

PAID HOLIDAYS

Ten paid holidays a year for all employees, regardless of length of service.	Ten paid holidays a year for employees who have thirty or more days of service.

PAID VACATIONS

One week after six months. Two weeks after 2 years. Two weeks, plus one week's bonus, after 15 years.	One week after one year. Two weeks after 3 years. Three weeks after 10 years.

ANDRE	THE UNIONIZED COMPANY

WORK UNIFORMS

Free uniforms supplied to all employees.

Free uniforms supplied only where required.

CAFETERIA SERVICE

Complete cafeteria service subsidized by Company at an annual cost in excess of $100,000.

Lunch counter run by outside concessonaire, without Company subsidy.

FUNERAL ALLOWANCE

Three-day payment for absence because of funeral in immediate family.

No provision in Union contract.

JURY DUTY ALLOWANCE

Payment of difference between amount received for jury duty and regular week's pay.

No provision in Union contract.

MEAL ALLOWANCE

$2.00 allowed for supper money if employee works two hours overtime in the evening. Hot meals usually available in dining room.

$2.50 allowed for supper money if employee works 3 hours overtime in the evening. No restaurant service available.

WASH-UP TIME ALLOWANCE

5 minutes at end of shift.

No provision in Union contract.

MINIMUM PAYMENT IN CASE OF BREAKDOWNS

Minimum of 4 hours paid, unless previously notified not to report for work.

No guarantee except carfare.

SAFETY SHOES

Andre pays one-half of cost.

No provision in Union contract.

ANDRE	THE UNIONIZED COMPANY

PRESCRIPTION SAFETY GLASSES

Andre pays full cost for employees who benefit by their use.

No provision in Union contract.

EMPLOYEE ACTIVITIES

Andre gives financial sponsorship to employee activities such as bowling, softball, Christmas parties, etc.

None.

MERIT INCREASES

More than 500 merit increases have been granted thus far this year.

None.

SENIORITY

Andre has a long-established policy of plant-wide seniority. Any employee transferred to another department always retains his, or her, Company seniority.

Union contract requires strict departmental seniority. If a department is eliminated, or reduced in size, employees who are transferred go to the bottom of the list in their new department and are the first subject to layoff.

The members of Local #34 at the Unionized cookie company pay dues of $8.00 per month. They have been paying dues for the past twenty years.

Andre benefits are provided without a Union, without Shop Stewards, without a Business Agent, without Union dues. They clearly speak for themselves.

VOTE: "NO UNION!"

Sincerely,

O. M. Barnes
Vice President

September 18

ANDRE COOKIE COMPANY

To All My Andre Friends:

I know you will permit me a personal word, a note, written because this Union subject is really so personally important to all of us.

A few days ago, one of my very good friends, a member of a Union, said to me: "You know, something goes out when a Union comes in--the sort of old 'family feeling' isn't there any more."

It seems to me that my friend has put his finger on something mighty important! Somehow, in spite of all our normal gripes and grumbles, we are here because we want to be associated with Andre. None of us really want to lose that sort of inexplainable "homey" feeling that we have always had here. I know that I don't--that you folks who have grown up with us don't--and that those who have come with us in recent years don't--want that feeling lost.

Believe me--and I honestly mean this--you don't need a Union here!

Sincerely,

O. M. Barnes
Vice President

September 19

ABWA LOCAL #34

ATTENTION ANDRE EMPLOYEES:

In answer to a recent letter sent to you by the Andre Cookie Company dated September the 16th.

The Company asks you to examine for yourself benefits you are now receiving. This very day you have received your weekly earnings from the Andre Cookie Company. Examine its contents with your family needs carefully. Are you receiving a fair week's wages for the services you have rendered for the past forty hours?

Andre Cookie Company has the audacity to tell you to examine somebody else's working conditions and wages and they also pretend that we have a cookie company in our Union with far worse conditions than the Andre Cookie Company. IMPOSSIBLE AND RIDICULOUS IS ALL I HAVE TO SAY.

Mr. Barnes does not name the Company. We have no Company in our Union with the conditions that he tried to explain to you.

Why doesn't he name the Company? It is very obvious. We have no such Company.

There is no doubt in my mind that the Andre Cookie Company, Mr. Barnes in particular, is getting desperate when he resorts to such cheap tactics by not being specific and in indulging in subterfuge.

In conclusion may I restate to the Andre Cookie Company --I DARE YOU TO NAME THE COMPANY YOU MADE REFERENCE TO IN YOUR LETTER SENT TO YOUR EMPLOYEES ON SEPTEMBER THE 16TH, and then we will prove that the statements you make are nothing but fabricated falsehoods.

Vincent Anderson
Business Representative

September 20

ABWA LOCAL #34

ATTENTION ANDRE EMPLOYEES:

Local #34's answer to Mr. Barnes' fictitious letter
dated September 16, and Mr. Barnes' letter dated September
18.

Now that they have dared to name the cookie company
that Local #34 represents, here are the true facts
comparing the Brown Company Contracts and Andre's poor
wages and conditions.

First let me state to the Andre employees that you have
no guaranteed wages or conditions presently with the Andre
Cookie Company. There is not one single condition—
Pension, Share-the-Profit Plan, Wages, Holidays, Bonuses or
anything else that is guaranteed to you that the Company
cannot take away from you at any time they see fit.

FOR EXAMPLE:

Andre's Bonus
In 36 years Andre failed
to pay a bonus in seven
of the years.

Brown's
Brown paid their bonus for
every year.

MERIT INCREASES
Andre claims to have given
increases totaling 500.
What happened to the other
700 people and how much of
an increase did they get?

Through a Union Contract all
employees get the increases.
No favorite groups.

SENIORITY

No definite established
system of seniority.

UNION'S FEELINGS TOWARD
SENIORITY
The Union Members working in
the plant decide whether or
not they want department
seniority. The Brown employees prefer department seniority, and that is what they
get. Not any seniority the
Company wants to give them.

VACATIONS

1 week after 6 months –	1 week after 1 year –
2 weeks after 2 years –	2 weeks after 3 years –
2 weeks plus one week's	3 weeks after 10 years.
bonus after 15 years.	

Now for the comparison on wages that the Andre Cookie Company, particularly Mr. Barnes, failed to put in his letter dated September 16.

At this very moment the Union is negotiating wages and other working conditions with the Brown Cookie Company. We have already refused 15 1/2¢ per hour increase. The Company has also offered us an improvement on our vacation plan and many other benefits too numerous to list in this letter. Listed below are the rates and wages of the Brown employees—not including the present offer of $6.00 additional a week. Compare these wages with yours.

BROWN COOKIE COMPANY

Cooks	$5.97
Cooks' Helpers	5.30
Operators	5.52
Spinners	5.97
Helpers	5.30
Receivers	5.40
Shipping Room Packers	5.40
Laborers	5.18
General Helpers	5.12

Fraternally yours,

Vincent Anderson
Business Representative

September 20

ANDRE COOKIE COMPANY

TO YOU, AS AN ANDRE EMPLOYEE

The Senate hearings some years ago exposed the "goings-on" in the Amalgamated Bakery Workers of America.

The complete, official Government report of every word of this testimony is available in our Personnel Office. We urge you to glance through it and form your own opinions. It sets forth, far better than any words of ours, the entire picture of the activities of the officers of this Union and their associates. It clearly indicates what was said, and what was not said but hidden behind the Fifth Amendment.

What has all this to do with you? Simply this:

1. Over one-third of all the dues paid to Local Unions are sent to the International Union Headquarters in Washington, D.C. (It is the dues of the Local Union members that support and pay for International headquarters activities.)

2. Testimony at the hearings indicate that Local Business Agents are guided by these International officers.

3. The International officers establish the general policies for the entire organization.

In his remarks at the closing of the hearings, the Committee Chairman said in part:

. . . if the interest of these laboring people, these people who are earning their money by the sweat of their brow, is to be protected . . . there will continue to be, in my judgment, a large question mark and suspicion that the integrity of the leadership of this union is not what it should be and what the working people have a right to expect.

Are YOU willing to pay for this type of representation? The choice is yours. Be sure to vote. We ask YOU to vote "NO"!!

Sincerely,

O. M. Barnes
Vice President

September 23

ANDRE COOKIE COMPANY

<u>TO YOU, AS AN ANDRE EMPLOYEE</u>

The business agent of Local #34 of the Amalgamated Bakery Workers of America who is seeking your vote is either:

Unbelievably ignorant of the wage rates in the union contract he himself has negotiated with the Brown Cookie Company or is resorting to deliberate falsehood to mislead you.

We have a copy of the current union contract with Brown.* Paragraph 8 of that contract lists the minimum hourly rates. The Brown Company tells us that, with a few individual exceptions, <u>these are the rates now being paid</u> in their plant.

Here they are:

JOB TITLES	What the Contract Says	What the Business Agent tells you
Cooks	$5.97	$5.97
Cooks' Helpers	5.13	5.30
Operators	5.27	5.52
Spinners	5.79	5.97
Helpers	5.13	5.30
Receivers	5.16	5.40
Shipping Room Packers	5.16	5.40
Shipping Room Laborers	5.03	5.18
General Helpers	4.95	5.12
Wrappers	4.76	4.91
Feeders	4.98	4.95
Checkers	4.55	4.95
Small Machine Operators	4.55	4.95
Packing Belt Supply Girls	4.55	4.95
Stock Case Packers	4.49	4.73

Draw your own conclusion. Do you want this man and his organization to represent you?

Sincerely,

Andre Cookie Company

O. M. Barnes

Vice President

*This copy is available in the Personnel Office for any employees who wish to examine it.

September 23
ANDRE COOKIE COMPANY

TO YOU, AS AN ANDRE EMPLOYEE

On Wednesday, September 25, you will have the opportunity to decide whether you want to be free to take your problems up directly with your Company or whether you want to give up that right to some outsider.

Today, you are free to work, or not, as you please. After September 25, if a Union comes in, you may have to stop work if the Union orders you to stop--or you have to cross a picket line to work and draw your pay. This cannot happen if you note "NO" in the right-hand box on the ballot.

You do not need a Union. You have never had to pay Union dues, assessments, or initiation fees to work here. If a Union later seeks a Union shop, you may have to. You have had steady employment and, even when work was slow, jobs were made for many of you.

This Union has many salaries and expenses to pay, and if it gets regular monthly dues from each one of you, plus initiation fees and assessments, its take can run into thousands of your dollars. Is this the real reason it is seeking unionization of this plant?

Do you think any Union--which deliberately, or through ignorance, makes such misstatements as were made in the letters handed out to you--is worthy of your trust?

It is more than just today that is involved:

1. Do you realize that you, as an individual, might be ordered out on a strike with which you are not in agreement?

2. Would you be called on to help picket some other plant?

3. Would you be assessed to support outside strikes?

4. How much do you really know about this organization that is seeking your support?

5. Has this Union told you--
   What your initiation fee will be?
   What your monthly dues will be?
   What fines you will pay if you don't attend meetings?

6. Have you carefully considered the qualifications
   of those Andre employees who are active in this
   Union Drive? It is reasonable to assume that
   these persons will expect recognition.
   Are they the persons you would like to have as
   Shop Stewards or Union officials?
   Are they the persons you would like to have make
   decisions <u>for you</u>?

We have suggested in this letter some of the questions
you should ask yourselves in deciding how you should vote.
Consider and examine carefully any promises or inducements
that the Union representatives hold out to you. Are they
promises or inducements on which they can possibly make
good?

And finally, remember this: that neither the Union nor
the Company will be allowed to know how you vote. Under
the law—even though you were persuaded to sign a Union
card—you have the right to vote "NO" in complete <u>privacy</u>.

Sincerely,

O. M. Barnes
Vice President

Do you wish to be represented for purposes of collective bargaining by—AMALGAMATED BAKERY WORKERS OF AMERICA, LOCAL 34, AFL-CIO?

Yes	No
	X

A VOTE OF "NO" IS A VOTE FOR YOURSELF!

September 20

ABWA LOCAL #34

<u>ATTENTION ANDRE EMPLOYEES</u>:   <u>THE ELECTION DAY IS NEAR</u>

You must make up your minds one way or another whether or not the Company under the present conditions it now operates is fair.   Your wage rates and working conditions are at this very minute unbearable to you.   How much longer can you stand this situation?   The cost of living has continually risen to the point where you must receive higher wages.   Not 500 of the employees but all of you must receive it.

Your Company in order to cloud the issue is attempting to character-assassinate anybody and everybody who is in opposition to the present Company Policy.   It would seem to me that you employees should stand up and be counted and say to the Company through your vote Wednesday, we don't believe you, Andre, and you have not been fair with us over the past years and we want to be represented by a good honest Union.   And Local #34 through its history has proven to all of its members who work in Bests, Brown, Ann Page Mayonnaise, Ann Page Chips, that it is a good Union and has given the people good wages and good working conditions and you must do the same for us.

Now, may I answer the Company's letter dated September 23, where the Company again in its desperate desire to win the election has again attempted to assassinate the character and the integrity of our business representative.   We say to you, the good people of Andre, to come up to the Union Office at your own convenience at 140 Westlake Avenue to examine the contracts that we have with the companies mentioned above.   Compare them with your present wages and conditions and see for yourselves what the Company has been taking from you every single week in wages and conditions. This Local Union on the average to its members is getting for them at least $30.00 per week more, with working conditions too numerous to mention in our letters.

Ask yourselves this one question.   If the Union could not do anything for you, why is the Company so desperate in trying to confuse the issues and assassinate the character of the officers of Local #34?   It stands to reason that your Company knows once the Union gets in and you have representation as a group, that the Company will no longer be able to run roughshod over the employees.

Why hasn't the Company put on its bulletin boards the recent settlements of contracts that Local #34 has made? Why hasn't the Company told you about the 89¢ a month pension they gave one of the employees? What happened in Room #64, where they are now attempting to bribe the people with a few cents increase? Why doesn't the Company treat you all alike? Why doesn't the Company show you all of the contracts by Local #34?

In answer to the charge by the Andre Company in reference to the Brown Cookie Company, may I at this time state emphatically that I admit the Brown Cookie Company contract is not as good as the Bakery Contracts, but analyze with me for a minute the reason why.

In the bread and cake industry, we have the vast majority of the plants organized. In the cookie industry at this time we have only Brown. One group of people trying to do for all of the cookie workers what the cookie workers should do as a whole.

I personally make you this promise, that if you organize, your conditions and wages and Brown's will be as good as the bread and cake and perhaps even better, but, I cannot do it alone.

Now, in reference to the statements by the Andre Company about the Brown contract of the charge they made that we don't tell the truth, let me say here and now to pay particular attention to the statement made by the Company, where they say we have a copy of the current Union Contract with Brown; paragraph 8 of that contract lists the minimum hourly rates which means that these are the least they can make. Why has Brown Company cooperated with the Andre Company? Because they know that once we consolidate both plants they will not be able to keep us down.

Most important for your consideration if the Union by merely being outside campaigning can get the raises for the people it has already got it for, what can it do for you when it gets inside and wins the election? This should be all too obvious to you.

Fraternally yours,

Vincent Anderson
Business Representative

4

THE ORGANIZING PROCESS

Carl Jung once observed that "The great decisions of human life have as a rule far more to do with the instincts and other mysterious unconscious factors than with the conscious will and well-meaning reasonableness."[1] All too often the same can be said for the decisions made by managers, union officials, and even employees in the heat of a union organizing campaign.

Managers often seem to respond emotionally to the first signs of a union organizing campaign. The instinctive management response often is, in the words of one corporate vice-president, to "do whatever is necessary to defeat the union." Not only can such a policy statement lead to illegal actions, in the form of unfair labor practices committed by the manager or overly zealous subordinates, but in some cases overzealous supporters have been responsible for multimillion dollar lawsuits charging "illegal conspiracy to violate the organizers' right to privacy, freedom of speech and freedom of association."[2] When the intention to resist unionization has been followed by illegal actions, subsequent short run decisions occasionally result in strategic errors that in the long run come back to haunt management.

Sections of this Chapter were originally published as, "Step by Step Through a Union Campaign," in July/August 1981, Harvard Business Review. Used with permission.

Union organizers also seem to make many key organizing decisions without adequate thought or planning, that is, without "well-meaning reasonableness." There are numerous cases where union leaders have attempted to organize a work place without counting the cost of the campaign and have had to bow out because of an inability to persuade enough employees to sign authorization cards. In other cases, they plunge into an election without understanding either the real concerns of the employees or the relationship between management and employees. Such actions not only cost the union financially, but lead to election losses which in turn raise questions about the very future of the labor movement.[3]

Even American workers frequently seem to make their decisions about how to vote in a union election on the basis of "instincts and other mysterious factors." One employee, when asked why he wanted a union, replied that "my minister told me unions are good." Such unreasoned support may partially explain why an increasing number of unions are decertified soon after certification.

It is the purpose of this chapter to show that the organizing process is not a mysterious nor even a sinister experience. Rather, it is systematic and quite comprehensible. If all participants have a better understanding of the process, perhaps fewer managers will be frightened by union organizing efforts and more union officials will make better use of their limited resources. American workers also may benefit by better understanding what is expected of them by those who seek their support in an organizing campaign.

STAGES OF UNION ORGANIZING

To some casual observers of organizing campaigns, the process is fairly brief--a few letters and handbills are exchanged and an election is held. As is true of most casual observers of anything, they fail to truly understand what they are seeing. There are at least seven stages of the organizing process. Although these stages overlap and not all organizing efforts follow any one pattern, there are common phases through which the organizing process evolves.

Target Identification. Someone must make the first move. Usually disgruntled employees will contact a local union office to learn how to organize a union at their place of work. Occasionally the union will make an unsolicited contact with employees at a work place, particularly if someone has decided that the work place is of strategic importance to the union or if it looks like an easy target. Once the potential target has been identified, the union official involved may do some preliminary research into the target and assign a representative to follow up the initial contact.

Interest Determination. It is important for the union to determine if the target is viable. If it is not, it is a waste of resources to actively pursue the target and a potential embarrassment for the union. A good union organizer will try to answer at least three questions during this phase: Which employees are interested in the union? Is there good employee leadership potential for the campaign? What company policies and practices may affect the organizing campaign?

Organization Development. If the union believes it has a viable target, it usually begins building an organizing committee. The potential leaders who were identified in the prior stage are now called together. A key objective of this phase is to educate the committee members. The emphasis will be on such subjects as the benefits of forming a union, the law and procedures involved in forming a union, and the issues likely to be raised by management in the campaign. According to one union official, "the ability of the committee to answer questions by other employees and to debate effectively determine whether the organizing campaign is won or lost." During this phase the committee members begin to contact other employees to determine their interest in the union and their willingness to serve on the committee.

Interest Building. Active solicitation of signed authorization cards now begins in earnest. Frequently management first becomes aware of the campaign during this period. This phase is usually marked by the campaign going public, with an exchange of leaflets, handbills, and letters. At some point in this phase the union may publicly identify the committee members as a way to protect them from possible disciplinary action by management. (Management cannot argue that it did not know who key supporters were.) Public identification also helps to build momentum in the drive for a majority of card signers. Although by law the union only needs 30 percent of the employees in the unit to sign cards in order to call for an election, most union organizers wait for at least 50 percent and usually 60-80 percent before announcing that they represent a majority of the employees. Once this announcement is made, the union usually will demand recognition as the bargaining representative for the employees. If management has a "good faith" doubt about the majority status and declines to recognize the union, the union will petition the National Labor Relations Board for recognition.

NLRB Hearing. As discussed in Chapter 2 the National Labor Relations Act does not require employee representatives to be selected by any particular procedure. However, the act does provide that one of the methods can be an election. In most cases the Board orders an election, but before an election can be conducted a hearing usually is held. The hearing officer will seek to answer the following questions: Is there a question of representation? Does the employer qualify for coverage by the NLRB? Is the union a labor organization within the meaning of the act? Do any existing collective bargaining agreements or prior elections bar the petitioner from representation? Is the proposed unit appropriate? Are there questions of eligibility of certain employees? Is there a sufficient showing of employee interest to justify an election? Once the questions have been answered to the satisfaction of the regional director of the NLRB, an election date is set.

The Campaign. The actual campaign usually is characterized by a steady exchange of appeals to influence the employees' vote, culminating in a formal election. During this period management must prepare a voters eligibility list for the NLRB and post notices of the election and a sample ballot in conspicuous places throughout the premises. The election is held 30 days after the NLRB order.

Postelection. Once the votes are cast and counted, any party who believes the Board's election standards were not met may, within five days after the tally of ballots has been furnished, file objections to the election with the regional director of the NLRB. If the objections are found to be substantial, a new election may be ordered or a hearing conducted to determine the validity of the objections. If no objections are filed or the objections ultimately are dismissed, the NLRB issues a certification of the results of the election and both parties prepare to negotiate their first contract.

THE FOUR T's OF ORGANIZING CAMPAIGNS

If the participants are to be well prepared for an organizing effort, they need to know not only the phases through which they will pass, but also the decisions they will have to make. Most decisions that must be made in a union organizing campaign can be generalized under the four T's: themes, talent, tactics, and timing. These categories are equally applicable for managers and union leaders.

Campaign Themes

There are three levels of decisions that must be made regarding management's themes. First, should management oppose the union organizing effort? In making this decision, managers should consider the costs and benefits of such opposition. The conduct of a campaign usually results in at least four short-run costs: legal services, lost employee time, reduced productivity during the campaign period, and loss of executive time. In a 1975 study, it was estimated that the per-employee cost for a company of 100 employees was $123.60, and for a company of 1,000 employees, $101.60 for a total of $101,000.[4] Since these calculations assumed an average rate of $3.50 per hour plus $1 for fringe benefits, and since the current average hourly earnings for private, nonsupervisory employees is $7.55,[5] the campaign costs are considerably higher today.

In addition to the short-run costs, there are long-run costs such as the effect on the employee-management relationship. If the union wins, what will be the effect of the campaign on the union-management relationship? Will the union respect management for waging a tough fight or try to make it pay for its actions? To offset management's campaign, will union organizers have to make big promises that they will have to make good on during the first contract negotiations? What will be the effect of the campaign on the relationship between first-line managers and bargaining unit employees? If the union is defeated, will it be back next year? If the election is close, will the divided work force create an unstable labor situation? Will a more militant union seek representation next time?

The major advantages of remaining nonunion, as seen by managers, are the avoidance of strikes, lower labor costs, greater management flexibility that results in greater efficiency, lower turnover rates, competitive advantages in hiring, less managerial time spent in grievances and contract negotiations, and the satisfaction of certain emotional needs of top management.[6]

If management decides to oppose the union organizing effort, another decision must be made: What type of opposition should be mounted? These seem to be four basic campaigns that managers run.

Antiunion. Some companies, although probably a declining number, run a totally antiunion campaign. The theme of the campaign stresses the "evils" of unionism. Every effort is made to link unions with whatever else employees may think is bad. In the 1950s and 1960s some managers, particularly in the South, tried to tie unions to integration and civil rights. In more recent campaigns the connection is to alleged union corruption or communist connections.

Anti This Union. In some cases managers do not oppose all unions but "this one" in particular. In the words of one manager's letter, quoting from a speech by the union president, "This union has issued more strike authorizations and supported more strikes in the last ten years than any other union in the . . . industry." Later, in a captive audience speech, management reinforced the point that they were not antiunion, just this union in this company:

> A union has its place in our society in certain industries where people could not get any benefits, where people were ill-treated. But this company has had an outstanding record with our people and does not need a union.

Procompany. The procompany campaign is much less likely to attack the union or unions in general, but will stress the positive aspects of the company. Rather than running against the union's record, management runs on its own record. In one manager's letter, the stress was on how good the company's benefits were in comparison to a union plant:

> We believe you and your family should examine for yourselves the employee benefits of the only . . . company organized by Local #34. Here is a factual comparison of your benefits with [company name] compared with the benefits of the only . . . company organized by Local #34 for twenty years. . . .

The letter contained a comparison on 24 different benefits, ranging from holidays to cafeteria service.

You Have Rights But . . . In a few campaigns managers will run a very low key campaign in which employees are asked to vote against the union but are informed that it is really up to them. A typical letter is one that was written by the president of the company that tried to correct some union charges:

> You have the right to deal with us directly without the intervention of a union on any matter, both with respect to either present benefits or the consideration of any new or additional benefits. . . . We wish to make it perfectly clear, however, that you have the right to join a union. You have just as much right not to join.

Most management campaigns seem to be a combination of "anti this union" and "procompany" with an occasional element of the other two themes. Sometimes, what starts out as a "you have rights but . . . " or "procompany" campaign becomes a more "anti this union" campaign. Often there appears to be little attention given to a consistent campaign theme.

A third level of decisions involving the theme concerns what specific issues will be stressed in the campaign. According to Julius Getman's study of 33 elections, the average company campaign contains 30 issues and the union campaign 25, but employees usually recall only three company issues and between two and three union issues.[7] As John Kilgour suggests, "It is therefore imperative that the company identify those items central to the employees and not waste time and resources on matters that are not."[8]

In an "antiunion" or "anti this union" campaign, one frequently sees at least one of five very common issues stressed, and occasionally all of them. First, there is the strike record of the union. The objective is to raise the fear of potentially lost income and work place unrest among workers. Some firms make the point by illustrating how long it would take to recoup the lost income from a strike, given varying wage increases, or the amount of money that employees lose each day of a strike. Some companies like to focus on the specific strike record of the union. One company mailed a statement to all employees that listed all strikes called by the national union in the last five years. The list was four-and-one-half feet long.

A relatively common issue is corruption or abuses in the unions or in this particular union. One company stressed to employees:

> The Senate hearings some years ago exposed
> the "goings-on" in the [union's name]. . . .
> The complete, official Government report of
> every word of this testimony is avail- able
> in our Personnel Office. . . . It clearly
> indicates what was said and what was not said
> but hidden behind the Fifth Amendment.

Some firms reportedly make use of various clipping bureaus that claim they can produce "the criminal record of anyone in the labor movement, going back 27 years."[9] Frequently the information they use to smear unions is from the McClellan Hearings in the late 1950s—hardly relevant to a current organizing campaign. Some managers like to cite examples of union rules or punishments that appear autocratic or endangering of personal liberties. One manager found a case where a member was fined for "going to church instead of union meetings." The union meetings were on Sunday morning and the bylaws required any member missing three out of five to be fined $5.

Related to the issue of corruption or abuses is the issue of trust or union competency. Some managers try to identify campaign issues where the union has been in error, thus stressing the union's unreliability. It has been reported that this is the most common mistake of unions: basing a campaign on false issues.[10]

Another common issue is the cost of unions. This issue may stress such costs as strikes and rules that restrict members' behavior, but usually it focuses on the cost of dues, membership fees, and possible special assessments. Some managers like to mail employees two checks on payday, one reflecting the amount of dues that will be deducted each pay period and the other the amount of money each person could take home if dues had been deducted. In some cases unions have made the dues issues even more significant by raising dues during the campaign and failing to openly acknowledge it. In one campaign this allowed management to raise the question: "What will the minimum dues be next time?"

A very common issue is that unions cannot guarantee employees anything. In some cases there is an implied threat that existing benefits may be lost. As one management letter stressed:

> In the event that the union ever got into [company name], your company would only be obligated to "bargain in good faith." But all matters of wages and benefits would have to be bargained for. It is perfectly possible that in conceding one demand other existing benefits could be reduced.

In another communication in the same campaign, management pointed out the NLRB's position regarding "making promises of promotion, pay raises, or other benefits to influence an employee vote by a party capable of carrying out any such promises." The statement went on to note that "the law recognized that the union is not a party capable of carrying out any such promises. As a result, the law allows the union to make any promises it wishes because they cannot carry their promises out."

An issue that is occasionally stressed is the losing record of the union. One management letter proclaimed that "THE [union name] IS A LOSER'S UNION!" It went on to identify several recent elections within the industry that the union has lost. The letter concluded: "DON'T JOIN A SINKING SHIP!"

In a more positive campaign, managers stress their best side, often comparing their wages or benefits with firms that look less attractive. Companies may compare themselves with less-favorable area or industry employers, or if those two categories do not make the employer look good, they may stress how good they look relative to "other firms our size" or "other firms organized by this union." One particular benefit that employers like to emphasize is job security--particularly the absence of layoffs in the company's history or the growth of the company, which suggests future promotion opportunities and the unlikelihood of layoffs.

In some cases, management will stress how good the employee-management relationship is, how they are "one big happy family." This is usually combined with the assertion that we do not need an outsider intruding into our family affairs. If it is true, it can be an effective issue, but too often managers make such claims when most of the evidence suggests otherwise. One campaign that stressed the "homey feeling" at the plant never seemed to acknowledge that 50 percent of the family was leaving home each year and 60 percent had to belong to two families to support themselves. In other cases, employers stressed the desire to avoid outsiders (meaning unions), and then turned around and brought in outsiders in the form of consultants or lawyers to help them oppose the wishes of some family members.

A final issue that should be acknowledged is one that is occasionally used when all else has failed. Managers sometimes play upon the dislike that many people have for change--any change--and their fear of the unknown. They may admit to the employees that "we have made a lot of mistakes but give us one more chance." This is usually combined with claims that "you can always elect the union next year if we fail," and "if you did vote the union in, you will probably be stuck with it as long as you work here."

Union officials must make the same basic theme-related decisions as managers. First, they must decide whether to pursue a lead or invitation. As discussed earlier, in most cases the union is invited in by a group of disgruntled employees. In other cases, the union may invite itself in because of what it sees as an easy target or one that is strategically important. However the union initially contacts potential members, its organizers need to consider the first impression they make. In one case, employees contacted eight different unions. In describing the one they chose, an employee said, "They didn't promise us the sky, they just told us that they would do anything to help and explained what they thought they could do for us, and how they would do it. Some of the unions promised so much that I just couldn't believe it. The [union's name] boys were straightforward and honest, and they didn't promise the moon."

Since so much has been made of the declining percentage of union victories, and since unions are having to become increasingly budget conscious in a period of high inflation, unions might be well advised to select more carefully their campaign targets. At least one large union has centralized the coordination of its major campaign, leaving the smaller campaigns to regional and local officials. In addition, criteria were established to screen proposals for organizing campaigns that included estimated investment or cost of the campaign (expected duration, staffing level, and per-day costs), the degree of industry control a successful campaign could create (a dominant position was sought and, if possible, a proprietary position as the only union engaged in collective bargaining with a multiplant employer), and ability of establish a strategic toehold and preserve options for later organizing activity. Although it was important to justify the costs in most campaigns, if the campaign was felt to be vital to the union's interest, cost did not prevent the union from obtaining approval from its president.

Unlike management campaigns, there appear to be few variations in themes, but considerable variation in issues stressed. The basic theme is almost always the short-comings of management and the need for organizing as a way of forcing management to deal with these problems, that is, strength in unity. Although in many campaigns there may be attention focused on the general benefits of unionism, most of the effort is devoted to identifying specific short-comings of management and how this particular union can redress these shortcomings. In other words, the key is to find an issue. Most campaigns seem to fall in four broad categories of issues: compensation, poor management practices, worker control, and job security.

Compensation

In the words of one veteran union organizer, "Wages are an issue in any campaign, it's just a matter of degree." Frequently it is simply a question of inadequate or un-competitive pay. In one case, two employees who were working nights and weekends to make enough money to pay their bills contacted several unions to see what could be done about their situation. Some employees in this plant had not received an increase in several years.

Occasionally the wage issue is difficult to sell. In one campaign, even though unionized employees at another company plant were receiving from $1.60 to $3.00 more per hour, the wage issue did not catch. According to one of the organizers involved, "Evidently these people can't imagine rates . . . being from $1.60 to $3.00 more than theirs; it's too far out." In another case, the wage issue proved difficult because certain workers would not admit that they were low paid or that they had not received a wage increase in years.

In addition to the issue of wage levels, there frequently is an issue to be made over confusing or subjective wage systems. For example, merit systems are often perceived as being influenced by favoritism. In one plant where 500 out of 1,200 employees received a merit increase, an issue became "what happened to the other 700 people. . . . Through a Union Contract all of the employees get the increases. No favorite groups." Also, incentive systems can create an issue. In the company just described, prior to an organizing campaign 50 employees met with the personnel manager to complain that as a result of a change in the speed of a conveyor, only on one day in several months had they been able to meet the new standard, and never had reached the level where incentive earnings became effective. No action was taken on their complaint.

Gaps in benefits or poor administration of benefits can be a major issue. According to one labor consultant, "The most volatile [benefit] from a union organizing standpoint is lack of long-term disability insurance. . . . Where an employee is disabled and not adequately compensated, the union organizer is given a highly emotional rallying cry of 'Remember what happened to poor old Joe'." [11]

In a relatively large financial institution's organizing campaign, a key issue became the absence of an employer-paid hospital and medical care program. Although smaller firms in the same area had such a program, it was opposed by the firm's largest stockholder on the grounds that the good of the country would be served best if everyone paid their own medical bills. An inadequate pension plan became a key issue in a large manufacturing plant. The union raised the question of "Why hasn't the Company told you about the 89¢ a month pension they gave one of the employees?"

Job Security

When employees feel their jobs are threatened, it is not unusual to see an organizing effort occur. In some cases where an acquisition has occurred, particularly where the business has been locally controlled and now a conglomerate purchases the operation, employees often have real fears about the degree of commitment the new management will have to the business and especially to the employees. In other cases, a new management team may raise fears in employees' minds. Will the new managers be as interested in employees as was the prior management team? Where technological changes are occurring that downgrade people's skills and raise the possibility of fewer workers needed, it is common to find employees more receptive to an organizing appeal. When there are layoffs, some employees become particularly concerned about job security, especially if the layoffs do not take seniority into account. The common interpretation of such layoffs is that management is showing favoritism.

Poor Management Practices

A variety of management practices can become good union organizing issues. Perhaps the most common is inconsistency by some managers in handling such matters as discipline, wage increases, and promotions. Too often a few or even an individual manager can be responsible for a large number of disgruntled employees. A major issue in one campaign was the factory superintendent who had complete authority over the production work force. It was felt that he played one employee against another, and that any employee who went over his head would be fired. In another case a very successful manager, from a profit standpoint, was viewed as autocratic and often unfair in his treatment of people. Even though annual turnover in his department was 35 percent, the highest in the company, top management's response was "I know [manager's name] has problems with people, but with his performance . . . I think we'll just have to live with his people problems."

Another issue predicted by management actions concerns trust of management. In one large organizing campaign, a key union issue was that management could not be trusted. Not only did managers violate the National Labor Relations Act by committing several unfair labor practices, but managers used incorrect information about the union in some of their letters to employees, which the union was able to refute.

Worker Control

In this period in American history, people want a greater say about conditions that affect them. This is particularly true in matters of work.[12] Some unions seem to be successful in attacking the lack of participation that employees have in the area of wages, hours, and working conditions. In one campaign, the union attacked a "complaint review board" for lack of worker representation. It claimed that "The scales of justice will . . . be balanced . . . with equal representation by having a grievance committee, which is composed of workers from among your own ranks, elected by you." Later the union attacked the lack of employee input into compensation decisions, claiming "We trust that after November 16 . . . intelligent management will sit down across the bargaining table with an intelligent elected union committee and negotiate a workable contract which cannot be broken by either party."

Campaign Talent

A second fundamental set of campaign decisions that top management should make is who should be involved in the campaign. One decision involves whether to bring outsiders, such as special consultants or lawyers, into the campaign. Not only should the cost of such services be considered, but also the impact that such talent can have on the campaign. In some campaigns the outsiders become an issue, particularly when the union knows their usual tactics or fees. As pointed out earlier, the outsider can reduce the effectiveness of management's claim not to need an outsider in the employee-management relationship. An additional consideration is the relationship between the personnel office and the outsiders. In one case where a consulting firm was used, top management reportedly fired its personnel manager, who had 18 years service with the company, allegedly because of his opposition to some of the consultants' tactics. Less than two months before the election, management dropped the consultants and had to borrow an "expert" from its parent company. Certainly if management plans to go to the brink of an illegal campaign and yet not commit any unfair labor practices, and if the managers in decisionmaking positions have never been involved in a campaign, then good legal advice is essential.

Once management has resolved the issue of the outsider, decisions must be made regarding the insiders to be used. At what level should the campaign be controlled? Some firms allow local personnel to control, whereas in others a corporate personnel team takes charge. Should one person make most decisions or should a committee be appointed? Should line managers or personnel control the campaign? What role should first-line managers play? Some firms seem to try to sell first-line management on the idea that it is their jobs that will be dramatically changed if the union is successful. Who should handle various group meetings or write letters to the employees?

The choice of people to meet with employees can be critical. In one company the president was chosen to meet with all employees since he was well liked. Over the years the company had used the president to communicate with employees whenever there was good news to report as a conscious way of strengthening his relationship with the employees. After a captive audience speech in which he urged the employees to vote against the union, several came to him and apologized for those who were creating trouble for his company. In another campaign an assistant personnel director was used and in one meeting, after being asked why the company did not pay its employees more, he replied, "If you want more money, go out and get yourself an education like I did." According to an internal union memo, "This really ticked the whole bunch off--signers and nonsigners. We hope they'll keep using him."

A fundamental decision that union leaders must make in any campaign is who and how many people to assign to the campaign. Unfortunately for some unions, little thought is given to the qualifications of organizers. One director of organizing who had thought about the organizers to be assigned to a key southwestern campaign described the traits he liked in an organizer: "Sincere, dedicated, willing to work long, hard hours, and has a pleasant personality and a southern accent. Northerners think it's amusing and Southerners can't understand anyone who talks faster than them." As more and more women and minorities enter the work force, it becomes increasingly important that unions be sensitive to these changes when choosing organizers.

According to a top union official, the decision on how many organizers to use in a campaign is affected by such factors as:

The geographical area over which the employees are spread. The larger the area to be covered, the more organizers needed.

The number of simultaneous campaigns. If the union is involved in several campaigns at once, it can assign fewer organizers to any one campaign.

The employer's labor relations policies. More organizers are used in campaigns where the employer has a reputation for violating the law.

The stage of the campaign. Fewer people are needed in the early stages.

As indicated earlier, the key to a successful union campaign is the in-plant organizing committee. According to one union official, weekly meetings of the committee "turn interested employees into organizers on the job." Not only does he want committee members organizing on the job, but also making house calls, helping to obtain a list of all employees, gathering information on company policies, and communicating information to and from employees.

Frequently unions are trapped into using as key members of the organizing committee the employees who initially contacted them. In one campaign a key organizer became one of management's best issues. He not only was rude in his approach to some employees, but also provoked a fight with a fellow employee on company property while passing out union literature. Employees who are respected by many employees, willing to take personal risks, and are mobile, such as maintenance employees, seem to make good organizers.

In some cases unions make use of outside groups to help in an organizing effort. Sometimes union organizers find it useful to invite local politicans to meetings as a way

of increasing interest. Contact with the local police
department may be helpful should the police be called by
the employer to break up some union activity near the
plant. In areas where various churches are strong, support
from priests and ministers can be helpful at breaking down
worker resistance to unions.

Campaign Tactics

Once the overall theme and who will be in charge of the
campaign have been decided, management attention should
focus on the tactics of achieving its overall plan. Common
tactics include letters to employees and in some cases re-
tired employees and family members, leaflets, small group
meetings between top management or first-line supervisors
and employees, identification and conversion of informal
employee leaders, captive audience speeches, posters, hand-
books, and buttons. The decisions regarding which tactics
to use should be influenced by the need for variety and impact as well as what can be done within the constraints of
a budget.

Another set of tactical decisions involves the use of
unfair labor practices to stall the election. Some employers know that the penalties associated with committing unfair labor practices are quite mild, usually a cease-and-
desist order and, even in the case of discharge, eventually
reinstatement with back pay. Since such orders can take
months and even years to process, it is quite possible for
management to effectively destroy an organizing effort or,
at the very least, signal to employees the relative
ineffectiveness of the union in dealing with management.
Before undertaking such actions, management should
recognize several disadvantages. First, if the unfair
labor practices are severe enough, management may be
ordered to bargain with the union. Second, the long-range
effect may be to enhance the chances of much more
restrictive labor legislation. Third, it provides a major
issue for the union to use in its campaign, that is,
management cannot be trusted. Fourth, such actions may
reinforce prounion sentiment by convincing employees of the
need for a union to help protect them from such practices.

In some cases employers find out quite late that an organizing effort is under way and use appeals to give themselves more time to mount a campaign. In other cases managers want to postpone the election until a more suitable
time. This is done mostly in cases where employment is
somewhat seasonal. Occasionally managers want to stall the
election until a particular time of the year so that if the
union wins, the contract will expire at a time that is to
management's advantage. In other cases, managers will stall

in the hopes of discouraging workers in their organizing efforts. Although many of the stalling campaigns postpone the election only a matter of months, one company stalled the election for two years and a contract was not reached for two more years. At least one southern campaign reportedly took 12 years from the time the union won the election until a contract was signed; all in all, it was a 14-year effort.[13] Clearly the use of such tactics has some of the same disadvantages as those cited for unfair labor practices, plus raising the issue of justice delayed being denied.

One aspect of the NLRB procedures that should be carefully studied by both management and labor is the hearing to determine the appropriate bargaining unit. Both unions and managers have a substantial interest in the composition of the bargaining unit, particularly regarding whether it should be a broad unit, such as all retail stores in an urban area, or narrow, such as one individual store. The composition may greatly affect the outcome of the election since both parties may have reliable sources of information about the intention of employees long before a secretballot election is held. Occasionally managers make shortterm decisions about who should be included in the unit based solely on how they are likely to vote. If the union wins, management may regret having ceded these people to the union. Even if the union loses, employees who thought of themselves as management but were categorized by management as members of the bargaining unit along with hourly employees, may feel sold out by top management, thereby creating a morale problem. Many small units may mean that labor and management are constantly involved in negotiations, but that no single unit can close down the entire operation with a strike. One large unit may reduce the time spent in negotiations, but it makes it possible for the entire operation to be shut down by a strike.

Another tactical decision that top management needs to consider prior to a campaign is how it will deal with the first evidence of an organizing effort. If the first evidence is a demand for recognition based on authorization cards, without prior thought a local manager may accidentially recognize the union. Usually the first evidence is finding a union leaflet or spotting someone passing out leaflets either on or near company property. The reaction of some managers is to prevent such activities on company property. Yet, if management has not established a non-solicitation rule in advance and applied it in all cases, including charitable _organizations, the union cannot be denied such access without committing an unfair labor practice.

Another set of tactical decisions concerns the period immediately after the election. If the union wins the election, will management agree to bargain, refuse to bargain, or bargain very tough either as a way of breaking the union or appealing the NLRB's earlier decision regarding the bargaining unit?* If management wins, what will it do about key union supporters? Will management introduce immediate changes in wages, hours, or working conditions so as to correct deficiencies before another election, or will it avoid such changes as a way of punishing employees or to avoid conditioning employees to expect such improvements after each organizing campaign?

Many of the tactical decisions faced by unions are similar to those described for managers. This includes not only the methods for communicating with employees, but also bargaining unit composition. There are, however, some unique decisions that must be made by union leaders.

A major set of decisions concerns the use of authorization cards. First, how should they be solicited? Some organizers prefer to solicit them individually through one-to-one contact by committee members either in their department, at home, or through small group meetings. Others are willing to allow the cards to be attached to leaflets that are distributed. Whereas the latter tactic is much less personal, it is a quicker way to reach everyone. A second card-related decision is if and when to present the cards to management and ask for recognition. Although it is possible to go directly to the NLRB and schedule an election if 30 percent of the unit have signed cards, most organizers prefer at least 60 percent and frequently a higher percentage. Also, some organizers prefer to approach management before going to the Board, even though it is most unlikely that management will recognize the union without an election. According to one union official, the employer often responds to the demand for recognition with a wage increase to demonstrate that the employees do not need a union to obtain such benefits. They know that the NLRB is much less likely to declare such an action an unfair labor practice before the petition is filed. For the union, this not only prevents the employer from saying that if the union has not filed its petition a raise would have been possible, but it also benefits the workers and gives the union the opportunity to claim, "look what we got for you and we are not even certified yet."

---

*As indicated in Chapter 2, one of the few ways a regional director's decision regarding the bargaining unit can be reviewed by the full Board is for management to refuse to bargain with the certified union and raise the bargaining unit issue as a defense.

Another tactic that some organizers use, particularly when confronted with a management that commits unfair labor practices, is to file many unfair labor practice charges in an effort to harass and increase the legal costs of the employer. According to one international representative, "nothing could be more frustrating and costly to an employer."

In large units, it can become difficult to keep track of who has and has not been visited or talked to. Some unions make use of a card system and record such information as employee name, department, shift, social affiliations, gripes about work, attitude toward the union, and date of the housecall. These data can be useful in developing a department diagram of the plant so as to better identify how widespread the committee and supporters are within the plant.

A final tactical issue for unions relates to after the election. If the union wins, does it push for a strong first contract as a way to justify itself to the new members, or does it try to settle quickly and moderately so as not to push management into a union-breaking posture? Does it push for significant economic gains or settle for smaller gains with a strong union security clause so as to assure its survival at the work place? If the union loses, should it try again in 12 months? What should be done to reassure its supporters that they will not be abandoned during the next few months?

Campaign Timing

As with political elections, momentum and timing are important factors, and yet they are often overlooked by managers. Only in one campaign studied did managers consciously consider momentum, and then only after the campaign was well under way. For weeks the union would attack various management practices and management would respond by "correcting the union." In one union attack, the leaflet concluded "we will await your reply." The vice-president of personnel acknowledged that when he read that sentence, he knew that he had been conducting a reactive campaign. From that point on he took the initiative by raising his own issues and ignoring the union's issues. Ultimately the union began to react to his issues. One very successful union organizer indicated that his policy was never to react to company literature. Instead we would take the initiative in developing issues and rely on the in-plant committee to get the workers to discuss the union's issues rather than management's issues.

A well-organized campaign schedules in advance the tactics it plans to use. This is particularly true if one is trying to build momentum and wisely schedule the time of top management. One company reported that as soon as the date for an election was set, a management committee met to develop a detailed campaign schedule. They began by deciding what activity they would like to have as the last thing before the election, and then worked backward for the remaining four weeks. As discussed earlier, some companies will use NLRB procedures to stall elections so as to provide themselves with sufficient time to mount a campaign or to hold an election at a time they feel is advantageous to them in terms of both an election and contract negotiations.

There are a few unique timing decisions that unions need to consider. For example, when should leaflets first be distributed? Although they may generate some interest early on, they also tip management off to the campaign. In one campaign involving only 40 employees, the union organizers were involved for six months and had a majority signed up before ever handing out leaflets. It was not until the first leaflet was handed out at the plant entrance that management had any idea that there was union activity in its plant. Even then it believed that the large majority of its employees did not want a union. Six weeks later the union won by a 32 to 5 vote.

Another timing decision is when to set up a permanent employee organizing committee. According to one union director of organizing:

If the potential leaders necessary to form a representative Volunteer Organizing Committee cannot be found, the organizer might as well acknowledge the strong possibility that he will not be able to conduct a successful campaign. There is no reason for wasting time and money if influential employees cannot be interested in the union or are opposed to it. Once the organizer has that information, the site survey is complete. He is ready to recommend that the organizing effort be dropped or to call his potential leaders together in a first meeting to form a Volunteer Organizing Committee.

Once the committee has been established, another decision is when and how to make it public. Some unions use buttons to identify the committee. In the same union described above, the director of organizing liked to

pop the committee out all at once. My favorite method is to use leaflets, like posters, with pictures of the committee on it. It's great with the employees. How many times in a worker's life does he get his picture anywhere? When he graduates from high school, when he gets married, and when he joins the union is the third!

This technique has the added advantage of providing protection to the activists since it cannot be argued that management did not know who the leaders were. Also, it weeds out those members who are not committed enough to have their roles revealed to management. A disadvantage is that it may become necessary for each new leaflet to show more pictures so that the campaign does not appear to be stagnant.

NOTES

[1]   Carl Gustav Jung, <u>Modern Man in Search of a Soul</u> (New York: Harcourt, Brace, 1950), p. 69.

[2]   Urban C. Lehner, "As Union Organizers Get to Millidgeville, Ga., The Mayor Holds an Unusual Welcoming Party," <u>Wall Street Journal</u>, February 29, 1980.

[3]   Labor on the Defensive," <u>Forbes</u>, February 20, 1978, pp. 44-48, and "Are Unions Losing Their Clout?" <u>U.S. News and World Report</u>, October 4, 1976, pp. 29-32.

[4]   Woodruff Imberman, "How Expensive is an NLRB Election?" <u>MSU Business Topics</u>, Summer 1976, p. 15.

[5]   U.S. Department of Labor, Bureau of Labor Statistics, <u>Employment and Earnings</u>, April,1982, p. 108.

[6]   Fred K. Foulkes, <u>Personnel Policies in Large Nonunion Companies</u>, (Englewood Cliffs, N.J.: Prentice-Hall, 1980), pp. 58-61.

[7]   Julius G. Getman, Stephen G. Goldberg, and Jeanne B. Herman, <u>Union Representation Elections: Law and Reality</u> (New York: Russell Sage Foundation, 1976), pp. 74-76.

[8]   John G. Kilgour, "Responding to the Union Campaign," <u>Personnel Journal</u>, May 1978, p. 242.

[9]   Ron Chernow, "The New Pinkertons," <u>Mother Jones</u>, May 1980, p. 58.

[10]   T. M. Rohan, "Would a Union Look Good to Your Workers?" <u>Industrial Workers</u>, January 26, 1976, p. 41.

[11]   Thomas M. Rohan, "Would a Union Look Good to Your Workers?" <u>Management Review</u>, June 1976, p. 53.

12   Lawrence Ingrassia, "Nonunion Workers are Gaining Status, but so far the Talk Outweighs the Action," <u>Wall Street Journal</u>, July 24, 1980.

13   <u>Wall Street Journal</u>, February 14, 1978, p. 1.

5

ANATOMY OF A
MANAGEMENT CAMPAIGN

TABLE WARE PLASTICS, INC.

It was the afternoon of November 9, 1976. The union election was only one week away, and Dick Thornquist, vice-president of administration at Table Ware Plastics in Burlington, Massachusetts was feeling the effects of the company's eight-month campaign against the United Paperworkers and Cartonmakers of America (UPC). If the campaign failed, Thornquist's job could be dramatically changed over the next few months.

After reviewing the stack of union materials that had been issued in the last few days, Thornquist turned his attention to the week ahead. His campaign to keep the union from organizing Table Ware had gained momentum, but he realized the importance of keeping such a campaign under control. Before tomorrow's 10 o'clock meeting of his planning committee, he had to decide what action, if any, should be taken during the last week of the campaign.

Table Ware Plastics

Company Background

Table Ware Plastics was founded in the 1950s by Daniel Goldman, who was then in his early thirties. Described as "a fighter, but quiet, sensitive and likable," Goldman had a keen eye for business opportunities. While managing a branch of the family business, Goldman had noticed the counterman at a roadside ice-cream stand trying to build a banana split in a tall waxed cup. After some thought, Goldman bought a small plastic extruder and set up a one-line operation in a corner of the family plant; among other things, he made dishes for banana splits. In the first year he sold $65,000 worth of his products. Soon thereafter he incorporated Table Ware Plastics and it became a subsidiary of the family holding company, Jersey Paper Corporation. By 1966 hourly employment had reached 150 and, with strong sales prospects, Goldman moved Table Ware to a 20-acre industrial site in Burlington, Massachusetts.

Although Table Ware charged a slightly higher price than its competitors, its reputation for quality had attracted many fast food chains as customers, including McDonald's, which accounted for 10 percent of Table Ware's sales. As sales continued to increase, reaching approximately 33 percent of Jersey Paper's total sales of $170 million, new plants were added in Dorchester, Massachusetts, Greenville, New Hampshire, and Griffin, Georgia. By 1976 total hourly employment at Table Ware was 745, with approximately 528 employees located at Burlington.

All of Table Ware's plants and all but two of Jersey Paper's facilities were nonunion. However, several minor organizing attempts by unions, including the Teamsters, had been made at the Burlington plant. According to Thornquist, "I think we may have been losing touch with our people because we were growing too fast. Maybe we were beginning to look vulnerable."

In 1973 Thornquist tried to determine if the company was indeed vulnerable. He surveyed employees at Burlington to find out their specific problems and what they considered to be issues that needed the attention of management. His survey showed workers to be concerned about such matters as the lack of training programs and clear company objectives, inadequate shift differentials, poor communication about benefit programs, unfairness of certain supervisors, the retirement-income plan, the employee appraisal system, quality of supervision, and the lack of coordination and planning; finally, employees were anxious about being at the mercy of first-line supervisors. A summary question asked workers whether they were treated too easily or too harshly; answers indicated that most thought that people were treated too easily.

Thornquist began to deal with some of those problems. One year later he conducted another survey to see if things had improved. Over 90 percent of the employees had filled out the first questionnaire; a considerably smaller percentage completed the second. Responses, however, were not dissimilar. Thornquist was convinced that people in personnel lacked credibility with the work force and that there were some problems between the hourly employees and the supervisors. Although Thornquist recognized the importance of these problems, he was more concerned that management's improvements had not been perceived by the work force. Consequently, he began a concerted effort to keep the work force better informed about what was done for them. Any good news for the employees came in letters from the president of Table Ware Plastics, Dan Goldman.

In addition to the employee surveys, other innovative personnel programs were tried. These included an attractive subsidized cafeteria that could be rented by employees for a nominal fee; off-hour access to the WATS line; a three-step grievance procedure in which the final step involved appeal to a complaint review board consisting of all corporate vice-presidents; a $25 bonus for recruiting a new employee; a $50 attendance bonus; a tuition-aid program for both full-time and part-time employees; access to the company's purchasing department for the purchase of brand-name appliances at discount prices; and free popsicles. Such advantages for employees were in addition to traditional benefits: ten holidays each year; vacations of one to four weeks; a pension of $2.50 a month for each year of employment; shift differentials; time and a half for overtime (after 7.5 or 37.5 hours); double time for Sunday work; three to five days of sick leave; and insurance coverage for death and dismemberment, accidents and sickness, and basic and major medical costs. The company paid all employee premiums and part of those for dependents.

Benefits amounted to approximately 24 percent of payroll, which was lower than the industry and national averages. Although wage rates at Table Ware averaged $3.25 per hour and were a little below industry and national averages, they were competitive in the Burlington area. Total payroll costs were approximatelt 20 percent of sales. Again, Table Ware was slightly below t e i dustry average.

In the mid-1970s the Burlington work force was primarily composed of semiskilled workers. Approximately half of these workers were women. The Burlington plant was also characterized by a large number of young employees. One factor contributing to the youth of the work force had been the 1971 change in which the B shift (3 p.m. to 11 p.m.) had been split into two four-hour periods (3 p.m. to 7 p.m.; 7 p.m. to 11 p.m.). Approximately 80 percent of those on the B shift worked only four hours, thus making it possible for many high-school students to work. A major reason for the shift change had been Goldman's concern that many local young people were dropping out of school for economic reasons. Of the 100 part-time employees, 80 percent were students. Consequently, the average age of part-time employees was 19, whereas the average age for full-time employees was 29. As a rule, there was a heavy turnover of part-time employees in June; a second round of turnovers occurred in September as summer replacements returned to school.

1976 Burlington Organizing Campaign

During the first week of March 1976, one of the older maintenance mechanics, whom Thornquist had befriended on several occasions, came to his office and informed him that another employee, Walt Belanger, was circulating a petition on behalf of the United Paperworkers and Cartonmakers of America.

Immediately, Thornquist called a meeting with Goldman and three company vice-presidents. The purpose of the meeting was to inform top management of the organizing activity and to begin planning for a possible campaign. Thornquist proposed that they find out exactly what was going on and then arrange for their attorney, Larry Bennett, to meet with all first-line supervisors to acquaint them with the legal problems of an organizing campaign. If a campaign was to be run, Thornquist wanted a planning committee of six people to assist him in managing it: Garry Roberts, the plant manager; Jane Neal, director of corporate communications; Tom Gentry, personnel manager; and three production managers. He also requested the use of the corporation's art department for the duration of the campaign. The executives agreed to all of Thornquist's requests. Although some executives proposed to do anything necessary to defeat the union, their ultimate decision was to opppose the organizing effort but not even "go to the brink of what was legal."

That afternoon, Thornquist met with his committee. After bringing them up to date on the day's activities, he asked his committee members to begin talking with first-line supervisors immediately in order to find out what was going on within the work force. They scheduled another meeting for the next morning, agreeing to meet at 10 a.m. each day during the campaign in order to review the events of the prior day and plan their actions for the rest of the day.

The next morning the committee began to set up daily meetings with first-line supervisors. During the first of these meetings, Larry Bennett advised the supervisors as to the legal "dos and don'ts" of a campaign. In addition, the committee members stressed that the supervisors were the key to success in management's campaign. It was to be the supervisors' responsibility to provide daily feedback to the committee on the status of the organizing effort. In one of the early meetings, supervisors were asked to classify each of their employees as a union supporter, a company supporter, or indifferent. The results showed 60 percent to be company supporters, 10 percent union supporters, and 30 percent indifferent.

While the first supervisory meetings were being held, arrangements were made with an outside printer to print and deliver posters and leaflets with a one-day lead time. A detailed campaign plan began to be formulated.

On March 23, 1976 Thornquist sent a memo to 12 top managers with a general plan of action to counter serious union activity. His memo advised managers how to respond to such initial organizing efforts as rumors, leaflet handouts, demands for recognition, and requests for an election. It also contained a two-page summary of the plan of action to be pursued during a "real organizational drive." A key feature of the memo was an outline of tactics to be used; these included daily supervisors' meetings, information booklets for supervisors, small group meetings with employees, daily planning committee meetings, and letters to employees. The campaign letters would stress such issues as "exposé of union," fringe benefits, security, the union record, and individual wage records. In addition, Thornquist's memo included a recent article from a trade journal that told why their industry was particularly vulnerable to unionization.

Key Union Organizers

During the first few weeks of the organizing effort, it became clear that two employees, Maxwell Blackburn and Walt Belanger, were very active in the union's behalf. There were rumors that Blackburn had made the initial contact with the UPC. His father and grandfather had been strong union members; when he had been hired 18 months ago by Table Ware, it was the first time in his life he had ever worked for a nonunion employer. He was described by one management official as "steeped" in unionism.

Although Blackburn was rumored to have been the instigator, Belanger was felt to be the leader in the organizing effort. He had been hired as a maintenance mechanic in December 1972, while in his late twenties. He was an outgoing man who became very active in the company's after-hours sports program, ultimately serving as volunteer sports director. Over the past 18 months, however, Belanger's supervisor, Albert Baird, felt Belanger's attitude had deterioriated. For example, in December 1974 he had received a $.15 per hour merit increase but had refused to sign his evaluation form, saying that he deserved $.25. During 1975 he had applied for worker's compensation for an industrial accident. In March 1976 still had not been approved; although one doctor had diagnosed the injury as having occurred at work, another had attributed it to an old football injury. While Belanger was away from his job, recovering from his injury, he had been seen in a hardware store buying supplies to work on his house.

There were increasing complaints that Belanger had carried his interest in sports over to his working hours. He had been seen visiting parts of the plant at times when his duties did not require his presence in those areas. Some supervisors complained that Belanger was interfering with the employees in their departments.

In spring 1975 Belanger had been warned about his activities during working hours, and he had agreed to change. Although he gave up his role of sports director, he soon reverted back to his old behavior. According to his supervisor, he began to "hold back" in performing certain repair jobs and frequently "took twice as long as it would normally take to do any job." His supervisor spoke to him again and indicated that he might hope for a supervisory job if he would "square away" and break his "bad habits," but Belanger later commented, "They're going to have to take me as I am. I'm not going to change my ways."

In an effort to help Belanger change his attitude, Thornquist enrolled him in a special course in interpersonal relationships at company expense. By December 1975, however, when his performance was reviewed, his supervisor refused to recommend a merit increase and recommended to Thornquist that Belanger be discharged. Thornquist declined to fire him. By March 1976 Belanger had become the most visible union organizer in the plant.

On April 26, 1976 Thornquist sought out Belanger to inform him that he had heard rumors of Belanger's union activity:

> Walt, I think we have leveled with each other over the years and I'd like to be straight with you now. There's a rumor going around that you're trying to get signatures to bring in a union. I want you to know that I'm not asking you whether this is true. Even if it is, you have the right to do it; but if it is true, I just want you to know that you can only get signatures through this kind of solicitation during nonwork hours.

When Belanger started to deny his involvement, Thornquist added, "Walt, I told you: I'm not asking you whether you are involved or not. In fact, I don't want to listen to your comments on it." For the next half hour they talked about Belanger's feelings toward his supervisor and his worker's compensation case.

The next day Thornquist confronted Blackburn, telling him that he had "heard a rumor about his activities and merely wanted to let him know that he had heard it and that he wanted to make sure he understood his rights and restrictions in this matter." Again there was a strong denial in spite of the fact that Thornquist emphasized that he did not want to hear such denials. After a few minutes of conversation, Blackburn stated:

> My foreman is the best boss I've ever worked for. He has always been fair to me. And this company has treated me very well since I've worked here. I've been through it before and I'd be foolish to try to do any organizing in a plant like this.

Start of the Letter Campaign

By late April Thornquist could feel a change in the attitude of the work force. A walk through the plant or a visit to the cafeteria gave him a strong sense of increasing tensions. It seemed to him as though the employees were beginning to measure their words and were cautious about whom they talked to. On April 28, 1976 Thornquist broke his silence. In a letter to all employees, he urged them to be skeptical of those asking for signatures:

> We urge you to ask those employees who are asking you to sign the cards the following questions:
>
> 1. What are the actual (not promised) rates being paid by companies in this area who have this union?
>
> 2. Tell us how this union will insure our security and what is the record of security of those companies who have this union?
>
> 3. Why are you trying to organize our company? What will you gain personally?
>
> After they have given you their answers, we suggest you check these questions out on your own to make sure of the facts. You can get these facts by contacting your foreman or me.

Remember these cards mean that you will be authorizing outside people to deduct money from your pay and can guarantee you nothing in return.

You cannot be forced to sign one of these cards; you have the right to ask for the return of your card even if you have signed it.

If you are refused the return of your card, you can report this to the labor relations board.

We strongly urge you not to turn your future and the future of your friends over to outsiders. Table Ware is a healthy company, let's keep it that way.

On May 3 Thornquist received a memo from one of the first-line supervisors who complained that Belanger, while on company time, had asked four of the employees to sign union cards. The supervisor adamantly requested that Thornquist take action so that he could do his work in peace without future interruptions from Belanger. Later that day, Thornquist issued a written warning to Belanger.

The same day, Thornquist sent a letter to all part-time employees encouraging them to consider the impact of a union:

As our Part-Timers, you have some special questions to be answered. I suggest that you ask the union organizer the following questions:

1. If the United Paperworkers Union came into our plant, would a part-time worker have to pay the same initiation fee as a full-time worker?

2. If the union makes its members pay regular monthly membership dues of $6.00 a month or $72.00 a year, would a part-time employee have to pay the same amount as a full-time employee?

3. Do any of the other companies in this area who have contracts with the Paperworkers Union provide regular part-time jobs? If they do, how many?

4. Can the Paperworkers Union guarantee me any wage increases or additional benefits?

Thornquist concluded by stating, "In my opinin you are better off without any union here at Table Ware Plastics. Think this over carefully. Again, I urge all part-time workers, as well as all our other employees, to refuse to sign any union cards."

During the next few days, the UPC handed out a variety of leaflets at the plant gates. One leaflet identified 11 other plastic manufacturers whose employees belonged to UPC. Another stressed that there would be "no initiation fee for any employee now working for the company" and that "dues are only four dollars a month and one dollar of that stays with your local union." The leaflet closed:

> Remember . . . the law protects any benefits you now have. One thing to keep in mind is that if the union does not do the job for you, you can vote them out the same way you voted them in, but you have to wait one year. Sign the enclosed card, and we will petition for an election in the very near future.

This leaflet was accompanied by a flyer answering such questions as: "What will my dues be with the UPC-AFL-CIO?" "Will I have to pay any initiation fees?" "How will our union contract be negotiated?" "Who is the union negotiating committee?" Other leaflets stressed the "dues" employees were paying to Table Ware in the form of "lost benefits."

On May 16 and 17, Thornquist responded to several of the earlier union leaflets (see Exhibits 5.1 and 5.2 in the Appendix to this Chapter). Over the next few weeks the union and management issued still more letters. The union stressed the advantages of "contract protection" and the "pay, security, and human dignity" that could be achieved through collective bargaining. Management responded by emphasizing the "sound and _independent_ relationship that has been built up over the years."

In late June campaign boredom seemed to set in among the workers. Whereas employees had been excited about the campaign during its first days, supervisors were reporting that now they were beginning to be turned off. Both the company and the union were accused of "playing games" and "acting pretty silly." Some supervisors felt that the company was beginning to lose the respect of its employees. One employee summed it up when he told a member of management, "We thought you were above this sort of thing."

After June 30 the campaign became much more general. The UPC attacked Table Ware's complaint review board for unequal representation:

> The scales of justice are rather unbalanced when a Table Ware _worker_ faces a large corporation with approximately 20 plants and offices throughout the country.

Your best protection is working under a United Paper-workers and Cartonworkers contract. The scales of justice will then be balanced . . . by having a <u>grievance committee</u>, which is composed of workers from among your own ranks, <u>elected by you</u>. This committee would be accompanied by an international representative from UPC.

Thornquist responded with a defense and an attack of his own (see Exhibit 5.3 in the Appendix to this Chapter). One week later the union's material focused on Thornquist alone:

WELL.....WELL MR. "DICK" THORNQUIST!

You have been writing letters to the workers of Table Ware Plastics in answer to the leaflets distributed by the UPC representatives.

We do not wish to reply to some of your letters, especially the ones that refer to the UPC constitution, as we are willing to let the UPC constitution speak for itself, and, incidently, we are proud of the UPC constitution as it was voted on by the membership of UPC--"Nothing dictatorial about that Mr. Dick."

Speaking of facts "Mr. T" and your contention that UPC is not telling the truth, <u>let us discuss pensions to start with</u>. If you want your employees to have all the facts "Mr. T," why not tell your employees how much of a pension credit you have in the profit sharing fund?

Is it more than the $100.00 per month pension that your employees will receive after 40 years of service?

"Let's not be tricky******Dick"
"Just make a fair comparison."

An immediate response from Dan Goldman (see Exhibit 5.4 in the Appendix to this Chapter) was followed by an open letter from the union to Goldman:

Your recent "undated" letter that was sent to all your "<u>Fellow Workers</u>" of Table Ware Plastics was worthy of study and worthy of a reply.

<u>First</u> we would like to clear up one point that you repeatedly stressed in your letter and this is--Yes we are professional union representatives. This we are quite proud of . . . but . . . <u>May we now ask you a question</u> . . . Do you hire professional people to represent you--<u>Such as attorneys--professional sales people--and last but not least--professional industrial relations representatives</u>?

The reason we are here at Table Ware Plastics is due to a request of a large number of your "Fellow Workers" who have requested us to assist them in bargaining as an equal with you and your associates.

Is this an unfair request on the part of your "Fellow Workers"?

You, along with Mr. Thornquist continue to stress that the "outside professional organizers" are giving out a lot of lies and misstating the facts.

Was it a lie . . . was it a misstatement . . . was it degrading . . . to ask Mr. Thornquist . . . how much pension credit he had in the profit sharing fund?

We feel that your "Fellow Workers" would like to know this . . . so that they could compare this with their pension credits (40 years times $2.50 equals $100.00).

Was it degrading to inform Mr. Thornquist that we are proud of our constitution? While Mr. Thornquist was attempting to convey to your "Fellow Workers" that they would have to pay initiations--dues and assessments to the union when our constitution is quite clear on this subject.

May we ask . . . Does Table Ware Plastics pay dues or fees to any of your trade organizations and/or any other organizations?

In conclusion, Mr. Goldman, "The only product we have to sell is . . . 'Real Responsible Trade Unionism' and without this product your "Fellow Workers" have nothing to say on wages . . . insurance . . . pensions . . . fringes . . . and the related cost to each item, and an opportunity to elect their own committee and sit across the bargaining table with you and your hired professionals as an equal, the same as millions of other 'Trade Unionists' do.

We will await your reply!

During the next few weeks the union distrubuted leaflets that criticized, among other things, the company's pension plan and its group insurance plan.

On September 6, 1976 Thornquist sent a new letter to all employees. It began, "We have not responded for many weeks to the propaganda that the United Paperworkers Union has put forth, and we would not now answer their latest leaflet except for the fact that this time they have gone beyond their 'half-truth' approach and have directly given you false information: it is only to this that we will direct ourselves." The letter then identified the Table Ware medical benefits that have been understated by the union.

September 17, 1976 was Table Ware Plastics Family Day. Approximately 4,000 peole toured the plant and offices, watched the production and printing lines demonstrate how Table Ware products were made, received sample packs of products and colorful brochures, ate a truck full of hot dogs and two trucks full of ice cream, watched clowns, enjoyed musical entertainment and children's rides, and took part in a variety of contests. The festivities were handled by approximately 150 employee volunteers.

Demand for Recognition

On September 21, 1976 Table Ware Plastics received a letter from an official of the UPC. The union now claimed to represent a majority of employees at the Burlington plant. The letter also indicated that the union had filed a petition with the NLRB. Goldman immediately wrote to all employees. He informed them of the petition and indicated his conviction that the "overwhelming majority of our employees do not want any outside union in this plant." He promised to keep them "fully and accurately informed of any and all developments."

During the next few weeks the planning committee did some research. A major thrust of the effort was to examine as many UPC contracts as possible. In addition, members of the committee telephoned companies with UPC contracts and asked about their experiences. Extensive research into the strike record of the union was begun.

Daily meetings with the first-line supervisors also were renewed as a way of staying in touch with what was going on. In addition, Thornquist used the meetings to stress that the union was not fighting against the company so much as against the first-line supervisors, and that the existence of a union would change the nature of their jobs. Since many of the supervisors were related to or lived in the same neighborhood as many of the hourly employees, Thornquist believed that they could have a major impact on the work force. According to him, "the supervisor is the difference. That guy will make it or break it for us."

In late September Thornquist began to meet with hourly employees in groups of 12 to 15 for approximately an hour. He stated the company's opposition to a union and responded to questions. The first-line supervisors also were encouraged to hold frequent meetings with their employees to answer questions. To help them prepare for such meetings, Thornquist distributed a six-page memorandum with detailed information as to the items that should be discussed with employees concerning the union drive. In his memorandum he stated: "Although we wish to operate within the restrictions of the law it is imperative that you make your people aware of the great and possible dangers to them and their security if an outside union came into our company." The day before he had sent all supervisors a memorandum specifying what legally could and could not be said in discussions with employees. This four-page memo discussed, in some detail, 14 different arguments that could be presented to employees "to persuade them to keep the union out."

On October 3, 1976 Thornquist issued a new memo to all foremen. This was in response to some of the questions that had arisen in their daily meetings. Four major points were stressed: the union promise that bargaining will begin with wages and benefits at their current levels is not necessarily true; individual bargaining for raises will be prohibited under a contract; even though more part-timers means more people paying dues, the union is dedicated to the principle of "40 hours a week" and usually insists on full-time employees only; although union representatives can "make all kinds of promises" during an organizing campaign, company representatives cannot.

Walt Belanger again came to the attention of the planning committee on October 4, 1976. He was given a written warning for driving his car across a railroad track on plant property while the crossing gate was down, thus violating a standing rule of the company. Although he was one of ten employees who reportedly engaged in this violation on October 4, the supervisor told Dick Thornquist that Belanger was the only employee he had recognized.

Reports of Belanger "talking union" during working time continued. On one occasion, an employee became so enraged at Belanger's persistence that he went after him with a length of pipe and had to be restrained. The employee was given a written reprimand for his part in the affair. In another instance, Belanger tried to give a union pamphlet to an employee who was working. The employee swung at Belanger and knocked all of the pamphlets to the floor. Belanger received a written warning from Thornquist for soliciting on company time. At about the same time, another employee with several relatives working at Table Ware wrote to Thornquist complaining that Belanger and other organizers had approached her at home in the midst of a birthday party for one of her children. When she told the visitors that a party was in progress, they replied, "That's good! We can talk to the whole family."

In an October 5, 1976 memorandum to all employees, Thornquist clarified a major piece of "misinformation" being given by the union. It related to the union's contention that "if a union were to come into your company,

you would be guaranteed that you would keep your current
rates of pay and benefits, and the union would negotiate up
from there." Thornquist pointed out that "this is not
true" and that the company's only obligation was to "bargain in good faith." While he acknowledged that wages,
benefits, and working conditions were "matters of negotia-
tion . . . no agreement has to be reached." He concluded
by quoting the National Labor Relations Act itself: "The
section [8(d)] expressly provides . . . that the obligation
to bargain does not include any obligation to agree to a
proposal or require the making of a concession."

On October 6, 1976 Table Ware employees received a
short letter from the Paperworkers:

> Just recently we petitioned the National Labor
> Relations Board for a secret ballot election. Upon
> your voting for the United Paperworkers and Carton-
> makers we will sit down with your elected committee and
> the company to negotiate your first union contract.
>
> Your employer was notified by the National Labor
> Relations Board as to our intentions. They were also
> sent copies of "Notice to Employees" from the National
> Labor Relations Board to be posted inside the plant.
>
> We are attaching a copy of this notice because your
> employer did not post it. Although it is not required
> by law for the company to post this notice, we feel you
> should know your basic rights under the law.

Almost immediately, management posted the "Notice to
Employees" along with a statement that indicated:

> We have not yet met with the Board to determine any
> specific dates for the election to be held: this
> meeting will take place next week--at which time we
> will pass the information on to you.
>
> Although we felt it was too early to put up the
> National Labor Relations Board "Notice to Employees"
> before having this meeting, we are pleased that the
> union took it upon itself to send out this notice to
> you prematurely. This gives us the opportunity to
> point out a couple of very important items noted on
> this official memorandum.

The statement took specific issue with the following quote,
which was labeled as an unfair labor practice: "making
promises of promotions, pay raises, or other benefits to
influence an employee vote <u>by a party capable of carrying
out any such promises</u>." The statement went on to note that

"the law recognized that the union is not a party capable of carrying out any such promise. As a result, the law allows the union to make any promises it wishes because they cannot carry their promises out."

NLRB Hearing

On October 11 at the regional office of the NLRB in Boston, company and union representatives met with an NLRB hearing officer and quickly agreed to have the Board conduct the election on November 16, 1976. The only issue on which management anticipated disagreement with the union was the inclusion of 25 so-called lead men in the bargaining unit. Because these employees had some supervisory responsibilities, management thought they would be loyal to the company and therefore asked that they be included in the unit. The union offered no objection. After the meeting, Thornquist sent letters to all employees informing them of the day's events. He ended the letter by urging employees to "vote No on November 16."

Once the date of the election was set, employee interest in the organizing effort seemed to grow. Thornquist sensed that some of them were surprised that enough signatures for an election had been obtained. He also felt that many employees were thinking "if there is that much dissatisfaction, maybe I should look at the union again." Management's response was to develop a detailed campaign schedule. The committee began by deciding what activity would be most effective in the days right before the election. From this point, they worked backward for the intervening four weeks.

One of the first things the committee did was to identify five of the hourly workers who were considered "thought leaders." Informally, the committee tried to convince these people that it was not to their benefit to join the union. They tried to do this by raising questions in the minds of these workers about the union through conversations, letters, and posters. In addition, they helped the thought leaders anticipate union answers to questions; where possible, they pointed out unsatisfactory answers.

In the past, management usually had given wage increases at the end of the year. In many years the practice had been to announce a wage survey in October, to review individual wages at the plant in November, and to announce specific wage changes in December. However, the company had been very careful to vary this timing. In October 1976 management spread the word that the employees at the Dorchester plant would receive a $.25 per hour increase in January, but that the Burlington people would not be given an increase because the election was under way. The underlying message was clear; management could not give a wage increase without becoming vulnerable to a charge of unfair labor practice.

Management's Renewed Letter-Writing Campaign

On October 13 management's letter-writing campaign began to gain speed with a letter from Goldman to all employees, which emphasized questions they should ask the union (see Exhibit 5.5 in the Appendix to this Chapter). A few days later Thornquist sent a letter to all employees describing UPC organizing failures (see Exhibit 5.6 in the Appendix to this Chapter). The same day, posters began to appear in the plant emphasizing the theme that the UPC was a "sinking ship."

Later the same day, the union responded with a letter identifying several new UPC contracts in which

> Our new members received an average of 22¢ per hour increase in their hourly rates of pay. In addition, they received higher fringe benefits and improved working conditions. We have never, and we repeat, we have never, negotiated a new or first contract in which our new members received less or the same hourly rates of pay and fringe benefits prior to workers voting for us to represent them.

Management immediately countered with a poster reporting that the average "pay and benefits" increase in the UPC contracts reported in their letter was approximately "26¢ per hour," whereas for "the past five years the average increase in wages and benefits for Table Ware employees has been over 33¢ per hour." They urged, "Compare these and remember--to obtain these increases you have had no dues to pay, no fines to pay, no layoffs, no strikes, and no initiation fees!"

On October 25, 1976 Thornquist mailed a new letter that addressed the position of part-time employees under a UPC contract:

Want Some Interesting Figures?

9000

is the approximate number of people employed in 19 UPC-organized companies.

0

is the exact number of regular permanent part-time employees in these plants.

Do these figures indicate a group which is <u>really</u> interested in providing part-time work for people who cannot work full-time?

... <u>The UPC has made no provisions in any of these con-tracts to help you or other part-time employees.</u>

Thornquist went on to discuss the benefits of Table Ware's split shift program. He concluded: "Your vote can help insure the continuance of this program. On November 16, please vote. VOTE NO TO THE UNION!"

On October 27 the UPC issued an off-the-shelf handout identical to one that had been issued on May 16, except for the fact that minimum dues were now to be $6.00 a month, not the previously reported $4.00. Management immediately posted signs showing the May 16 handout, the October 27 handout, and a large question mark with the words, "What Will the Minimum Dues be Next Time?"

During the next week a number of union letters and leaflets appeared. An October 30 letter pointed out the higher benefits received by union employees over nonunion employees as reported by a recent Bureau of Labor Statistics study: "It shows that union employees received $1.78 more per hour than workers in nonunion places." Three days later the union informed part-time employees that "you will have equal representation after the union wins on November 16, 1976." It also reported that "approximately 31,000 is the number of people employed in 201 UPC, AFL-CIO plants in New England and many of these <u>companies employ part-time workers.</u>" UPC concluded by asking the company to identify the 19 companies referred to in its October 25 letter. The next day an open letter responded to Goldman's October 13 letter:

Your letter of October 13, 1976 sent out to all your employees certainly deserves a reply on behalf of at least a majority of your employees who have signed authorization cards for UPC, AFL-CIO.

In the second paragraph of your letter of October 13, 1976 you ask many questions as to cost--strikes--promises--and job security. We believe we have already published in a leaflet on October 27, 1976 what the cost of joining the UPC will be--so why are you so vague about this question?

On strikes--our record is quite clear as Article 11, Section 2 of our constitution provides for a 2/3 majority vote by secret ballot of those union members present and voting. Do you have this type of democracy on your Board of Directors?

To the best of our knowledge the union has made only one promise to the workers of Table Ware Plastics and that is--fair, honest and firm collective bargaining, something you are trying to <u>deny</u> your workers with your vagueness and innuendos.

When a majority of your workers at Burlington show a desire of joining UPC--is it wrong that we should have the names and addresses of your employees--the same as you have? Certainly if you can enter the homes of your employees by mail or in person--is it wrong for us to do the same?

In the first paragraph of the second page of your October 13, 1976 letter you state in part--quote--"To give you all the facts, so that when you vote on November 16th you will make your decision on the basis of all <u>the facts</u>."

We are not ashamed of our record and whether you like it or not we readily admit that we are not perfect. So let's look at some of the company facts--facts which up to now have not been published. Contained in the proxy statement issued December 27, 1975, it lists one Mr. Daniel Goldman as holding 101,267 common shares of stock as of November 22, 1975. It further lists Mr. Daniel Goldman as receiving aggregate remunerations of $55,000 with a total amount of $42,924.79 in the company's "Employees Profit Sharing Plan."

The first paragraph on page 3 of the proxy statement issued December 27, 1975 explains in part the "Employees Profit Sharing Plan" and may we quote in part from the above proxy statement--"The plan provides for contributions solely by the company of an amount determined <u>at the discretion</u> of the <u>Board of Directors,</u> <u>but not less than 10% of the profits</u> before taxes after deducting 20% for return on capital and surplus." End of quote.

This is real good Mr. Goldman--you get dividends on your stock--20% of your capital investment--and not less than 10% of profits for profit sharing.

Do your employees get an equivalent return in dollars and cents for their investment--their labor, which of course is all your employees have to sell.

We will not argue with success, Mr. Goldman, but why not tell your workers the entire story.

We trust that after November 16, 1976 intelligent
management will sit down across the bargaining table
with an intelligent elected union committee and
negotiate a workable contract which cannot be broken by
either party.

Within the next three days, three more union leaflets
appeared. The first, an open letter from a member of the
organizing committee, emphasized the desirability of "the
right to express free personal feelings without reprisal
and the need for better working conditions at Table Ware."
The second letter again tried to reassure part-timers that
"your job will be fully protected," and stressed that there
really were "more important matters" to discuss than these
"rumors" that "cannot be pinned down to any one person or
persons. But we fully realize that you are too intelligent
a group of workers to fall for any rumors of this nature."
The letter attacked the merit-rating, sick-leave, and bonus
systems and promised that after November 16, 1976, "the
union fully intends to correct these situations by working
with your 'elected' committee to give all workers a fair
deal." The third letter discussed employee insurance and
pensions:

What do you full-time workers have to look forward to
with a union?

To have full insurance coverage for you and your family
at no cost to you--rather than paying approximately 8¢
per hour for family coverage as you do now.

What do you have to look forward to as you get older
and want to retire?

Don't you want to have a say in the amount of pension
benefits you will receive at retirement--and don't you
want to be covered by insurance during your retirement?

Not until November 8 did Thornquist respond. In his
first letter he identified five New England UPC plants that
had closed down and then contrasted them to Table Ware's
job-security record. The second letter (see Exhibit 5.7 in
the Appendix to this Chapter) included a four-and-one-half-
foot list of all UPC strikes since July 1971. The list
identified each company and gave the number of its employees, the UPC local number, and the details of the strike.
The same day, management posted signs stating how much
money employees could lose for each day of a strike.
    The union issued a letter to all students working under
the "school works program [who] may have no interest in the
coming union election [and] may soon be leaving Table Ware

Plastics to further your education." It asked them to vote for "better working conditions for those of us who may spend the rest of our lives at Table Ware . . . more and better insurance for workers and their families . . . higher and better pension benefits so that those of us who will be remaining at Table Ware can look forward to a life of <u>dignity and respect in our declining years</u>." The letter was signed by the six members of the union organizing committee.

As the last week of the campaign began, Thornquist began to wonder if his campaign was approaching overkill. The supervisors had reported that his last two letters, particularly the one regarding strikes, had generated a lot of talk among the employees. In addition, the supervisors were still estimating that 60 percent of their employees would vote against the union, 20 percent would support the union, and 20 percent were uncertain.

The basic question before Thornquist was whether to continue the strong push of his campaign during the last week. If he did so, he had to choose his tactics carefully. He still had several posters, brochures, and letters that could be used. Among these materials was a booklet with questions (and answers) that employees commonly asked about union elections; a list of Table Ware benefits; a letter comparing recent local UPC contracts with recent wage and benefit improvements at Table Ware; and a brochure summarizing Table Ware's medical-insurance program. In addition, Thornquist had to decide if a preelection speech by Dan Goldman should be included in his plans, and if so, the best content and time for the speech to be given had to be considered.

THE FINAL WEEK

During the last week of the campaign Thornquist kept a relatively low profile. On November 13 he issued the booklet with answers to frequently asked questions about union election. It was accompanied by a letter that concluded: "Your vote will determine your future and the future of your friends and fellow employees at Table Ware Plastics. This is why you need all the facts before you vote. Once you have all the facts, I am confident that you will vote 'no' on Thursday."

The same day, the UPC mailed a letter that contrasted the 1976 $.05 per hour wage increase with Dan Goldman's 1976 income of $55,000 plus $40,256 from the sale of real estate previously leased to the company. The letter emphasized, "Now you can see how well the Goldman family was taken care of. How much of this vast sum of money did you get?" Management quickly responded by listing the 1975 earnings of each UPC officer and representative on bulletin boards throughout the plant; the total was $2,241,547.46.

On November 14 and 15 Dan Goldman held four separate meetings in the plant cafeteria to address all employees. In his emotionally charged speeches Goldman asked each employee to take a hard look at the company's record before voting.

On November 16, 1976, out of 519 eligible employees, 502 voted: 53 votes for the UPC and 449 for no union. Nine days later, after the regional director of the NLRB had certified the election results, the company organized a victory celebration for all plant employees. Also, Goldman wrote a letter of "personal thanks" to all employees in which he announced plans for an attitude survey and the formation of a task force of hourly, administrative, and supervisory people to study the results and recommend programs and policies that "will make Table Ware an even better place for all of us to work."

Postelection Developments

Although management had decided to treat the six members of the union organizing committee like all of the other employees, two of these six never came back to work after the election. A third, who had decided to vote against the union in the last week of the campaign, was encouraged by management to remain at Table Ware. A fourth employee also decided to remain. In January 1977 Maxwell Blackburn informed his supervisor that he had a chance to take a job with Western Electric. Management, in the words of one executive, "accepted his resignation very quickly." The situation regarding Walt Belanger was more complicated.

In December 1976 Belanger had received a performance review in which he was given a "very good" for job knowledge, "consistently good" for quality of work, "fair" for quantity of work, and "poor" for initiative, attitude, and potential. His supervisor, Albert Baird, also had written, "I believe that he has the worst attitude toward the company of any employee I have met." Consequently, Belanger was denied a merit increase. He immediately filed an unfair labor practice charge. On February 25, 1977 the regional director of the NLRB ruled that the charge was without merit.

In March 1977 Belanger came to Baird in order to discuss a matter of importance. Belanger reported that his life and the lives of members of his family had been threatened by another employee, Harland Wing. The two men had had differences over the union in the past. Belanger claimed that Wing had accused him of "turning him in" to management for conducting a selling business "on the side," in addition to his regular duties in the warehouse. When the matter reached Thornquist, he talked with Wing and received an entirely different story. According to Wing, Belanger had approached him first and he had told Belanger to leave him alone. Belanger had then asked Wing if he was threatening him and followed Wing out of the warehouse, continuing to badger him. Wing then claimed to have sought out his supervisor and asked him "to get Belanger off my back." The supervisor reportedly "thumbed Belanger away" and reported the incident to higher management at once. Other witnesses could testify only to the fact that they had heard Belanger's question, "Are you threatening me?"

Shortly after the Wing incident, David Kenzel, a member of the building maintenance crew who had been in the hospital undergoing an operation, had visited the plant a few days before coming back to work and had talked to Belanger. On his first day back on the job, Kenzel sought out his supervisor and reported his conversation with Belanger; he claimed that Belanger had stated "They're going to make you a janitor." The supervisor assured Kenzel that this could not happen and reported the incident to Thornquist. Belanger's version of the story was that he had met Kenzel a week or two prior to his return to work, but that they had only exchanged a greeting. He did acknowledge, however, that in January, before Kenzel went to the hospital, he had seen Kenzel experiencing a seizure; he had then suggested that Kenzel "takes a job on light duty, or a janitor's job, something easy on you until you feel better."

Since the mechanical maintenance department had to do much of its work when the plant was not operating, Saturday overtime was inevitable and was available to everyone in the department. Although it was not mandatory, 18 or 20 of the 24 employees in the department regularly worked Saturday overtime; the others were excused by personal choice.

For a number of years, Belanger had been rebuilding his home. Consequently during 1975 and 1976, with the approval of his supervisors, he had been relieved of the overtime assignments usually given to the maintenance mechanics.

In early 1977, Belanger resumed overtime work. Each employee who was scheduled for overtime usually was notified on the preceding Friday. On Friday, March 4, Albert Baird specifically instructed Belanger not to come in for overtime the next day. When Belanger appeared at the plant ready for work the next morning, he was told to go home. Belanger left the premises at once. Baird reported the incident to Thornquist on Monday.

The same sequence of events occurred the following weekend. The denial of overtime for Belanger on both Saturdays had come from the vice president of manufacturing. He told Baird that he felt justified in denying premium overtime pay to an employee who was such a problem for the company. Supervisors not only had complained to him about Belanger's attitude and behavior, but also had asked that he be discharged. In the past, management occasionally had withheld overtime opportunities because of poor attendance, misconduct, or a poor attitude on the job.

On Monday, March 14, Baird approached Thornquist and told him of Belanger's actions on Saturday. As the conversation ended, Baird asked, "How much longer do I have to put up with this?"

The next day Belanger was fired. He immediately filed an unfair labor practice charge with the NLRB, claiming that he was discharged because of his involvement in the UPC organizing campaign. After several months, the regional director of the NLRB ruled in Belanger's favor and ordered him reinstated. Table Ware management appealed the decision to the full Board, which ultimately upheld management's discharge.

ANALYSIS OF THE TABLE WARE PLASTICS CAMPAIGN

This chapter illustrated a well-planned management campaign in which the company's clear objective was to remain nonunion. Not only can one readily observe many of the tactics, talents, and themes that management used in such a campaign, but also the more elusive issue of timing becomes apparent.

Management Campaign

Themes

From the very beginning, it is clear that management intended to oppose the union organizing effort. The broad theme seemed to be a combination of "anti this union" and "procompany." Initially, management tried to raise questions about the costs to employees of unions. Management's objective was to raise sufficient doubts in the minds of the work force so that the union would not obtain enough signatures to call for an election. Since there is a relatively large turnover of employees at the beginning and at the end of the summer, management also attempted to postpone an election. If the election was to be held, management preferred that it be held after this turnover period. It was possible that many of the part-time employees were less loyal to the company than were the permanent employees.

Although management stressed some positive reasons for voting for the company, most of its campaign literature stressed reasons for voting against the union. During the latter days of the campaign, management seemed to place particular stress on three issues: the strike record of the union, the loser image of the union, and the vulnerability of part-time employees should the union win at Table Ware. Other issues that were stressed throughout the campaign included job security at Table Ware, the fact that the union cannot guarantee that management will continue the same level of benefits as in the past, and the role of the union as an outsider versus the company as "one big happy family."

Tactics

Management placed a great deal of emphasis on letters to employees. Management believed its most effective letters were those of October 20 ("The UPC is a loser's union") and November 8 ("The Paperworkers Union is strike happy"). Both had the effect of raising questions about the union's effectiveness. The November 8 letter was made even more effective by the dramatic four-and-a-half-foot long enclosure.

One reason that the company's letters were so effective is that it was not something new for employees to receive letters from Dick Thornquist and Dan Goldman. Several years ago the company consciously set up Goldman as the "messenger of good news." Because he personifies the Goldman family and their relatively paternalistic approach to employees, the employees responded to him quite well. He was an effective spokesman for management and generated considerable employee confidence.

Another effective tactic was the use of small group meetings. Not only were there daily meetings for the planning committee but there were also regular meetings with first-line supervisors and the workers. These meetings served to convey management's concern for their people as well as allow employees to ask questions, thereby enabling them to feel that they were being heard. Management spent considerable time preparing for these meetings, developing memos to outline the kinds of issues that should be discussed and the kinds of answers that should be given.

Although the company's tactics were legal, in a few situations they closely skirted the edge of legality. For example, the withholding of a wage increase during late 1976 and the April confrontations with Belanger and Blackburn were carefully planned and documented to defend against possible unfair labor practice charges.

Talent

The company made very good use of two groups of workers: first-line supervisors and informal group leaders who were chosen from the work force. It is clear that the first-line supervisors became the communications vehicle for top management. The supervisors were in daily contact with both the workers and top management during much of this campaign. The "thought leaders" or informal group leaders may not have become strong advocates of the company's position, but they remained unsympathetic toward the union's effort.

From the start, management signaled its commitment to remain nonunion with the involvement of key people in the organization. Not only were vice presidents and even the president involved from the beginning of the campaign, but Thornquist was given key staff and operating people to help him during the entire camapaign.

Timing

From the outset of the union's efforts, management played for more time. First, there was an effort to prevent the union from securing enough signatures for an election; when that failed, management tried to postpone the election until after the summer.

It is important to recognize the fact that initially management took a reactive stance. It responded to charges raised by the union and raised very few issues of its own. According to one company official, it was not until Thornquist and Goldman had been personally attacked that management realized that it was merely reacting to the union. It was the final sentence on the open letter to Goldman that opened management's eyes. When management saw the statement "we await your reply," it realized what was happening. From that point, management rarely responded to specific union charges, choosing instead to raise issues of its own.

Union Campaign

It appears that the union was unable to find an effective issue to use during the campaign. Early in the campaign it seemed to stress the general benefits of unionism. In an effort to identify the company's vulnerability, a variety of charges against Table Ware were then levied. The company's pension program, grievance procedures, and merit increases were criticized. None of these issues seemed to sufficiently disturb the workers. In an effort to create interest, the union finally resorted to attacks on well-respected, well-liked company personalities. Such attacks most likely resulted in loss of credibility for the union, or at least created sympathy for the managers.

Tactics

Although the union's use of leaflets and letters was extensive, none of these publications seemed to be particularly outstanding or to have the potential to strongly affect the work force. Many of the early leaflets and letters were standard materials, applicable to any campaign. The house calls and one-on-one meetings were not particularly effective, given Belanger's lack of popularity with the work force. All in all, the union's tactics were unimaginative and gave the appearance of "going through the motions." About the best that can be said for the campaign tactics is that they were legal.

Talent

The leadership of the union organizing effort was ineffective. Not only was it a very small organizing committee (six employees), but the use of Belanger as a key figure in the organizing effort actually proved to be detrimental to the union. Although he was very mobile within the plant, he lacked the tact necessary to deal effectively with the work force. By failing to discharge Belanger during the campaign, the company not only avoided being charged with an unfair labor practice, but also allowed Belanger to sabotage the union's organizing efforts.

Major Management Decisions

It is important to understand that during a campaign, management must make a number of important decisions. The most important decisions that had to be made by Thornquist and his colleagues when Table Ware became threatened with unionization included:

When to acquaint top management with the news of an organizing effort;
Whether to oppose the organizing effort or do nothing about it;
Whether to use an outsider, such as an attorney or consultant, or handle the campaign internally;
Who should comprise the planning committee;
What tactics could be used most effectively;
What issues should be raised;
What position to take regarding the NLRB hearing (whether to go for an immediate election or attempt to buy time);
How to handle the wage increase for the Dorchester plant;
Whether to use a captive audience speech or decline to

use a preelection speech; and

How to deal with the union and its key members after the election.

Plan of Action

As of November 9, 1976, Thornquist was faced with several courses of action for the final week of the campaign: employ several carefully chosen tactics, including a preelection speech by Goldman for a "big finish" by management; do nothing during the last week; or focus exclusively on the preelection speech by Goldman.

Some observers feared that Thornquist had oversold his case and, therefore, should take a low profile during the last week of the campaign. A danger of the low-profile option was that management might lose momentum and peak too early, as in a political campaign, and thereby allow the union to enjoy the big finish.

Others felt that the company should do everything it could to defeat the union during the last week of the campaign, including a last-minute emotional appeal by Goldman. If the speech was to be used, timing was important. It must not, under any circumstances, be allowed to violate the NLRB's 24-hour rule.

In considering a plan of action, it was especially important to address the question of what to do after the election. If the union wins, should management attempt to frustrate the union in bargaining in hopes that a decertification petition would be filed? How will management go about developing the kind of relationship that it wants with this union? On the other hand, what should management do if the union is defeated in the election? Should it overtly or covertly punish the members of the union organizing committee, particularly Belanger? Should it reward the work force for voting against the union? To do so might set a dangerous precedent. At Table Ware, management's immediate reaction was to conduct a new employee survey and to give employees some responsibility for implementing corrective action in the hope that any future organizing efforts would not be successful.

Why Was Table Ware the Target of an Organizing Effort?

Management believed that Blackburn and Belanger invited the union into the plant. It did not believe that there were sufficient grounds for unionization at Table Ware. The vote, as well as the foremens' estimates of worker support, seemed to indicate that this assessment was correct. This appears to be a case in which one disgruntled employee created a great deal of difficulty for management by pulling a union into the plant, albeit into a "no-win" situation.

SPECIFIC MANAGEMENT RULES

After reviewing the incidents in a successful company campaign to resist union organizing, it may be helpful to summarize some common legal "can" and "cannot" rules for managers who actively seek to resist a union campaign.* The following rules are not meant to be exhaustive and are listed with the following warning: NLRB rulings on various subjects are not constant. What is legal one day may be a violation of the law at a later time. With changing Board membership and policies, specific rulings occasionally are reversed or modified. Consequently managers should approach any list of cans and cannots with caution.

Can

Express opinions about unionism or about a particular union that are not threatening or coercive.

Prophecy "that unionization might ultimately lead to loss of employment . . . where there is no threat that the employer will use its economic power to make its prophecy come true."

Prevent nonemployee organizers from distributing union literature on company property if they have other channels of communication by which to reach employees and if the employer does not allow other nonemployees to distribute materials on company property.

Prohibit distribution of literature by employees during work time and in work areas.

Prohibit oral solicitation of authorization cards and/ or union support during work times.

---

*Although the author takes full responsibility for interpretation, this section is based on the following sources: Charles J. Morris (editor), The Developing Labor Law (Washington, D.C.: Bureau of National Affairs), 1971; National Labor Relations Board, A Layman's Guide to Basic Law Under the National Labor Relations Act (Washington, D.C.: U.S. Government Printing Office, 1971); and National Labor Relations Board, Summary of the National Labor Relations Act (Washington, D.C. U.S. Government Printing Office, 1971).

Prohibit employees from wearing union emblems where it is necessary for the maintenance of production and discipline and where it may be a legitimate precaution against violence.

Describe prevailing wages and benefits at other organizations in ways that are literally true but very misleading.

Stress the likelihood of strikes if it is relevant to the strike record and claims of job security of the union in question.

Remind employees that the selection of a union will not automatically produce any wage or benefit increases.

Change employee wages and benefits during a campaign if a valid reason unrelated to union activity can be established.

Change employee wages and benefits during a campaign if the employer had previously told the employees of its decision.

Take disciplinary action for good cause related to the maintenance of order and efficiency against a union supporter.

State its position on whether employees should vote for the union.

Listen to unsolicited employee comments about the union or its affairs.

Cannots

Threaten loss of employment.

Threaten close of operations, including moving or going out of business.

Threaten reduction in pay or benefits.

Threaten loss of promotion opportunities.

Threaten or perform acts of violence to discourage support of a union.

Promise to give special wage increases, benefits, or other consideration in return to opposition to a union.

Engage in electioneering at the polling place.

Make captive audience speeches, including question-and-answer sessions, 24 hours before the election.

Prohibit solicitation during nonwork times.

Adopt for the first time a no-solicitation role at a time of "intense union activity."

Prohibit the wearing of union buttons that are not provocative and do not alienate customers.

Supply employer campaign badges that place employees in the position of declaring themselves as if they had been interrogated.

Engage in "misrepresentation or other similar campaign trickery, which involves a substantial departure from the truth, at a time which prevents the other party or parties from making an effective reply, so that the misrepresentation, whether deliberate or not, may reasonably be expected to have a significant impact on the election."

Engage in campaign dirty tricks such as issuing antiunion materials over the signature of popular employees.

Portray unionization as inevitably giving rise to violence and strikes.

Warn that they "could make negotiations last a year and therefore another election would be necessary."

Create an atmosphere of fear by portraying the selection of a bargaining agent as "futile."

Imply that existing benefits may be diminished or discontinued if management is forced to negotiate with a union, especially when such statement is accompanied by unfair labor practices.

Withhold previously promised benefits claiming that you are trying to avoid committing an unfair labor practice.

Question or interrogate individual employees about their sympathy for and affiliation with the union when it is coercive in light of surrounding circumstances (time, place, personnel involved, information sought, and employer's known preference may be considered).

Conduct individual interviews with employees in the employees' office or at employees' homes for the purpose of urging them to reject the union or determining the extent of union support.

Engage in surveillance of employees using either supervisors, other employees, or outsiders, or give the impression of being engaged in surveillance.

Encourage or create an atmosphere of violence.

Reproduce ballots and other NLRB documents, especially where the effort either directly or indirectly suggests to the voters that the Board endorses a particular party,

Condone violence on the part of antiunion employees.

Use supervisors or people closely identified with the employer as election observers.

Promote the formation of an employee association and encourage it to apply for certification.

Libel or slander union officials.

Transfer workers to areas or jobs where the intent is to separate those who support unionization from those you think may not.

Ask employees at the time of interviewing for a job whether they have been union members or support unions.

Claim that you will not deal with the union.

Assist employees to withdraw union membership.

Ask employees about the identity of the leader or instigator of the organizing effort.

Incite racial or religious prejudice by inflammatory campaign appeals.

APPENDIX

Exhibit 5.1

Table Ware Park, Burlington, Massachusetts 01803
TABLE WARE PLASTICS, INC.
A Division of Jersey Paper Corporation

To: All Employees

Last week the outside union organizers handed out leaflets to some of you as you were attempting to come to work.
We did not intend to make any wide response to this first
leaflet. However, these outside organizers are persistent
in their attempt to gain a new "account" and have again im-
posed upon you another leaflet. We now feel that we should
clarify and emphasize a few of the points raised by these
leaflets.

UNION LEAFLET #1

In this first letter the union organizers made the
statement that they would gain nothing tangible by union-
izing your company. They stated that all the union gets
out of it is "the satisfaction of knowing that we have
helped more people to a better way of life." However, just
two paragraphs before this statement these same organizers
make the contradictory comment that "the union is not in
business to put a company out of business because <u>we would
lose as much as the company by losing membership.</u>

AND REMEMBER, MEMBERSHIP MEANS DUES

In this initial leaflet the union does make a statement
with which your company agrees: "Rates of pay are based on
what the company can afford to pay." They are right; union
or no union your paycheck comes from your company and is
based on your company's ability to pay and your ability and
willingness to do your job.

UNION LEAFLET #2

It is interesting to note that only now after the union
has obvious difficulty in its organizing attempts does it
tell you that you, as a current employee, will not pay an
initiation fee. Why not earlier? This second leaflet also

114

says that you should note from the attached flyer that "the dues are only $4.00 a month." One word, however, was noticeably left out: the attached flyer actually said, "minimum dues are $4.00 a month." We called four local companies that are unionized by the United Paperworkers and Cartonmakers and found that their actual dues are $6.00, $6.00, $5.50, and $5.50/month.

This leaflet also implied that our part-time program for workers has been good for Table Ware. We agree wholeheartedly. This program has been very good over the years for both Table Ware and for the hundreds of part-timers who have taken advantage of this Table Ware Program. No such program is good unless it works to the mutual benefit of all parties involved; and this one has.

The union organizers also made a statement in this leaflet that should be further clarified. They want you to believe that if the union got into your company that the law would guarantee that you keep all the benefits you now have and would get more. That simply is not true. In the event that the union ever got into Table Ware, your company would only be obligated to "bargain in good faith." But all matters of wages and benefits would have to be bargained for. It is perfectly possible that in conceding one demand other existing benefits could be reduced.

In the last analysis, your company would have to decide what it could and would do.

The fact that the union has finally come out into the open is a clear indication that their "secret" attempts to pressure you into signing cards have failed. We urge you again (and hopefully for the last time); do not sign these cards and turn your future over to "outsiders."

Exhibit 5.2

Table Ware Park, Burlington, Massachusetts 01803
TABLE WARE PLASTICS, INC.
A Division of Jersey Paper Corporation

To: All Employees

The United Paperworkers and Cartonmakers Union have again distributed another leaflet asking you to sign authorization cards.

It is our contention that you are not getting the full facts. You are entitled to get all the facts, and not just those which the outside union organizers choose to give you.

In my opinion the second leaflet most recently distributed by the union shows that the union is not willing to give you all the facts.

1. Note in the leaflet distributed by the union yeaterday, the union organizers say that there will not be an initiation fee charged to those employees who are now working for the company. But the union did not give that information until the company began to raise questions about how much the union initiation fees and dues would cost the employees of Table Ware Plastics.

2. As for union membership dues, the Union's leaflet of May 16 says that dues will be only $4.00 a month, and of that, $3.00 is sent to the International Union and $1.00 stays with the local union. The union gave you only a half-truth. What the union did not tell you is that under the Paperworkers' International Constitution, the Local Union's monthly membership dues must be at least a minimum of $4.00 every month. The union failed to tell you that under the International Constitution every local union is given the option of deciding how much more than $4.00 a month they should charge for membership dues. (Constitution of United Paperworkers' and Cartonmakers, Article XII, Section 3.)

We have checked some of the companies in this area which have contracts with the Paperworkers Union, and we found that actual regular monthly membership dues, of those we called, run $5.50 per month ($66.00/year) to as much as $6.00 a month ($72.00/year).

3. The union also failed to tell you that part of every member's monthly dues goes into the Paperworkers Strike Fund which can be used to support strikes at other companies. (The International Constitution, Article VI, Section 4.)

4. The union failed to tell you that the International Union can require members to pay general and special assessments on top of the regular monthly dues. (Paper-

workers International, Article IV, Section 7. I think you should know what you are letting yourself in for if the union came in here.

5. Article XII, Section 3 of the International Constitution says that any member that fails to pay dues or assessments may be expelled from membership--"without a hearing!" We don't think that is a fair procedure.

6. The union failed to tell you that if an employee works as little as 40 hours in a given month he would have to pay his full monthly dues even though he was out sick for more than 3 weeks. (International Constitution, Article XII, Section 4).

7. If you had a local Paperworkers Union in here, you would not be able to make your own decisions. When the local union reached an agreement with a company, that agreement cannot take effect until and unless it is approved by the President of the United Paperworkers and Cartonmakers Union.

All of these facts are taken from the union's constitution and they are all facts that the union would like to conceal from you.

The union organizers also made a statement in this leaflet that should be further clarified. They want you to believe that if the union got into your company that the law would guarantee that you keep all the benefits you now have and would get more. That simply is not true. In the event that the union ever got into Table Ware, your company would be obligated to "bargain in good faith." But all matters of wages and benefits would have to be bargained for. It is perfectly possible that in conceding one demand other existing benefits could be reduced.

If you cannot trust the union paid organizers to give you the full truth when they are asking you to sign authorization cards, how can you trust them in the future?

Do not sign any cards.

You do not need this union.

You will get a fairer future at Table Ware Plastics.

Exhibit 5.3

Table Ware Park, Burlington, Massachusetts 01803
TABLE WARE PLASTICS, INC.
A Division of Jersey Paper Corporation

"BALANCE THE SCALES? IN FAVOR OF WHOM?

This morning the United Paperworkers and Cartonmakers presented some of you with a very interesting suggestion about "balancing scales."

The idea of "balancing the scales" is interesting because it assumes that, right now, the scales are unbalanced, and assumes that the union would provide justice and sympathetic treatment to all employees. The fact is that almost all formal complaints have been _solved_ to the _satisfaction_ of our employees by their supervisors and personnel people WITHOUT HAVING TO GO BEFORE A COMPLAINT REVIEW BOARD. And the vast majority of those that _do_ reach the Review Board _are_ solved to the employee's complete satisfaction. (We realize that this system _or any system_ cannot resolve every problem to the complete satisfaction of every individual.)

LET'S IMAGINE THIS SITUATION

"Table Ware decides to hold Company meetings on Sunday mornings. You decide you can't because it interferes with your church services. Table Ware fines you $5.00 for not attending the meeting. You complain and refuse to pay. Table Ware then brings legal suit against you and forces you to pay the fine."

Sounds ridiculous, doesn't it? Because you know by past experience it would never happen in this company.

However, this actually did happen with a member of the United Paperworkers and Cartonmakers.

HERE IS AN ACTUAL CASE!

For going to church instead of union meetings on Sundays, Mrs. Mary Ellen Benson of Milwaukee was fined $5.00 by the United Paperworkers and Cartonmakers Union some time ago.

The union brought suit against Mrs. Benson for not complying with union by-laws which required any member missing 3 of 5 meetings be fined $5.00.

Mrs. Benson was quoted as saying that the union meetings came on Sunday morning at the same time her Church held services. The hapless Mrs. Benson ended up paying the find <u>and</u> court costs because she said she couldn't afford to quit the union and be out of a job.

ADD THIS TO ANOTHER EXAMPLE OF THE UNION'S
ATTITUDE TOWARD INDIVIDUAL RIGHTS!

A Continental Can employee-a woman--was discriminated against by her union leaders (again, UPC). Nobody listened to her, not even a grievance committee of union officials. UPC is now being sued by the National Labor Relations Board for discriminatory practices and UPC members' dues will foot the bill for it.

The list of examples goes on, almost endlessly. Union members have been fined for exceeding production quotas set by the union--for not performing picket line duty--for bringing unfair labor charges against the union--for petitioning to oust the union--for charging a union official with misconduct--and for other violations of the union by-laws.

It's a matter of looking at the record . . . <u>both</u> sides of the record. Table Ware Plastics has a complaint procedure that <u>does</u> work, <u>has</u> worked, and <u>will</u> work for <u>each</u> and <u>every Table Ware employee</u> who wants to use it.

Do not be fooled by the collection of half-truths and misleading statements that the union has made and will continue to make.

The union cannot guarantee anything more for you than what Table Ware Plastics is <u>already</u> doing.

Exhibit 5.4

Table Ware Park, Burlington, Massachusetts 01803
TABLE WARE PLASTICS, INC.
A Division of Jersey Paper Corporation

Dear Fellow Workers,

In the 15 years since Table Ware Plastics was founded, I have watched our company grow and prosper. In all these years, one of the basic beliefs of Table Ware Plastics that has been demonstrated by action over and over again is that of respect for people as individuals. We have made every effort to practice this belief in our day-to-day business affairs.

Last Friday, July 7th, the professional organizers of the United Paperworkers and Cartonmakers Union were at it again, passing out leaflets.

This time, however, these outsiders showed their true colors by resorting to degradation of character, in attacking Dick Thornquist, one of our most respected and loyal employees, calling him, "Tricky Dick."

Like you, Dick is an employee. He started at Table Ware twelve years ago as our Personnel Manager and worked his way up to Vice President. He is a man who has worked diligently over the years to improve the position of all Table Ware employees and, as many of you know, he has bent over backwards to help scores of people with both their work and their personal problems. He has been personally responsible for giving many of our people a "second chance" when they needed it.

Unfortunately, the union is now using this kind of political smear tactic.

The outside professional organizers have been hanging around the streets near our factory for a long time, trying to sell you a bill of goods. I promise you that we will do everything within our legal power to prevent these people from infecting our company and our employees with the kind of moral character that is capable of this type of unfounded and degrading personal attack.

For if they are capable of doing it to one person, they will certainly be prepared to do it again to anyone who stands in the way of their achieving there own selfish ends.

Some of you have expressed your feelings that you are getting tired of being constantly besieged, first by union leaflets and then by your company's responses.

I apologize to you that you must go through this but I know you appreciate the fact that we cannot stand by and allow so many of their false and misleading claims to go unchallenged.

The law requires that we tolerate their activities. But we do not have to tolerate their code of decency . . . or lack of one.

Sincerely,

Daniel Goldman

Exhibit 5.5

Table Ware Park, Burlington, Massachusetts 01803
TABLE WARE PLASTICS, INC.
A Division of Jersey Paper Corporation

Hello,

On Thursday, November 16th, the National Labor Relations Board will conduct a secret ballot election in our plant. I am glad that this election is to take place to give you and your fellow workers the opportunity to decide whether you wish to retain your rights as free individuals by voting NO against the union or whether you are willing to transfer your rights to this outside Paperworkers Union.

There are many questions you should ask about the Union, such as: How much would this Union cost me if it came into our plant? What is this Union's record for strikes? Can the Union guarantee any of its promises? What can this Union do for my job security? Your Company has the answers and will present them to you in the next few weeks.

You should also review the record of your company by asking questions such as: How has the Company treated the employees over a long period of time? Has the Company been fair? What is the Company's record for keeping its promises? How do the wages and benefits at Table Ware Plastics compare to the wages and benefits received by employees in other companies in our line of business? And, most important, what is your Company's record for giving employees steady work and job security, and no layoffs?

The Union will be giving you leaflets and letters, they may also come into your home at night. Some employees are unhappy about the fact that the Company has to give the Union a list of names of our employees and their addresses. I apologize for that, but the National Labor Relations Board requires us to give that information to the Union. We must comply with the law.

The Union will look for any little thing which it can exaggerate or distort in the hope of getting your vote. You must make sure that you get the truth. I hope that the Union representatives will be more honest with you than they have been in some of the leaflets they have previously passed out and in the statements they have made.

Don't be misled into making your decision on the basis of any one or two isolated things. You owe it to yourself to make your decision on the basis of the total package of wages, benefits and the type of family company-employee relationships which you enjoy here at Table Ware.

Our company intends, in the next few weeks, to give you all the facts, so that when you vote on November 16th, you will make your decision on the basis of ALL THE FACTS.

If you have any doubts about the accuracy of any statement, whether made by a Union representative or by your Company representative, you should ask for further information. We will answer every question and hope the Union will do likewise. In addition, you should feel free to get further answers from the National Labor Relations Board or any documents which may apply.

I urge you to think carefully about the issues, Your job and your security are involved.

I am confident that on November 16th, you will vote FOR YOUR COMPANY and vote NO—against the Union.

Sincerely,

Daniel Goldman

Exhibit 5.6

Table Ware Park, Burlington, Massachusetts 01803
TABLE WARE PLASTICS, INC.
A Division of Jersey Paper Corporation

October 20, 1976
Hello,

Here are some important facts you should know about the Paperworkers Union--facts that prove that

THE UPC IS A LOSER'S UNION!

FACT #1: The UPC has <u>not been successful</u> in organizing one single plant in this state in the past two years.*

FACT #2: Time after time the UPC has tried--and failed-- to organize Jersey Paper Corporation employees in its other plants. Now they have come to Burlington, hoping that you are not as smart as other Jersey Paper employees--hoping that you will believe their stories and let them in.

FACT #3: Dixie Cup Company--our competitor--had its plant in Easton, Pennsylvania organized by the UPC almost 40 years ago. Yet the UPC has <u>failed to organize</u> every other Dixie plant in the country. Obviously Dixie employees learned from the mistake made by their fellow workers in Easton.

FACT #4: A year and a half ago the UPC tried to organize our competitor--Solo Cup Company. The union was <u>overwhelmingly defeated</u>.

These are documented facts. But you won't hear them from union organizers because they don't want you to know about their many, many failures.

THE UPC IS A LOSER'S UNION!
DON'T JOIN A SINKING SHIP!

Please vote <u>for your company</u> on November 16. Vote <u>NO TO THE UNION</u>.

Sincerely,

Dick Thornquist

---

*Source: Bureau of National Affairs

Exhibit 5.7

Table Ware Park, Burlington, Massachusetts 01803
TABLE WARE PLASTICS, INC.
A Division of Jersey Paper Corporation

November 8, 1976

Hello,

THE PAPERWORKERS UNION IS STRIKE-HAPPY
READ A DIRECT QUOTE FROM U.P.C. PRESIDENT JONES!!

"This union has issued more strike authorizations and supported more strikes in the last ten years than any other union in the paper industry.

"In fact, it has occurred to me, and is a matter of record, more strike authorizations have gone out involving more people, in the 28 years I have been an international officer, over my signature, than any other person who ever held office in the paper industry. This, of course, was the result of the policies of the Unions that I served as an officer, but I helped formulate those policies and it was my signature confirming them in the most meaningful way."
(Quote taken from an official speech made by the President of the U.P.C.)

WHAT IS HE TELLING YOU ABOUT YOUR FUTURE?

This man is <u>bragging</u> about the large number of UPC-organized strikes. He is <u>happy</u> that thousands of UPC members have been out of work on strike—that his union caused its members to lose wages for weeks and sometimes months. He is <u>proud</u> that his signature put people out of work, companies out of business.

And he is <u>relaxed</u> because DURING ALL THOSE STRIKES HE GOT HIS PAYCHECK EVERY SINGLE WEEK.

Do you want this man or his successor dictating your future?

Do you want to depend on HIM for job security, for next week's paycheck, for money to take care of your family week after week?

Do you want to be one of the thousands out of work that he brags about in his next speech about his strike-happy union?

On November 16, tell him . . . . NO strikes, NO work interruption, NO dues, NO fines . . . NO UNION. VOTE NO.

Sincerely,

Dick Thornquist

6

ANATOMY OF A UNION CAMPAIGN

INTERNATIONAL BROTHERHOOD OF ELECTRICAL WORKERS* (A)

Organizing . . . should be called "union education."
If everyone understood that, everyone would be in a
union. It's as simple as that. We can't get people
jobs or help people keep them if they don't work, but
we can protect them and give them a chance to file
grievances if they're treated unfairly. But they've
got to be organized first. Everyone has their greed;
for some it's money, for others it's fame. For me, I
want electrical workers to be 100% organized.

Michael D. Lucas, IEBW Director
of Organizing

* Most of the names in this chapter have been changed.

International Brotherhood of Electrical Workers
Copyright © 1977 by the President and Fellows of Harvard
College. This case is a merger of the International
Brotherhood of Electrical Workers (A), (B), and (C) cases
originally prepared by Tommy Gilman under the direction of
William E. Fulmer. Reprinted by permission of the Harvard
Business School.

On a hot June day in 1973, 32-year-old Mike Lucas flew out of Washington, D.C.'s National Airport. He was on his way to take field command of the most difficult organizing campaign of his career. For the two years that he had served as director of organizing for the International Brotherhood of Electrical Workers (IBEW), he had been locked in an organizing campaign against a new American Communications and Electronics (ACE)-Kenmart plant in Albuquerque, New Mexico. In his opinion, the campaign had involved "every trick in the book, and then some." Now, with only four weeks before the election, he was moving into the field for the duration.

Mike Lucas had lost very few elections in the last two years. Nevertheless, the ACE-Kenmart campaign, more than any other, had become a critical test. He firmly believed that once he started a campaign, he had a responsibility to the employees involved, no matter how long it took. He often said that "A winner has many fathers, but a loser is a bastard." Come June 29, 1973, he had no intention of being in the latter category. Nor did he intend to abandon the Kenmart employees.

The IBEW: History and Background

The IBEW had been organized in 1891 as a craft union of 286 electricians. Its growth had been influenced by economic conditions as well as by an expanding jurisdiction. An early decision to organize telephone operators, plus a favorable economic climate, had led to membership of 110,896 by 1920. While the economy had been largely responsible for a membership decline to 56,349 by 1925 and to even less in the early 1930s, the emergence of the CIO-affiliated United Electrical Radio and Machine Workers of America (UE) in the late 1930s was an even greater obstacle to continued growth. In response to the UE's organizing efforts in the electrical-manufacturing industry, the IBEW had also begun organizing utilities and electrical-manufacturing plants. By 1940 membership had grown to 145,954; after massive organizing campaigns, especially in gas and electrical utilities, it had increased to 450,000 in 1950. The acquisition of an independent New Jersey telephone union in 1954 had strengthened that long-neglected jurisdiction and helped to expand membership to 735,000 by 1958. Despite this expansion and diversification, however, the IBEW remained strongly construction and craft oriented.

With over 950,000 members in 1970, the IBEW was the largest major union in the electrical industry, the second largest AFL-CIO-affiliated union, and the fourth largest American union. Relatively wealthy, it had total assets in 1970 of $229,347,983 (including pension fund provisions of

$190,651,654) and annual general-fund (the union account for
current income and expenses) receipts of $63,554,057; per-
capita taxes and initiation fees contributed $51 million and
$5 million, respectively, to the general fund. Membership
was concentrated in the four traditional jurisdictions: con-
struction--150,000; telephone--80,000; utilities--175,000;
manufacturing--400,000. However, rapid technological
changes in the electrical/electronics field had widened the
IBEW's scope to inlcude industries such as radio, television, recording, railroads, and government.

The IBEW was governed by detailed constitutional procedures and a quadrennial convention. Union administration
was the responsibility of various elected and appointed
officials. The top three elected officials (the international president, secretary, and treasurer), as well as the
appointed directors and staff representatives of the seven
industry and five support departments, had their offices at
national headquarters in Washington, D.C. At the district
level, 12 elected regional vice-presidents provided service
to the local unions, with the help of appointed district
representatives. At the local level, the 1,677 business
managers were the chief administrative officers who handled
local problems. An additional organizational level was
composed of a nine-member International Executive Board,
elected from districts not identical to vice-presidential
districts. The board served as a judicial board, hearing
union members' appeals from presidential decisions.

Organizing Process

Reflecting its commitment to growth, the IBEW had consistently allocated around 20 percent of its general-fund
expenses to organizing. In 1970 this was almost $4 million,
exclusive of organizers' salaries, and was relatively high
in comparison to other unions' organizing allocations.

Prior to 1970, organizing could be initiated by the
local business managers, the regional vice-presidents, the
department directors, or the international president,
although most major campaigns were undertaken by the industry departments. Acting on information received from the
commercial press, from friendly companies, and from employees voluntarily seeking the union, the directors decided
when and where to organize, which staff representatives
would run the campaign, and which additional reps would
best be able to assist with the campaign. Since each campaign used up part of the department's resources, directors
learned to choose campaigns carefully in order to justify
the expense of "going in." There was, however, greater
target flexibility in electrical manufacturing, where only
25 percent of the potential members were organized.

At the 1970 convention, IBEW President Charles H. Pillard had stated that in the future the major portion of organizing funds was to be used in the electrical-manufacturing and telephone industries. At the same time, he announced a new policy that limited the manufacturing department to conducting only "major campaigns."* Leaving the smaller, "minor" campaigns to the regional vice-presidents and the local business managers, the director of the Manufacturing Industry Department could concentrate on campaigns to organize national employers.

In 1971 Pillard strengthened the organizing focus by creating a new Organizing Department at the international level. This new department was charged with organizing drives in any and all industry jurisdictions where: the scope was too large for a single district to staff; the campaign involved more than one district; the union was following a national employer across the country for national bargaining purposes; or the regional vice-president had requested, and the president had approved, organizing assistance in locations of specific interest to the Brotherhood. The new department would have sole responsibility for major campaigns. In April 1971 Michael Lucas, the 30-year-old assistant director of the Manufacturing Department, was appointed as the first director of organizing.

Initial Activities

As the stack of <u>Wall Street Journals</u> on the glass coffee table in his office indicated, Lucas read various business publications because he was convinced that "companies love

---

*"Major campaigns," those that involved substantial potential costs, were approved on a project basis by the IBEW president. The criteria used to screen proposals were estimated investment and cost of the campaign (expected duration, staffing level, and per-day costs), degree of industry control a successful campaign would create (a dominant position was sought and if possible, a proprietary position as the only union engaged in collective bargaining with a multiplant employer), and ability to establish a strategic toehold and preserve options for later organizing activity. While it was important to justify the costs in most campaigns, if the campaign was felt to be vital the the IBEW's interest, cost did not prevent obtaining approval. In recent years, use of these criteria allowed the IBEW to win approximately 50 percent of more than 250 annual NLRB elections.

to brag about their expansions." Such publications frequently helped him identify targets; however, Lucas had learned of Kenmart's decision to build in Albuquerque from the business manager of the IBEW's San Carlos, California local. Soon after becoming director of organizing, Lucas had asked the IBEW Research Department for more information on the company.

Lucas learned that Kenmart had been founded in 1944 in San Francisco by Kenneth Johnson and Martin Richards. The purpose of the company was to design, develop, and manufacture custom-made electronic carrier systems for telephone companies, using solid-state technology to produce the key component, Pulse-Code Modulation Carriers. These PCMs made it possible to carry two or more voice signals point to point simultaneously over a pair of telephone wires. The company was successful and eventually moved to larger headquarters in San Carlos, California and opened a small plant in Burnaby, British Columbia. Both locations were organized by the IBEW. Since management was described as pro-union, labor relations were peaceful.

In 1959, American Communications and Electronics (ACE), a firm with a strong antiunion reputation, acquired 100 percent of Kenmart's stock, and Kenmart became a wholly-owned subsidiary of ACE's manufacturing division, Electric Manufacturing Company. In 1968 ACE ranked in the top 50 of the Fortune 500 with sales of $3 billion and employed 161,000 people systemwide. Kenmart, which employed 3,500 people, contributed $80 million in sales. By 1968, Kenmart had expanded beyond multichannel carrier systems to produce microwave radio systems, mobile radio and television equipment, and telemetering and supervisory control systems. By this time, it had built two additional Canadian plants in Rimoulski, Quebec and Saskatoon, Saskatchewan.

In June 1971 Lucas asked Orville Tate, a district rep for the Albuquerque area, for further information about Kenmart's Albuquerque project. After examining newspaper files, Tate reported that a site-location consulting firm had recommended Albuquerque, a city of 300,000 people 65 miles south of Santa Fe. Civic development groups had become interested in continuing the industrial expansion begun by corporations such as Singer, Levi Strauss, Farrah, Ampex, and at least four other electronics plants (all but one, nonunion). These groups had arranged for 40 acres of land to be bought from the University of New Mexico for $390,000 and for four local banks to pick up $4 million of city-issued bonds; Kenmart provided $2 million. In November 1970 construction began on the 200,000 square foot plant that was expected to begin production of microwave relay parts and other electronic components by late summer 1971. Designed to be an "expandable" plant, employment was planned to increase from 1,000 in mid-1972 to 2,000 in 1975

with a payroll of $20 million, "the biggest thing to hit
Albuquerque in years." Tate toured the plant, which was
being build by IBEW construction members. He found the
layout identical to that of the San Carlos plant.

Once Lucas had received Tate's report, he realized that
because Kenmart was "going in big, into an antiunion area
and at minimum wage," the Albuquerque plant had the potential to be an alternate source of production for the San
Carlos plant. With all of the other Kenmart plants organized by the IBEW, there was a great possibility that this
would become a "runaway" plant. Lucas decided that he had
to go after it to protect the other Kenmart bargaining
units. In addition, he felt that the district would benefit from the boost that a "showcase" contract would give.
According to Lucas, "I needed something to crack the town
open; something large and industrial." Emphasizing the
five other IBEW-ACE bargaining units and the potential
erosion of the San Carlos-Kenmart unit if Albuquerque
remained unorganized, Lucas requested and received permission from President Pillard at the end of June to begin
a major campaign.

In September Lucas assigned staff organizer R. W. "Rojo
Red" Purcell to be the chief organizer of the Kenmart campaign. Expecting a long and bitter battle, Lucas chose
Purcell because, at 55, he had been organizing since the
1930s and had "seen it all." A Texas who spoke some
Spanish, Purcell had all the traits that Lucas liked in his
organizers. He was sincere, dedicated, willing to work
long, hard hours, and had a pleasant personality and a
southern accent. "Northerners think it's amusing," Lucas
had observed, "and southerners can't understand anyone who
talks faster than they do."

The number of organizers Lucas used on a campaign
depended on a number of factors:

The size of the unit was not as important as the size
of the geographical area over which the employees were
spread.

The number of simultaneous campaigns determined the
number of reps available.

The employer's labor-relations policies greatly influenced the number of organizers necessary. For example,
because Lucas felt that Electronic Systems, Inc. never
violated the law, he used fewer organizers on those
campaigns.

The stage of the campaign was also important, with less
manpower needed at the beginning; because of this, Purcell
began the campaign by himself.

The Site Survey

After arriving at Albuquerque, Purcell contacted the IBEW workers who were working on plant construction to find out if they knew any of the 40 hourly employees who had been hired to date. Purcell discovered that few of them knew the hourly workers. He soon realized the reason for this and wrote to Lucas in his weekly report:

> The company had made arrangements to have the employees and the construction guys come to work and quit at different times. Also, they had arranged to have different break periods which made it hard to make any acquaintances. Further, when our guys would start conversations with employees there was a very attentive supervisor, office person, or engineer around. Finally, we did get a few names and addresses and started making contacts. The IBEW steward who was instrumental in getting the contacts was laid off by the contractor very shortly, in spite of protests of the local union. It was obvious at the outset that the company intended to operate this plant nonunion and remarks heard being made by engineers, office, etc., indicated the strong animosity toward the necessary evil of having to tolerate our construction guys.

Once he had the names of some employees, Purcell began to make house calls. Unlike many other organizers who used handbills or letters to determine if there was any initial interest in union representation, Lucas was of the opinion that such tactics were useless in creating employee interest and only served to alert the employer of the impending campaign. Intead, he had established a policy of making house calls on individual employees to gather general information about the organizing target, to determine what feelings the employees had toward the union, and, if the employees were favorably disposed, to ascertain whether they would provide good leadership for the potential organizing committee. The purpose of these first visits was not "to push the union too much." On repeat visits the organizer would seek more detailed information about the employer and the work force and explain unionism more fully.

By mid-September Purcell had met several employees, most of whom had reacted very favorably to the idea of a union. A few had been union members before and most appeared disappointed with Kenmart wages: a hire-in rate of $1.70 that rose to $1.95 at three months. Although Purcell was not attempting to get authorization cards signed, he picked up eight nevertheless. During the rest of September, as the number of employees increased, Purcell continued to make house calls and to meet with as many employees as possible. Realizing that most of the now 100 or so hourly employees were 20 to 22 years old, of Indian or Mexican descent, and Catholic, he began working with officials of the Albuquerque IBEW construction local to arrange meetings with "those of that church who are favorable and influential." In addition to his weekly reports, Purcell kept in touch with Lucas by phone, calling on an almost daily basis.

Kenmart management, apparently aware of the union's presence, put out an elaborate employee handbook in mid-September (which explained employee benefits) and began daily supervisors' meetings from 10 a.m. to noon. The purpose of these meetings was unclear to Purcell; he described them to Lucas as "instructions on how to keep employees misinformed."

By the end of September Purcell had determined that there was enough employee interest to set up a permanent organizing headquarters and an employee organizing committee. Usually this decision was made after the organizer evaluated many house calls and recommended to Lucas that the campaign continue. As Lucas wrote in a training document for organizers:

> If the potential leaders necessary to form a representative Volunteer Organizing Committee cannot be found, the organizer might as well acknowledge the strong possibility that he will not be able to conduct a successful campaign. There is no reason for wasting time and money if influential employees cannot be interested in the union or are opposed to it. Once the organizer has that information, the site survey is complete. He is ready to recommend that the organizing effort be dropped or to call his potential leaders together in a first meeting to form a Volunteer Organizing Committee.

The Kenmart situation was so important that Purcell knew the campaign had to continue. He decided to call the critical first committee meeting for October 1, 1971.

The Volunteer Organizing Committee

Lucas often told his staff that the Volunteer Organizing Committee was the key to a successful campaign.

> I use the same strategy for every election—house calling, educating, building a committee of in-plant people. Just educate the people to the benefits of being union. It's the communication, the education, that is really important. When you've got them educated, you've won the election. I build myself a committee very quietly and only start ballyhooing it when I

have that. I sure don't want to start raising red
flags at the bull without any picadors. The issues
will change for every election, but the committee is
always the key. The ability of the committee to answer
questions asked by other employees and to debate effectively determines whether the organizing campaign is
won or lost.

Recognizing that the in-plant committee was the rep's
only communication to workers on the job, Lucas's policy
was to use weekly committee meeting to "turn interested employees into organizers on the job." He wanted to educate
the employees on the benefits of collective bargaining and
the law regarding employee rights and election procedures.
A crucial part of the education process was to inform these
employees about union dues, initiation fees, fines, and
assessments. Lucas's organizing experience had taught him
that most employers quickly cite reasons for unorganized
workers to remain nonunion. He wanted his organizers to
openly acknowledge such issues by explaining the facts and
the law to the committee and by providing materials that
would help them communicate the truth to their fellow workers on the job. He also wanted the committee to establish
a communication system between the employees and the reps,
make house calls, help obtain employee lists, and gather
information on the employer's policies.

Purcell's first Volunteer Organizing Committee meeting
on October 1, 1971 attracted 15 people; all but four signed
cards and gave the names of other employees who might be
interested. Encouraged, he started weekly meetings to continue educating and building the committee while he continued to call on the new names and on those who had shown
previous interest. He used a "house call book," compiled
by the Organizing Department especially for the Kenmart
drive. The book helped him present the advantages and
benefits of unionism in general and of IBEW in particular.
During his house calls he explained the law, answered questions about the IBEW and its membership, and compared the
organized San Carlos plant to the unorganized Albuquerque
plant.

After returning from each house call, Purcell filled
out a three-inch by five-inch "contact report card" on each
individual. He included specific data such as name, department, shift, and date of the house call, as well as information on the employee's social affiliations, gripes
about work, and attitude toward the union. Purcell then
used this information to fill out a "target diagram" of the
plant. This was a layout of the plant by departments, indicating the number of employees on each shift and the number of union supporters in each. This diagram enabled
Purcell to pinpoint the active supporters and gave him an

invaluable indication of how dispersed the organizing committee was and what kind of communication system was being formulated. By mid-October, although he was still educating the committee and not actively soliciting cards, Purcell has 35 cards out of an estimated 225 employees in the production and maintenance unit and had committee members in eight of the ten functioning departments.

Two of the employees who had attended the first organizing committee meeting but had not signed cards apparently told management about the meeting. Immediately afterward, supervisors began to question employees about who was involved. In addition, vague rumors that Kenmart had hired a consulting firm to do "efficiency ratings or something of that nature" began to spread. However, the company took no visible action until the end of October; then supervisors began strictly enforcing rules regarding talking and openly questioning employees about union activity.

In the first week of November, the first discharge took place--"an excellent committeeman" who had been Purcell's first employee contact and who had, as Purcell reported to Lucas, "been on the move in the plant talking union." The discharged employee was told that he talked too much, did not do his job, and made too many mistakes. Fearing that the discharge foretold what he could expect from the company, Purcell instructed all card signers and committee people to keep written records of questionable activity by supervisors. If unfair labor practice charges were eventually filed, such records would provide evidence to support the case.

Purcell soon began weekly mailings to card signers regarding the committee meetings. Although he felt that interest continued to be strong, expansion of the committee suffered because employees found better paying jobs and quit Kenmart. Nevertheless, by November 11, 1971 the committee was up to about 25 out of an estimated hourly force of 300.

In mid-November Kenmart management, having allowed the daily two-hour supervisory meetings to drop to two or three per week, returned to daily meetings and started "close surveillance" of suspected union supporters. As Purcell related to Lucas, many committee people were moved from their normal jobs to isolated areas where they were not able to talk to other employees. Several supervisors and engineers, desperate to find out who attended the union meetings, ordered employees to give them a list of supporters. Other supervisors told employees that they already knew who the supporters were. One employee was made a supervisor after he bragged that he had turned in a list. Purcell reported to Lucas that "interrogation" was occurring regularly. He concluded, "It looks like it's going to get hairy."

After the first shipment of electronic components from Albuquerque in mid-November, employment began to rise again. It was estimated that by December there would be 500 hourly employees. By December 10 the organizing committee had expanded to more than 30 and over 100 cards had been signed. It was then that Purcell felt ready to begin active solicitation of authorization cards by the committee on a unitwide basis, that is, to "open up." He decided, however, to wait until after the traditional lag of Christmas and the New Year.

As Purcell was deciding when to open up, Kenmart management began to accelerate activity. Purcell reported that early in December some committee people and card signers were interrogated about their union attitudes and activities and were then reassigned to less populated work areas. At rest and lunch periods, a supervisor, foreman, or engineer usually sat at every table and was present wherever the employees gathered.

On Friday morning December 10, the company started discharging employees. By the end of the day, 30 people had been fired. According to Purcell, a supervisor was stationed at the head of each work line; every 15 minutes or so, he would walk down the line, put his hand on a worker's shoulder, and tell the worker that it was best for both the employee and the company if he or she did not work at Kenmart any more. Purcell identified 12 of the 30 people discharged as "good union supporters." The next week another 30 were fired. Purcell reported to Lucas that the "overwhelming majority" of the discharged employees had recently received satisfactory reviews and yet they had been fired for "poor quality and poor quantity." A few other employees were fired sporadically throughout the rest of December and into early January, including the personnel manager who, after 18 years of service with ACE, had been given a 30-minute notice.

Using the records he had told the employees to keep concerning questionable company conduct, Purcell spent the rest of December gathering information for unfair labor practice charges. He filed these in early January, alleging Section 8(a)(1), (2), and (3) violations. Also during December, he managed to obtain copies of some of the material being used in the supervisory training program. His report to Lucas described this as "canned material with some innovations of their own."

Perhaps the most important development during December was that Purcell developed an inside contact who confirmed the consulting firm rumors. The contact, a technician who had been one of those fired in December, had approached Purcell for help after his discharge. Within a few days, apart from Purcell's effort, the technician had been rehired as a supervisor as a result of protests from several

Kenmart engineers. The employee reported back to Purcell
that he had learned at his first supervisor's meeting that
John Gibson and Associates, labor relations consultants
from Chicago, had been hired by Kenmart in the fall of 1971
to conduct the campaign against the IBEW. Gibson and two
associates conducted the daily supervisors' meetings.
Among other things, the supervisors were told at these
meetings how to keep daily reports on their employees and
to record their attitudes toward the union. Employees who
favored no union received a plus, and a plus with a circle
around it if they were strong supporters of the company.
Employees who were union-minded received a minus, with a
circle around it if they were active union supporters. A
question mark indicated that the supervisor did not know
how the employee felt. Gibson made it very clear that
question marks would not be tolerated for long. Apparently
the personnel manager had been discharged because he disagreed with Gibson's tactics. Purcell, in reporting this
information to Lucas, commented:

> Minus some way to stop these cunningly planned and
> tightly organized company tactics, getting a majority
> would be next to impossible. I have suspected, but
> never seen, a program quite this well put together.
> Mike, I don't claim that I've seen it all, but in 25
> years I have never seen one put together with the
> detail we see here.

Leafletting and the Release of Authorization Cards

As 1972 began, the union campaign was not progressing
as well as it had in the latter part of 1971. Purcell continued to hold weekly meetings, but the committee had been
drastically reduced by the discharges and the quits; no
further cards came in until mid-January. Most of his time
was spent locating witnesses and cooperating with the NLRB
agents in the unfair labor practice (ULP) charges. Kenmart
reportedly delayed the investigation by refusing to let the
agents talk to any supervisor without an attorney present
and would permit no affidavits to be taken. In addition,
the company announced an $.11 general wage increase, sent
letters to employees regarding the union's card signing
(see Exhibit 6.1 in the Appendix to this Chapter), and
reportedly held antiunion meetings during the week of
January 30, 1972.

To combat this, Lucas proceeded on three different
fronts. First, he asked the IBEW Legal Department to check
whether Gibson and Associates had filed, as required by
law, with the Department of Labor and had declared their
yearly income from labor consulting. Second, he assigned

two additional representatives to the campaign, Kenneth Lax in January and Richard Crabtree in February. Third, in response to Purcell's evaluation that the union was not able to reach enough employees through the 25-member organizing committee, he altered his usual campaign strategy of using leaflets and handbills only after the election petition had been filed and proceeded to have some printed. In addition, Lucas changed another aspect of his usual campaign procedure: instead of having authorization cards solicited individually by committee members in their departments, he now permitted the cards to be released by attaching them to the leaflets.

Purcell and the members of the organizing committee handed out the union's first leaflet, with authorization cards attached, at the plant gates the week of February 27. The 11-inch by 17-inch leaflet stressed the endorsement of unionism by past American leaders (see Exhibit 6.2 in the Appendix to this Chapter). Following Lucas's policy, these and other leaflets and handbills were always of good quality and were sometimes professionally printed.

During the following weeks, Purcell continued to mail announcements of the weekly meetings to card signers and interested employees. Because of the release of the authorization cards, he focused on educating the committee about the law regarding distribution and solicitation rules. He and the other representatives also continued to make initial and repeat house calls and cooperated with the NLRB. In general, Purcell tried to gain back the momentum that had characterized the campaign before the December discharges. To do this, he informed area AFL-CIO officials of his situation and asked for any influences they could exert. He then began to attend meetings of the IBEW construction local as well as those of the Building and Construction Trades Council and the Central Labor Council; he arranged visits to his weekly meetings by local politicians who enjoyed labor's support; he contacted a local minister who was prolabor; and he spoke with the presidents of the local firefighter's union and the police association. The police offered to "assist with some of the problems out where you leaflet." Despite these efforts, neither the committee nor the number of signed cards grew. Most employees even seemed afraid to discuss the leaflets that were handed out at the gates every two or three weeks by the hard-core committee members.

In April the NLRB regional office issued a complaint on the charges filed in January. This meant that the regional office had decided to hold a hearing on Purcell's unfair labor practice charges. Purcell immediately printed up leaflets announcing the favorable decision and reproduced about 50 copies of the complaint for circulation in the plant; both were well received by the workers. The com-

plaint, together with the presence of the state attorney-
general (who was running for the U.S. Senate with AFL-CIO
endorsement) as a speaker at a weekly meeting, seemed to
renew employee interest in the union. Consequently, by the
end of April, Purcell had again become hopeful. He wrote
to Lucas, "Now 'if' the company doesn't bust us again with
more discharges maybe we'll begin to move again." He and
reps Lax and Crabtree, plus district rep Tate who was on
loan for the campaign, joined together to renew their
efforts to enlarge and educate the committee, hoping that
most of the fear had been eliminated or at least subdued.

Lucas, having learned from the Legal Department that
Gibson and Associates had never filed the necessary papers
with the Department of Labor, lodged an official protest
with the assistant director for the Office of Labor-Management and Welfare-Pension Reports on April 20, 1972. Upon
discovering that Kenmart had not yet registered to do business in the State of New Mexico, Lucas also considered the
possibility of filing suit for evasion of taxes with the
State Corporation Commission. (Eventually, he decided
against filing.)

Purcell and the other reps continued to concentrate
their efforts on building the committee and obtaining more
signed cards, allowing leafletting to be done primarily by
plant employees. Management's response was to post "security engineers" in the parking lots and various management
officials on the top of the building to take the names of
those on the leaflet line.

By this time, activity with the NLRB had intensified.
Several more charges involving discriminatory discharges
and discriminatory solicitation rules were filed by
Purcell. Also, the regional office, for only the second
time in its history, was authorized by the NLRB in Washington to seek a 10j injunction against Kenmart.* Perhaps
more important, Purcell had obtained a full list of employees by department. This was a tremendous aid in assessing
the strength of the campaign, since he could see how support was spread out across the plant and concentrate house
calls where they were most needed and promised to be the
most productive.

Although the company sporadically discharged some
employees during the spring, including some card signers,
those employees who most actively supported the union were

---

*10j injunction--an order to cease and desist from
activities that would cause irreparable harm or damage.
Here it would require Kenmart to stop all activity that
discriminated against union support, i.e., discharges, etc.

not reprimanded or discharged. It appeared, as Purcell wrote to Lucas, that the company had changed its tactics and was "starting with the sugar promotions." In at least one case the promotion backfired; an employee continued to help the union after being promoted. This employee used pay phones outside the company to report everything he knew about the company's campaign plans.

Hiring at Kenmart remained strong all through the spring, especially for the second shift. By the end of May, unit employment was estimated to be over 500. Consequently, Purcell and the other reps used the department list and increased their house calls. In addition, Purcell brought in the business manager and his assistant, as well as the chief steward from the San Carlos local, to attend committee meetings and to call on several influential but undecided workers in the four days that these officials were free to help with the campaign. Because the wage differential between the organized San Carlos plant and the unorganized Albuquerque plant was so great (an average $2.00 per hour lower in Albuquerque, with the highest paid tester in Albuquerque receiving less than the janitors in San Carlos), many employees did not believe the San Carlos rates when the organizers told them. Purcell felt that the facts would be more believable if they came from the people who actually worked in San Carlos.

On another front, the campaign suffered a big disappointment. In June the regional office of the NLRB agreed with Kenmart to set the original ULP hearing for September and to allow the federal judge in the 10j injunction proceeding to base his decision on the transcript of the NLRB hearing. This September date represented the third postponement of the hearing. In spite of his frustration, Purcell continued to deal with the NLRB concerning subsequent charges on which no complaint had yet been issued. He also prepared for the September discharge hearing.

Leafletting by the union continued on a weekly or biweekly basis with occasional flare-ups between the leaflet line and Kenmart management. On one occasion when leaflets were being handed out at the guard gate (between the parking area and the plant), management called the police. Purcell instructed the leaflet line to stay put and risk getting fired, arrested, or both. When the police arrived, they refused to arrest or break up the leafletters. Purcell reported to Lucas that he thought that incident seemed to "make a difference with many of the frightened employees."

The topics addressed in the leaflets and handbills during the spring and summer of 1972 had been developed carefully by the union to progress from general issues, such as "rights of employees to join unions" and "unions are good," to specific issues, such as wage comparisons with San

Carlos and the company's violations of the law (see Exhibits 6.3 and 6.4 in the Appendix to this Chapter). Management, with its steady stream of letters to employees, raised the issues of card signing, the cost of union membership, and the fact that Kenmart's wages were competitive for the Albuquerque area. Following Lucas's policy, the organizers never reacted to company literature. Instead, they sought to take the initiative in developing the issues and relied on the in-plant committee to get the workers to discuss the union's issues rather than those of the employer. Gradually the company began to answer some of the union leaflets. Also, they no longer prohibited handouts at the guard gate.

Breaking the Committee Out

By August 12, 1972 a status report from Purcell to Lucas on the campaign indicated the following:

number of employees (as of July 1972)	658
authorization cards signed	158
percentage signed	24%
card signers not contacted by house call	96
noncard signers with addresses to be house called	163
house calls in process	38

Purcell realized that the number of signed cards and the size of the committee were still growing and that the spirit of the campaign was more like what it had been before the first discharges in December. He decided that it was time to break the committee out into the open. He did this by giving each committee member an "IBEW Volunteer Organizing Committee" button to wear and a briefcase containing organizing materials to take into the plant, and by issuing an 11-inch by 17-inch leaflet with pictures of all 37 committee members. Although some supporters received verbal reprimands from supervisors, the signing of new cards seemed to increase.

The use of picture leaflets was one of Lucas's favorite tactics:

I pop the committee out all at once. My favorite way to do it is to use leaflets, like posters, with pictures of the committee members on it. It works great with the employees. How many times in a worker's life does he get his picture anywhere? When he graduates from high school, when he gets married, and when he joins the union is the third!

Once this approach has been used, however, it is necessary to follow it with more pictures on the next leaflet so the campaign would not appear to be stagnant. Purcell also used handbills framed with the names of committee members. In addition, he changed the meeting schedule so that committee meetings were held every two weeks, with regular meetings for all card signers held in between. In the meantime, he and the other reps continued to concentrate on the department list and house calls.

In early September the U.S. district judge ruled against issuing the 10j injunction against Kenmart, commenting that he "did not intend to be a personnel manager." The same month another union, the International Association of Machinists (IAM), lost a representation election at the nearby Ampex plant by a vote of 90 to 87, even though the IAM reps had claimed to have 70 percent of the Ampex employees signed up.

These developments prompted Purcell to conclude that he needed to expand the committee to 100, and thus he wrote to Lucas: "Have one committee member for every 10 people in the plant. If we can do that, and actually educate the committee, there's no way the company can win."

Although more than 160 house calls had already been made, Purcell and the other reps changed their house calling strategy slightly. They began by making appointments with card signers over the telephone for both initial and repeat house calls, and then just dropping in on employees who had not yet signed cards. In addition, Purcell stopped issuing leaflets and letters, except for those that dealt with issues needing immediate communication, such as NLRB activity. Instead, he began to hold meetings of department committee members, hoping to generate more activity through the small-group approach. By September 20 the size of the committee had risen to 41, double its size in July; although over 300 people had been signed up, only 210 were "still good." Purcell remained frustrated by the campaign. He reported to Lucas:

> You know what bugs me about this campaign? Wages are an issue in any campaign (it's a matter of degree). It doesn't appear to be that way here. Evidently these people can't imagine rates in San Carlos being from $1.60 to $3.00 more than here; it's too far out. Shift premium, overtime difference, or anything else just doesn't move these people as it should. There's fear, but I don't believe enough to hamper our campaign much, at this time. We're still looking for the "handle."

Meanwhile, although the IBEW Legal Department was pushing for an investigation of the charges filed at the Department of Labor against John Gibson and Associates, apparently nothing had been done. In late September President Pillard wrote directly to Secretary of Labor James Hodgson:

> I would greatly appreciate it if you could assign someone in your office to look into this matter personally as it appears that the Office of Labor-Management and Welfare-Pension Reports has either neglected to advise us as we requested or is unwilling or unable to carry out these investigations.

A week later Assistant Secretary Usery replied that he had requested the appropriate reports and that he was looking into the matter.

In October, because of some long-standing personal clashes that became more aggravated as the campaign proceeded, Lucas flew to Albuquerque where he reassigned one of his reps and gave Purcell a two-week vacation. Although Lucas had been in Albuquerque briefly in early August, this time he stayed for two weeks. He conducted morning staff meetings, during which the reps went over the campaign issues and the contact cards before making the house calls. He also held evening school for the committee members. Addressing a different issue each night, Lucas would explain it completely, often using slides to aid the discussion. He would then give the committee members "proof positive" so that they would have evidence to support their discussions the next day. Lucas also made house calls, concentrating on learning what issues most concerned the employees and locating the hard to find employees. According to Lucas:

> I'm the only department director to ever have done that --go out on house calls. Some of my staff thought it wasn't dignified enough, but hell, we're out here to win, not be dignified.

By mid-October the committee had grown to 47 members. Cards numbered over 250.

Despite the low level of company activity since the early summer, there were reports that Gibson continued to brief supervisors and had begun giving antiunion lectures to technician trainees who attended school for two weeks at Kenmart before becoming employees. In mid-October the company gave a general wage increase from $.10 to $.25 to most employees. These wage increases did not appear to hurt the union, which at the beginning of November had at least 50 committee members wearing IBEW buttons in the plant, despite frequent demands by supervisors that these buttons be removed.

Throughout the fall of 1972, the IBEW filed more charges with the NLRB concerning interrogations, threats, and discharges, even though a decision still had not been issued on the first charges filed in January. Finally, in mid-November the administrative law judge for the NLRB issued his decision on the September hearing and ordered, among other things, that 15 of the 24 discharged employees be reinstated with back pay. Purcell immediately reproduced the decision on a leaflet and distributed it to all shifts. The result was an upsurge in the signing of cards. The NLRB regional office also issued complaints on several other charges filed by the union. While Purcell was filing charges with the New Mexico Employment Compensation Agency concerning denial of unemployment compensation for several of the dischargees, President Pillard heard from the Labor Department that evidence presented in the NLRB hearing was being considered in the Gibson investigation, although nothing yet had been decided.

By the beginning of December, Lucas had assigned two more organizers to the campaign. By then, 330 employees had signed cards and 60 were on the Volunteer Organizing Committee. By mid-January, out of 900 employees, 400 had signed cards and 70 were on the committee. This increase in union support had occurred despite the high turnover, the increases in company hiring, and increased working hours (to 10 and 12 hours a day).

In January, Kenmart appealed the administrative law judge's decision concerning 11 of the 15 employees to be reinstated. This appeal to the NLRB in Washington served to further delay the Department of Labor's investigation of Gibson.

In spite of the temporary setback, Purcell did not let the return of four discharged employees go unnoticed. The leaflet (complete with individual pictures) read:

POSITIVE PROOF
THE FEDERAL GOVERNMENT
PROTECTS YOUR RIGHT TO ORGANIZE!

PICTURED HERE

. . . are four employees who were discharged by ACE-Kenmart back in December 1971.

IBEW filed charges—the Federal Government (NLRB) processed the charges. The Administrative Law Judge of the NLRB upheld the charges.

Now—these four employees are back to work and will be paid for all lost earnings back to December 1971.

Aside from these four: Anthony Montoya will be returned to work upon his discharge from Service--and paid for all lost earnings back to the time of his discharge at Kenmart.

Teresa Romero, Joe Terrazas and Stella Sena (Blackstone) do not desire re-employment but they will be paid back to the time of their discharge for all lost earnings.

The same NLRB Administrative Law Judge--rules that "NINE" other employees were discharged illegally--and are entitled to their jobs back with pay for lost earnings.

The longer the company delays reinstatement of these other Nine--the larger the back pay bundle grows.

Like we said before--Uncle Sam means business--And so does the IBEW.

Once again, leaflets became important to the union's campaign. After reprimands were given to employees who distributed leaflets inside the plant, another round of NLRB charges against Kenmart ensued.

The Majority Announcement

The union was rapidly acquiring enough signed cards to represent a majority of the employees. Lucas informed Pillard at the beginning of February 1973 that he would demand recognition as soon as he was sure of the number of employees in the bargaining unit. Signed authorization cards from 30 percent or more of the unit were needed to support a petition for an NLRB election. However, Lucas liked to have at least 60 percent, a clear majority with a 10 percent margin for error. With such a majority, it was Lucas's practice to go directly to the employer with a demand for recognition. Recognition was rarely granted, but the employer often responded with a wage increase in an effort to demonstrate that the employees did not need the union to obtain better working conditions. (Such unilateral actions by the employer were prohibited after a petition had been filed. Lucas did not want to make it possible for an employer to say, "The union and its petition made it impossible for us to give you a raise.") After an interval of a week to ten days, enough time to allow the employer to make such a gesture, Lucas would submit his petition to the NLRB.*

---

*Kenmart did not grant a wage increase.

Lucas had another reason for wanting a clear majority. An employer sometimes engaged in flagrantly unfair labor practices. When this occurred the NLRB would rule a fair election impossible. In such circumstances, the fact that enough cards had been signed to constitute a clear majority might pursuade the Board to issue an immediate bargaining order without an election.

The demand for recognition was made on February 22, 1973, by Purcell in a letter to Kenmart's Albuquerque general manager; the company immediately denied this demand (see Exhibits 6.5 and 6.6 in the Appendix to this Chapter). At the same time, an open letter from the general manager to his "Fellow employees" initiated a new series of communications emphasizing that the union only wanted "to get you as a dues-paying member without an election." The letter concluded, "I feel that a union is not in the best interest of all of us or for the future of our plant. If you have any questions at all, please feel free to contact your supervisor."

In the first week of March, Purcell petitioned for an NLRB election. The Board scheduled a meeting of all parties for the first week in April.

After the demand for recognition, both sides increased their campaign activity. Kenmart began holding "captive audience" meetings with groups of 25 to 30 employees. In these meetings, the bad aspects of unionism--high dues, strikes, and few results--were stressed. In addition, Kenmart reportedly continued to delay NLRB investigations. Weekly union leaflets continued to emphasize comparative wages with San Carlos. The "Truth Tape," a telephone message recorded by committee members, began in mid-March in order to keep employees informed of late-breaking developments, particularly NLRB action, and to "nip rumors in the bud." As usual, Purcell and the other reps continued to house call and double check all card signers.

During the week of April 8, 1973, the representation case meeting commenced at the NLRB. After two days, it was agreed that a "stipulated election" was to be held on June 29, 1973. At the hearings, Kenmart argued that 60 technical employees were supervisors and therefore should be excluded from the unit. Although such employees were included in other IBEW-Kenmart bargaining units, Purcell conceded in order to avoid more hearings and delays.

The remainder of April was taken up by an NLRB hearing on unfair labor practice charges filed against Kenmart in 1972 over alleged discriminatory discharges and distribution-solicitation rules. When not involved in the hearing, the union reps, including Joseph Mazaisz, who had been recently sent in by Lucas, tried to expand their majority by distributing leaflets that emphasized wages and Kenmart's legal violations, by making further house calls, and by holding weekly meetings for the committee and card signers. The company continued the captive audience meetings. During one of these meetings led by the assistant personnel director, a group of employees asked why Kenmart didn't pay more. The assistant director reportedly replied, "If you want more money, go out and get yourself an education like I did." Purcell reported to Lucas that "This really ticked the whole bunch off--signers and nonsigners. We hope they'll keep using him."

In May John Gibson and Associates were unexpectedly dismissed by the company. A personnel labor relations expert from ACE's Electric Manufacturing Division was then loaned to Kenmart.

In mid-May the first of eight "fact sheets" that discussed the union's dues, constitution, and other issues was distributed to supervisors by the company's new campaign manager. A leaflet also was issued to employees that included a cover sheet answering "Why the IBEW Wants You" (to pay $75,000 a year in dues), as well as articles attributed to the IBEW Journal. Purcell and the other organizers immediately checked the articles. They found that only part of one article came from the Journal, and it had been quoted out of context. They immediately sent the committee in to the plant with issues of the Journal to show how wrong the company's literature was.

During the first week of June, Lucas made plans to move to Albuquerque for the last weeks of the campaign. Purcell's latest report was on his desk. It indicated that the company "hadn't done all that much so far," even though the union had at least a 100-card majority. Purcell concluded: "I believe we're holding pretty good--but we've yet to see what happens when the company really turns loose. Maybe we can hold them and maybe we can't."

The Final Days of the Campaign

When Mike Lucas arrived in Albuquerque in June 1973, he immediately increased the union's efforts from a two- to a three-shift operation and increased leafletting from two to three times a week. He also gave the committee briefcases full of organizing materials and had them spend their free time at work discussing the union and the campaign issues. Lucas held the first "mass meeting," which 160 employees attended, to alert the workers to "the various gimmicks the company may use from now to election." As part of this effort he showed a strongly antiunion movie--Women Must Weep --and discussed its "biased" nature.

The union's main theme was successful: "You just can't believe what the company says." While "riding that one to the limit in leaflets," the union also established a telephone committee to call card signers to make sure they were not wavering, "pushed buttons pretty hard," and held general meetings for all three shifts.

Meanwhile, Kenmart was putting out two letters a week, distributing "Reject IBEW" buttons to its supporters (Purcell estimated that there were about 350 pro-IBEW button wearers as opposed to 146 company supporters), and continuing to hold captive audience meetings. Some of these meetings were attended by more than 100 employees.

During the week of June 17, the IBEW distributed a new leaflet every day, held committee meetings after every shift, called one general meeting, and continued to "push buttons." Three employees from the Burnaby plant, including the business manager, spent the week helping the reps and the organizing committee. The union's main theme continued to appear successful. This was especially true after the Burnaby people came in. The company had made statements regarding the Burnaby agreement that these employees claimed was misleading and false. The company's response was to express doubts that these people were really from the Burnaby plant.

In the final week, efforts reached a feverish pitch. Company captive audience meetings used the movie Cash on the Barrel Head with William Bendix (a movie Lucas considered less effective than Women Must Weep) and had a company vice-president speak to the employees. Many employees commented afterward that these meetings were dull. Kenmart continued to send daily letters to employees and to distribute the "Reject IBEW" buttons. The union also emphasized buttons and used the committee to counter management's letters, encouraging the employees to forget the issues Kenmart raised and to talk about the union's issues. The final count of cards against the list of eligible voters showed the IBEW leading by approximately 145 votes.

On June 28, the evening before the election, the IBEW held a pre-election victory party. Among those present was Father Ramon Aragon, the vice-general of the archdiocese of Sante Fe, director of Indo-Hispanic Affairs, and a supporter of the employees' efforts to organize. He made a brief statement at the party in which he claimed "New Mexico has become a dumping ground for corporations looking for low-priced labor." He also noted that the Catholic Church, in a Vatican document, had said:

> Among the basic rights of the human person must be counted the right of freely founding labor unions. These unions should be truly able to represent the workers and to contribute to the proper arrangement of human life. Another such right is that of taking part freely in the activity of these unions without the risk of reprisal.

The Election and its Aftermath

On June 29, 1973, the IBEW won the NLRB representation election by a vote of 407 to 358, with 20 challenged ballots. Representatives of Kenmart not only refused to sign the tally of ballots, but immediately filed objections with the NLRB regarding the IBEW's conduct in the campaign. It was alleged that eight specific actions, two concerning the improper intrusion of the Catholic Church into the campaign and six concerning union threats and coercion of employees both before and on election day (including offers to waive initiation fees), had interfered with the "laboratory conditions" necessary for the employees to exercise their right to a free choice. After investigation by a Board agent, the regional director issued his report on objections on September 19. The report ordered five of the allegations dismissed for lack of evidence and three sent to a hearing because of credibility conflicts in the testimony of witnesses. The hearing was scheduled for October 9.

Kenmart then filed exceptions to the regional director's report on objections with the Board in Washington. The company sought a review that would sustain its objections or, at a minimum, would include the five dismissed issues in the hearing. Because of extended delays by the Board in ruling on the exceptions, the hearing on objections was subsequently rescheduled for November 12. It was then postponed until December 3; again postponed until December 17, 1973; again postponed until January 8, 1974; and finally postponed indefinitely, pending the Board's decision. On March 7, 1974, the Board issued a decision and order, supporting the regional director's findings of September 19, 1973. The hearing was then scheduled for April 15.

On Friday, April 19, Lucas was deliberating over his alternative courses of action. The hearing on the objections had finally started on Monday, April 15, and was then in progress. During the previous week, Lucas and the other IBEW reps had asked all employees to sign new cards authorizing the IBEW to represent them in bargaining. These cards would be used to demand recognition from the company. They also had explained that should the new recognition demand be refused, employees would be in a position to implement an unfair labor practice strike against the company. A majority had signed the cards, a new demand had been made, and on Thursday, April 18, the company had informed the union by letter that the demand was denied. On Thursday evening, a meeting of all employees was held by the union; by a secret ballot vote of 270 to 35, the employees voted to strike. The time of the strike, as well as when the employees should return to their jobs, was to be determined by Lucas.

Lucas knew that going on strike had risks. While most of those at the meeting had voted for a strike, this vote comprised only 270 of the total 890 employees. It was not entirely clear that a majority of employees favored a strike, and the strike might fail to attract a majority of employees. Further, Lucas was not sure how long he could keep the employees out on strike even if a majority did strike at first. If that happened, Kenmart might convince the NLRB that they had a legitimate "good faith doubt" about the union's representation status, and the IBEW might lose its potential certification. That, in turn, would have long-term consequences for the protection of the San Carlos local since that bargaining unit might be completely eroded because of work transferred permanently to Albuquerque. Yet if most of the 890 employees were on the picket line, a strike would clearly demonstrate the union majority. Lucas felt that this was important to show to Kenmart management, as well as to the NLRB. Lucas wanted to leave no doubt that the union had a majority in the event that the regional director sustained the objections in the hearing and overturned the election, and the union then had to turn to Washington. Pressure was beginning to build among the employees "to do something," since it had been almost three years since the campaign began and a year since the union had won the election. A strike might release some of this tension. In addition, the San Carlos plant was in the fourth week of a contract strike; a strike at Albuquerque would serve to strengthen that local's bargaining position. Union officials from that local were pressuring Lucas to help them, especially since a small amount of work was reportedly being shifted to Albuquerque from San Carlos.

With all these factors foremost in his mind, Mike Lucas knew that he had to decide whether or not to take the employees out on strike, and if so, when and for how long.

Lucas filed unfair labor practice charges against Kenmart for refusing to bargain (8a5). He then called a strike for Tuesday, April 23, 1974. On the second day of the strike, over 70 percent of the employees refused to cross the picket line. By the third day, however, this percentage decreased to just slightly over 50 percent, so Lucas ordered the workers to return to work on Friday, April 26.

On July 31 the NLRB regional office dismissed the (8a5) charges. The IBEW's subsequent appeal to the Board was denied on September 27.

On August 5, 1974, the NLRB regional office issued a decision on the objections that had been filed by Kenmart in June 1973. All were overruled with no violations found against the union. Kenmart's demand that the election be overturned was denied. On August 30 Kenmart filed exceptions to this decision with the NLRB in Washington.

On December 5, 1974, the Board issued a supplemental decision and certification of representation, upholding the hearing officer's decision to dismiss the objections and certifying the IBEW as the bargaining agent.

On December 26, 1974, Kenmart filed a motion to reconsider with the NLRB.

On January 7, 1975, the NLRB denied Kenmart's motion.

Kenmart now had exhausted its legal procedures against the election and against the IBEW as the bargaining agent for the employees at Kenmart in Albuquerque. Thus, on January 14, 1975, representative Orville Tate requested the names of the company bargainers and the dates for meetings to discuss a contract. One week later he held elections for the negotiating committee. In May 1975, after delays and refusals by the company to provide information or to meet with the union, the union filed a refusal-to-bargain charge with the NLRB (8a5). In June the NLRB found the company guilty in a summary judgment. In July the company filed its intent to take the matter to the court of appeals, eventually filing with the ninth circuit in San Francisco.

On October 15, 1975, with the case pending in the circuit court, Kenmart's general manager unexpectedly offered to recognize the IBEW and drop the circuit court case—if the union would drop all outstanding unfair labor practice charges. Lucas agreed and negotiations began on October 20. A contract was tentatively reached. On December 22, at a union meeting in which officers of the local also were elected, the contract was rejected by a vote of 193 to 139, out of 1,500 employees in the bargaining unit. The low voter turnout caused union leaders to work hard to turn out more members for a second meeting that was held on December 29. This time the contract was ratified by a vote of 723 to 231.

On February 13, 1974 Gibson and Associates had informed the Department of Labor (DOL) that they had received $115,183.82 from Kenmart; nonetheless, charges continued against Gibson. In December 1976, the DOL informed the IBEW that on July 22, 1976, Judge Joel Flaum of the U.S. District Court of the Northern District of Illinois Eastern Division had issued a court order to Gibson to file reports for the fiscal years April 1, 1972–March 31, 1974. This was pursued further by the IBEW in order to obtain the reports for 1974–1976.

ANALYSIS OF THE IBEW CAMPAIGN

The Importance of the Campaign

Mike Lucas identified several factors that made this campaign particularly important to the IBEW: the new plant's potential as an alternate source of production for the San Carlos plant; the possibility of it becoming a "runaway" plant; and the need for a showcase contract in Albuquerque. Another factor that is not so obvious is the importance of this campaign to Mike Lucas's career. Recently appointed to the position of director of organizing, Lucas had already undertaken several major organizing efforts. To fail at such a highly visible campaign might not be well received by his union. Given his age, he could become an easy target for those who see him as a threat to their status within the union.

The campaign had strategic importance to ACE. It may have been the company's objective to provide additional leverage for itself in dealing with the IBEW on a corporate level. By building a new plant in Albuquerque and operating it nonunion, management had the ability to shift production from union plants to this nonunion plant, thereby minimizing the power of the union. A second possible objective was the development of a low wage manufacturing facility. Because wages average $2.00 an hour less in Albuquerque than in San Carlos, it was possible for the company to save approximately $4 million a year in the early 1970s ($2.00 x 1,000 employees x 52 weeks x 40 hours). This figure would increase to $8 million when employment reached its forecasted peak of 2,000. Not only did this represent a significant competitive advantage, but when viewed only in terms of dollars and cents, it also represented a good financial investment. Since ACE invested only $2 million in the plant to begin with and labor savings alone could produce $4–$8 million a year, a very quick payback for the company could be enjoyed.

It appears that the company sought to accomplish both of its objectives: remain nonunion and operate as a low wage facility. These objectives, however, may be in conflict. If the company's primary concern was to alter the balance of power in dealing with the union, it would have made sense to do everything possible to keep Albuquerque nonunion, including the payment of high wages. On the other hand, if the company's objective was to maintain a low wage plant, it would have made sense to keep wages very low and run the kind of campaign that they did, in fact, run. In the future, the company probably would bargain very hard with the union to keep labor rates down. The actual campaign did little to minimize morale problems and it cost the company over $100,000 in consulting fees.

Why Was it so Difficult to Organize the Albuquerque Plant?

It is quite possible that the social environment in which this plant operated served as a significant deterrent to union organizing efforts. It is clear that Albuquerque was considered a nonunion town. Therefore, employees interested in the union would find little reinforcement of their views in the community. They would have few friends and neighbors who shared a similar interest. In addition, the local political structure as well as the press could serve as factors in discouraging unionization.

Given the fact that the work force was comprised of young people, Mexican-Americans, Indians, and women, many employees may not have planned to remain with their jobs for very long. The relatively high turnover reported early in this Chapter supports this speculation. Because these were often the first jobs many of the employees had, it was likely that they did not want to run the risk of alientaing their employer. Also given the nature of the area and the work force, it was possible that these people were fearful of losing their jobs. After all, jobs had not been particularly plentiful in this region and the workers could easily be convinced to consider themselves fortunate that they were employed at all. In light of these characteristics of the work force, it is quite possible that the workers would be distrustful of any outsider, whether management or union. Because the union came into the plant uninvited by the workers, there may have been suspicion, if not distrust, of such an outside force. This fear and distrust may have been heightened by management's response to the union organizing effort.

Another factor that may have contributed to the difficulty in organizing this plant was the low wage rates. There is almost a Catch-22 situation in dealing with low wage workers. Although they may have the most to gain in the long run by organizing and raising their wages, in the short run they have the most to lose. Not only is there the possible loss of income from strikes, but also the payment of dues represents a significantly larger percentage of take-home pay than is true in high wage plants. After all, almost any deduction from a $68 per-week salary ($1.70 x 40 hours) is significant.

It is also likely that the plant's status as a new startup made the organizing effort more difficult for the union. Not only was there relatively little time for management to create bad feelings and hostility among the work force, but the union had more difficulty in identifying the size of the work force as well as its key opinion leaders.

Management's response to the union campaign also contributed to the organizing difficulty. The use of NLRB procedures and unfair labor practices certainly delayed the union's organizing efforts.

In spite of the factors working against the IBEW, there were two strong factors working in the union's behalf: the IBEW and the company's response. Not only did Lucas have very capable organizers assigned to the campaign, but he is himself a very skilled organizer and administrator. In addition, he secured commitment from the top officials of the IBEW to see the campaign through. Consequently, both the workers and the organizers knew that once the campaign became difficult the union would not pull out. Management, on the other hand, may have been responsible for causing many workers to support the union. Even though the workers did not ask the union to come in, management, through its firings, its general harsh treatment of employees, and its distribution of leaflets that contained incorrect information, may have convinced some workers that it could not be trusted. Therefore, a vote for the union could be seen as a vote against management.

There is a possibility that the role of the Catholic Church in the Albuquerque area, as well as the police, may have strengthened the union's organizing efforts. The church leaders were able to break down some initial resistance and fear of the outside union, while the police demonstrated that they were not opposed to unions, and, in fact, could work together with the IBEW.

Management Campaign

As indicated earlier, management may have contributed to the union's relative success in this campaign by its own actions. Since these workers did not seem particularly union oriented, and were possibly even distrustful of such outsiders, management's relatively harsh campaign may have actually lessened its chances for victory over the union's organizing efforts.

From the beginning it seemed that management's campaign lacked real focus and direction. Although it was definitely an antiunion campaign, no clear issue was developed by management. In addition, there were several leadership changes during the campaign. The most effective tactic for the company seemed to be the use of early discharges. This tactic dramatically lessened the momentum of the union's organizing efforts and served to discourage workers from joining the union. Another effective tactic was the stalling of the election, as this allowed management to organize its own campaign and served as a signal to workers that the union was ineffective.

Union Campaign

Although the union was able to utilize Purcell's pains-
takingly laid groundwork, its campaign was hampered by an
inability to come up with a key issue. In general, the
basic strength of the union organizing effort seemed to be
its talent. The IBEW made use of the organizers, Lucas,
the police, the church, local politicians, and even the
actions of the NLRB. By publicizing the decisions of the
NLRB, the union sought to convey to the workers the impression that the government was on the union's side and
that ultimately it would succeed.

There are several minor areas in which the union's campaign can be criticized. For example, it is not clear that
the use of the San Carlos people was very effective.
Although it was important to communicate the differences in
wages and working conditions at the two plants, it is possible that the San Carlos workers were simply so far away
and from such a different background that this information
lacked credibility with the Albuquerque work force. An
alternative comparison between workers at the Kenmart plant
and local (Albuquerque) workers who had joined unions and
therefore enjoyed relatively higher wages and better working conditions might have been more effective for the union.
The use of local Mexican-Americans, women, and Indian union
members in this comparison group would have added to the
effectiveness and credibility of the union's efforts. The
campaign could have further targeted such nonunion minority
employees with special leaflets printed in Spanish.

The Union's Plan of Action

In June 1973 the plan of action for the IBEW was depen-
dent upon one's assessment of the success of the campaign.
Many observers who felt that the union already had the campaign won argued for taking a low visibility approach during the last four weeks. This approach involved door-to-
door contacts, telephone calls, and personal solicitation
during the workday. The basic objective was to avoid making mistakes and hope that the company would do something
during the last four weeks that would antagonize the work
force.

Other observers, less confident of a union victory,
argued for continuing to do the same things that the union
had done throughout most of the campaign: leaflets, meetings, and visits by San Carlos people. Still others, feeling that the union could still lose the campaign, took a
"high roller" approach. They argued for trying to provoke
an incident with management, possibly with solicitation or
distribution on plant property.

As was illustrated by the postelection developments, contingency plans for the period after the election should be included in any plan of action. The key questions for this campaign included: What should the union do once the election is over if management wins? Should the union continue to push the unfair labor practices? Should the union try to organize the plant one year from now? What about the appeal to the Department of Labor regarding the consulting firm? On the other hand, if the union wins, what should it do? Should it drop the unfair labor practice charges? What kind of contract should be sought with the company? What if management continues to stall even after the election? It is important to recognize that winning the election is not the end of the process.

SPECIFIC UNION RULES

After reviewing the incidents in a successful union organizing campaign, it may be helpful to summarize some common legal "can" and "cannot" rules for union officials who attempt to organize nonunion work places.* The following rules are not meant to be exhaustive and are listed with the same warning as stated in Chapter 5. Consequently, union officials should approach any list of cans and cannots with caution.

Can

- Discipline members, including suspension and fines, for violating union rules.
- Discipline members for filing a decertification petition.
- Have their supporters wear union buttons, badges, and T-shirts under normal circumstances.

---

*Although the author takes full responsibility for interpretation, this section is based on the following sources: Charles J. Morris (editor), The Developing Labor Law (Washington, D.C.: Bureau of National Affairs, 1971); National Labor Relations Board, A Layman's Guide to Basic Law under the National Labor Relations Act (Washington, D.C.: U.S. Government Printing Office, 1971); and National Labor Relations Board, Summary of the National Labor Relations Act (Washington, D.C.: U.S. Government Printing Office, 1971).

- Describe prevailing wages and benefits at other organizations in ways that are literally true but very misleading.
- Promise to waive initiation fees for new members if they support the union.
- Strike over management unfair labor practices and expect to have their members reinstated whether or not replacements have been hired.
- File a petition for a new election within 60 days of the anniversary date of an earlier election.
- File a new petition for an election within a year of the previous election if the new petition covers a broader, more inclusive unit.
- Solicit cards from employees during the one-year election bar.
- Visit employees in their home for purposes of soliciting union supporters.

Cannot

- Threaten an employee with physical harm.
- Engage in mass picketing to prevent employees from gaining entrance to work place.
- Threaten loss of employment for failure to support the union.
- Threaten loss of seniority rights for failure to support the union.
- Threaten loss of future promotions for failure to sign cards.
- Try to force the employer to discriminate against an employee for refusal to support the union.
- Discipline a member for using the protection of the NLRB or encouraging others to use it.
- Engage in electioneering at the polling place.
- Deliver captive audience speeches within 24 hours of an election.
- Engage in "misrepresentation or other similar campaign trickery, which involves a substantial departure from the truth, at a time which prevents the other party or parties from making an effective reply, so that the misrepresentation, whether deliberate or not, may reasonably be expected to have a significant impact on the election."
- Engage in campaign dirty tricks such as distributing alleged reports from rival union organizers that describe employees in insulting terms.
- Engage in acts of violence against employers or employees.
- Reproduce ballots and other NLRB documents, especially where the effort directly or indirectly suggests to the voters that the Board endorses a particular party.

- Engage in jurisdictional strikes or secondary boy-cotts.
- Libel or slander company officials.
- Incite racial or religious prejudice by inflammatory campaign appeals.

APPENDIX

Exhibit 6.1

INTERNATIONAL BROTHERHOOD OF ELECTRICAL WORKERS (A)

ACE-KENMART INCORPORATED
One Camino DeKenmart,
Albuquerque, New Mexico 87123 - 505-296-0551

J. T. Williams
Vice President and General Manager
Albuquerque Plant   January 21, 1972

Dear Fellow Employees:

Many of you have recently received literature from a union
asking you to sign cards authorizing them to bargain with
the Company on your behalf. First of all, let me make
clear to you that the federal law gives you the right NOT
TO JOIN unions as well as the right to join.

You cannot be forced to sign anything as the law clearly
defines that it is illegal for a union to threaten the
employee or any member of their families in any way. It is
also against the law for a union to try to have an employee
discharged for being against the union. In addition, you
have protected rights under the law which include that a
union may not restrain or coerce employees in the exercise
of their rights including the right to refrain from engag-
ing or joining any union.

In an effort to explain what is going on, let me tell you
that by signing a card you could be turning over to the
union for the indefinite future the right to represent you
on an exclusive basis, in all of your dealings with the
Company. You would be hiring the union as your agent. If
you hire them you will have to pay for their services in
the form of monthly dues, initiation fees, and perhaps
other special assistance, including "strike" funds and
fines. There is no way of knowing how much you would have
to pay the union if you hired it as your agent and this
would have started by you simply signing the card.

The union will press you to sign the card. <u>DO NOT</u> make the mistake of signing merely to get rid of the union organizer as it may merely encourage the organizer and probably increase the problem rather than get rid of it for you.

Remember, the union may tell you that there will be an election but by signing a card you might actually give away your right to vote in an election. In certain cases, the Labor Relations Board uses the card to compel the employer to recognize and bargain with a union without giving the employees a chance to vote. <u>Before signing a card</u>, ask yourself, "Am I right to run the risk that a union could be brought in without my ever being able to vote in an election?"

You cannot sign up with a union on a trial basis. You might think that if you decide after a while you didn't like a union representing you that you could always drop it. If you sign that card it would be difficult, perhaps impossible, ever to get out of it.

We have treated you fairly, honestly, and on a personal basis during this difficult start-up time. We shall continue to do so in the future. I think you will agree that an outside party, trying to come between us, has no place in our personal relationship.

Sincerely,

J. T. Williams

A part of American Communications
   and Electronics

Exhibit 6.2

INTERNATIONAL BROTHERHOOD OF ELECTRICAL WORKERS (A)
OUR CHURCHES AGREE - UNIONS ARE GOOD

Baptist Churches

"We recognize the right of labor to organize and engage in collective bargaining to the end that labor may have a fair and living wage, such as will provide and culture." (SOUTHERN BAPTIST CONVENTION.)

"We reaffirm the right of labor to organize into unions or to affiliate with national labor bodies." NORTHERN BAPTIST CONVENTION.)

Methodist Church

"We stand for the right of employers and employees alike to organize for collective bargaining and social action; protection of both in the exercise of their right; the obligation of both to work for the public good." (THE GENERAL CONFERENCE OF THE METHODIST CHURCH.)

"Collective bargaining, in its mature phase, is democracy applied to industrial relations. It is representative government and reasoned compromise taking the place of authoritarian rule by force in the economic sphere. In its highest form it is the Christian ideal of brotherhood translated into the machinery of everyday life." (GENERAL BOARD OF CHRISTIAN EDUCATION OF THE METHODIST CHURCH.)

Presbyterian Church

"Labor unions have been instrumental in achieving a higher standard of living and in improving working conditions. They have helped to obtain safety and health measures against occupational risk; to achieve a larger degree of protection against child labor; to relieve the disabled, the sick, the unemployed; and to gain a more equitable share in the value of what they produce." (BOARD OF CHRISTIAN EDUCATION, PRESBYTERIAN CHURCH, U.S.A.)

"The right of labor to organize and to bargain collectively with employers is clearly an inalienable right in a democracy, and has been so recognized by our government." (SYNOD OF TENNESSEE, PRESBYTERIAN CHURCH OF U.S.)

Catholic Church

"In the first place, employers and workmen may themselves effect much in the matter which we treat--(saving the workers from being ground down with excessive labor). The most important of all are workmen's associations . . . but it is greatly desired that they should multiply and become more effective." (LEO XIII.)

"What is to be thought of the action of those Catholic industrialists who even to this day have shown themselves

hostile to a labor movement that we ourselves recommended."
(PIUS XI.)

The Protestant Episcopal Church

"We are convinced that the organization of labor is
essential to the well being of the working people. It is
based upon a sense of the inestimable value of the individual man."

Jewish Synagogue

"The same rights of organization which rest with employers rest also with those whom they employ. Modern life
has permitted wealth to consolidate itself through organization into corporations. Workers have the same inalienable right to organize according to their own plan for
their common good and to bargain collectively with their
employers through such honorable means as they may choose."
(CENTRAL CONFERENCE OF AMERICAN RABBIS.)

Congregational-Christian Churches

"We stand for the replacement of the autocratic organization of industry by one of collective effort of organized workers and organized employers."

United Lutheran Church in America

"It is the right of every man to organize with his
fellow workers for collective bargaining through representatives of his own free choice. It is the day of both management and labor to accept and support conciliation and
arbitration in industrial disputes . . ." (BOARD OF SOCIAL
MISSION AND THE EXECUTIVE BOARD OF THE UNITED LUTHERAN
CHURCH IN AMERICA.)

The Disciples of Christ

"Be It Resolved by the International Convention of the
Disciples of Christ:
"That it is our conviction that workers should have the
right to self-organization, to form, join, or assist in
forming, labor organizations to bargain collectively
through representatives of their own choosing and to engage
in such activities as are within the limits of Constitutional rights for the purpose of bargaining with employers
and other mutual aid protection."

Evangelical and Reformed Church

"In order that the Christian principles of respect for
personality, establishment of brotherhood, and obedience in
the revealed will of God may find more adequate expression
in the economic order, we commit ourselves to work for . . .
the recognition of the right of employers and workers to
organize for collective bargaining, as a step toward the
democratic control of industry for the good of society."

Churches of the Brethren

"Laborers are always to be regarded as persons and never as a commodity. Industry was made for man, and not man for industry. Employees as well as employers have the right to organize themselves into a union for wage negotiations and collective bargaining." (BRETHREN SERVICE COMMISSION, CHURCH OF THE BRETHREN.)

WHO SAYS UNIONS ARE GOOD
AND WHO SAYS UNIONS ARE . . . BAD?

The company, of course, says unions are bad. They have a particular reason — for wanting you to believe unions are bad. PROFIT!

The company never bothers to tell you that every church in the country, the Federal Government, and every President since Lincoln--has taken a strong position favoring unions and encouraging workers to join and support unions. Do you think they would do that if unions were bad?

All other production and maintenance workers employed by Kenmart belong to the union . . . the company would have you believe they're bad.

If you will remain non-union the company tells you they'll think you are good.

BUT THEY'LL ONLY PAY YOU . . . half as much for being good . . . as they'll pay the San Carlos workers for being bad! How about that!

NOW FOR A LOOK INSIDE

The company officials have told you IN WRITING . . . that they came here . . . to get you . . . to produce their products for half the price they pay in San Carlos . . . for performing identical duties.

They haven't told you . . . that if you submit . . . the company could expect to reap extra profits of about four million per year for each thousand Albuquerque workers they employ. That's your donation. The company contends they pay you less because the cost of living is lower here . . . but we know of no Company official - Foreman - or Engineer who took a 50% cut when transferred here.

NOW FOR A CLOSER LOOK: Ever wonder where the supervisors disappear to . . . when they take off for a couple of hours . . . and why?

WE'LL TELL YOU! The company had HIRED and IMPORTED, a group of "GUYS" . . . from Chicago . . . called Labor Relations Consultants. The firm name is, John Gibson and Associates. We understand that in some places . . . John is called, "BIG BAD JOHN"! According to information he is required to file with the Federal Government, "BIG BAD JOHN" and his helpers charge around $250.00 to $300.00 per day for their services.

HERE IN ALBUQUERQUE-KENMART . . . their services consist of training supervisors and others on the techniques - of convincing you that UNIONS ARE BAD . . . the company is good . . . and you should be willing to work for half price.

In the meetings the supervisors are taught to repeat like a "Polly Parrot". . . Scare Words and Catch Phrases deliberately designed to frighten you away from the union . . . and keep you willing to produce more . . . work harder . . . and earn less.

Some supervisors are "Eager Beavers" . . . but some strongly resent being required . . . to "Stool" on those they supervise . . . who are fellow "Albuquerque citizens."

Most supervisors here, already know . . . that San Carlos supervisors belong to the union . . . they can not be required to commit acts contrary to their principles . . . or the law. And, they are not considered bad by the company. Many Albuquerque supervisors also resent being only worth half as much as the San Carlos supervisor.

ONLY BY FORMING A UNION . . . can Albuquerque-Kenmart workers have some say . . . about Wages, Quotas, Conditions . . . and, a recourse when injustices occur.

8717 Central N.W.   International Brotherhood
Phone: 294-1595   of Electrical Workers, AFL-CIO

Exhibit 6.3

INTERNATIONAL BROTHERHOOD OF ELECTRICAL WORKERS (A)

There Must be a Reason

Leaflet #13
ACE-Kenmart
Albuquerque
7/19/72 All Shifts

There must be a reason why ACE-Kenmart would be moved to dish out a 39¢ to 43¢ raise <u>now</u> and <u>guarantee</u> another 24¢ to 42¢ about 8 months from now — to <u>some</u> of its employees while maintaining "Poverty Level" — "Food Stamp" rates of pay for other employees.

It would appear on the face of it — that Kenmart is <u>the kind of company</u> — that takes advantage . . . the kind of company that will pay <u>disgracefully</u> low rates — if the workers will put up with it.

On the other hand . . . it appears if the employees will "<u>growl</u>" a little (like in Canada or San Carlos) the company <u>will</u> grudgingly come through.

IT'S A MATTER OF RECORD . . . That Kenmart workers who simply refuse — to let the company cram "Food Stamp" wages down them — are the ones getting decent wages.

IT'S A MATTER OF RECORD . . . That Albuquerque-Kenmart workers <u>earn less</u> working a 60-hour week — than a San Carlos worker doing the same job earns — in a 40-hour week.

THERE IS A REASON: San Carlos and Burnaby, B.C. workers are <u>organized</u> into IBEW. They are <u>united</u> — in demanding that ACE-Kenmart pay decent wages — and ACE-Kenmart came through.

Albuquerque-Kenmart employees <u>are not yet</u> so <u>united</u> — and ACE-Kenmart has given it to you <u>in writing</u> — that all they have in mind <u>here</u> — is to keep your wages up with <u>other</u> workers in Albuquerque <u>who are also</u> earning "Poverty-Level Wages."

LET'S TALK SOME MORE ABOUT THAT . . . AT THE MEETINGS . . .

THURSDAY

Night Shifts	2:00 p.m.
Day Shift	7:30 p.m.

WISHING WON'T MAKE IT SO: San Carlos and Burnaby workers did more than wish.

They recognized that ACE-Kenmart had to be gouged to make them pay decent wages — and they recognized that they needed help . . . they recognized that help would be available by joining the IBEW.

San Carlos and Burnaby workers showed good judgment and courage — from there on the record speaks for itself.

What will the record show in Albuquerque — one or three or five years from now?

WHATEVER THAT RECORD SHOWS . . . one or three or five years hence — Albuquerque workers will either bear the shame — or share the pride.

IT MAY DEPEND ENTIRELY — UPON WHAT YOU DO WITH THE ATTACHED CARD . . .

8717 Central N.E. International Brotherhood
Phone: 294-1595 of Electrical Workers, AFL-CIO

Exhibit 6.4

INTERNATIONAL BROTHERHOOD OF ELECTRICAL WORKERS (A)

<u>Are You Next?</u>

Leaflet #16
8/9/72
All Shifts

Some 750 Albuquerque workers have been employed by ACE-
Kenmart since September of 1971 and of that number <u>only</u> 600
remain.

WHAT HAPPENED TO THE MISSING 150?

The <u>sad</u> and often <u>tragic</u> fact is that 150 workers (<u>one</u> out
of <u>every</u> <u>five</u> employed since September) have been terminated by Kenmart.

As you well know, many of the former Albuquerque workers
were <u>discharged</u> for "reasons" <u>beyond belief</u> . . . and in
some instances for absolutely <u>NO REASON!</u>

For "reasons" such as: "long hair," "talking too much,"
"poor attitude," "couldn't get along with others" and "personality conflicts," many of your fellow workers have been
<u>discharged</u> by the Company.

Others have been hassled, harassed and frustrated to the
point they just couldn't take anymore . . . so they gave up
in <u>utter disgust</u> and quit!

Not one . . . we repeat, <u>NOT ONE</u> of the "missing 150" <u>ever</u>
had an opportunity to present <u>their</u> case, prior to <u>being</u>
discharged. Not one, <u>ever</u> had a fair and impartial hearing. Not one, could <u>ever</u> do <u>anything</u>, other than be marched
out of the plant by a supervisor . . . much in the fashion
as the "Viet Cong" <u>parade</u> American Prisoners through the
streets of Hanoi.

Should you allow this pattern to continue . . . one out of
every five of <u>you</u> . . . or 20% of <u>you</u> . . . will not be
employed by Kenmart one year from <u>NOW!</u> <u>One</u> out of every
<u>five</u> new workers hired won't last the <u>first year!</u>

<u>DON'T BE NEXT!</u> It doesn't have to be this way . . . and
<u>it's not that</u> way in San Carlos, California . . . Burnaby,
B.C., Canada or in any other place where <u>workers are pro-</u>
<u>tected</u> by an IBEW CONTRACT.

No one knows for sure how many Albuquerque-Kenmart workers have been unfairly or unjustly discharged, or pressured into quitting? But if it was only one . . . that was <u>one</u> too many!

<u>Don't be the next one</u>! Sign an IBEW Authorization Card <u>TODAY</u>!

The NLRB Hearing resumed this week in the Federal Building, with the Government continuing to present its charges and evidence against ACE-Kenmart.

It is expected that "COMPANY WITNESSES," T.J.W., A.W.S, C.Z., and many "supervisors" will "testify" within the next few days.

So, that you will know who "they" are . . . "they" will be the ones "all dressed up" . . . with a worried look . . . carrying a Bible!

DON'T MISS THIS WEEKS MEETING! A complete report on the trial proceedings . . . and a Very Special Guest from Washington, D.C.

THURSDAY MEETINGS . . . . .

Night Shift . . . 2:00 p.m.
Day Shift . . . . 7:30 p.m.

Plan <u>now</u> to attend the meeting this week and bring a fellow employee.

8717 Central N.E.   International Brotherhood
Phone: 294-1595   of Electrical Workers, AFL-CIO

Exhibit 6.5

INTERNATIONAL BROTHERHOOD OF ELECTRICAL WORKERS (A)

Charles H. Pillard
International President

Joseph D. Keenan
International Secretary

8717 Central N.E.
Albuquerque, N.M.

Mr. J. T. Williams
Vice President & General Manager
ACE-Kenmart, Inc.
1 Camino DeKenmart N.E.
Albuquerque, N.M. 87123

CERTIFIED MAIL

Dear Sir:

A majority of the employees of the ACE-Kenmart plant have signed cards authorizing the IBEW (International Brotherhood of Electrical Workers), AFL-CIO, to represent them in collective bargaining. On behalf of the IBEW Organizing Committee, the IBEW hereby makes a <u>continuing</u> demand for recognition as the exclusive collective bargaining agent for:

> All production and maintenance employees of ACE-Kenmart employed at the Albuquerque, New Mexico plant excluding guards, professional employees, office clerical, and supervisors as defined in the Act.

The IBEW believes that Kenmart is fully aware of the validity of the IBEW's majority status − particularly in view of the admissions made under oath during hearings conducted by the N.L.R.B. and the subsequent decision of the Administrative Law Judge finding Kenmart guilty of making illegal surveys designed to determine the extent of employee organization − and in view of Kenmart's continuing commission of unfair labor practices designed to destroy that majority status. However, in order to still any good faith doubt that Kenmart may allege, the IBEW is willing to prove its majority status as follows:

1. The IBEW will name a committee from among those Kenmart employees serving as members of the IBEW Organizing Committee to meet with a like committee named by Kenmart to prepare a list of all Kenmart employees eligible to be represented by IBEW;

2. The IBEW and Kenmart will then select a mutually agreeable, impartial third party, such as a priest or an agent of the N.L.R.B., to serve as Chairman of and Arbitrator to the joint committee. The person mutually selected shall be empowered to rule on all questions in dispute and his decisions shall be final and binding on all parties;

3. Once a list of eligible employees has been prepared and agreed upon by the joint committee, the IBEW will submit all current signed authorization cards to the impartial Chairman and Arbitrator of the joint committee. The IBEW will not be given access to the list of eligible employees nor will the company be allowed to determine the identity of the card signers. In privacy, the impartial Chairman and Arbitrator will compare the signed authorization cards to the list and will then issue his ruling as to majority status;

4. Once it is determined that a majority of Kenmart employees have, in fact, designated the IBEW as their collective bargaining agent, those employees eligible to join the IBEW will elect a Negotiating Committee from among themselves to immediately meet with the company to negotiate an IBEW Union Contract;

5. As per the IBEW policy, any contract negotaited can become effective only after acceptance by democratic vote of a majority of the eligible Kenmart employees.

6. There will be NO INITIATION FEES charged any Kenmart employee who joins the IBEW within 60 days following installation of the IBEW Local Union Charter;

7. There will be NO UNION DUES for any Kenmart employees until after an IBEW Union Contract has been negotiated and accepted by vote of the employees. At that time, Kenmart employees will set the amount of their own dues subject only to a minimum amount of fifty cents (50¢) per month plus the applicable per capita tax of $2.00;

8. Initially and at all times thereafter, Kenmart employees will elect their own IBEW Local Union officers from among themselves by democratic ballot and all employees will be afforded equal opportunity to seek office and support and/or vote for the candidate of their choice.

The IBEW Organizing Committee feels that the above proposal is extremely fair and protects the interests of all parties — employees and company alike — as well as meeting all requirements of the Law and National Labor Relations Act. Awaiting your early reply, I am,

Sincerely yours,

R. W. Purcell

cc: N.L.R.B.

This Certified Letter, Subscribed and Sworn before me this 22nd day of February, 1973,

———————————
Michael J. Ervin
Notary Public in and for the State of New Mexico, Beralillo County. My commission expires 10/25/76.

Exhibit 6.6

INTERNATIONAL BROTHERHOOD OF ELECTRICAL WORKERS (A)
ACE-Kenmart, Inc.
1 Camino DeKenmart N.E.
Albuquerque, N.M. 87123
March 1, 1973

Certified Mail
Mr. R. W. Purcell
International Brotherhood of Electrical Workers, AFL-CIO
8717 Central N.E.
Albuquerque, N.M.

Dear Mr. Purcell:

In response to your letter of February 29, 1973, your demand for recognition as the exclusive bargaining agent for certain of our employees without allowing them a secret ballot election is emphatically rejected.

This company has a good faith doubt of the validity of your union's claim of majority status, and has no independent information available to it to verify or substantiate that claim. It is our firm belief that a vast majority of our employees do not desire the intervention of your union in their employment relationship with this company. We have received reports of incidents where employees have signed authorization cards because of duress, coercion and misrepresentation. Under these circumstances, this company should not and will not do as you demand, which would amount to a forfeiture of the rights of all our employees to cast a secret ballot on this important question.

Your letter states that our employees will have the right to elect their own union officers "by democratic ballot." Why then do you suggest a procedure which would deny our employees that same "democratic ballot" on the most important issue involved — whether they want your union to represent them at all?

Your union apparently does not agree that our employees should be allowed the right to a secret ballot election, supervised by representatives of the National Labor Relations Board. Your union apparently does not agree that our employees have the right to exercise their free choice, unhampered by outside pressure, duress and coercion. Perhaps you believe, as this company does, that given such a choice, our employees will reject your union resoundingly.

To summarize, we will not recognize your "demand" for recognition since we have a good faith doubt as to your majority status; we will not consent to the meaningless procedures set out in your letter which do not provide for a secret ballot election. We will not take any action which will deprive our employees of the right to a secret ballot election if at least 30% of our employees want such an election.

Very truly yours,

J. T. Williams
Vice President and General Manager

cc: N.L.R.B.

7

THE USE OF OUTSIDERS AND UNFAIR LABOR PRACTICES

In recent years more managers have been turning to outsiders, in the form of consultants, to help them in
conducting campaigns to resist unionization. Although both
unions and managers have been known to resort to unfair
labor practices in various campaigns as a way of advancing
their cause, it is management that seemingly makes the
greatest use of outsiders and unfair labor practices in
organizing campaigns.

A common theme stressed by managers in many union
organizing campaigns each year is "we do not need an
outsider telling us how to run our business or interfering
with our one big happy family." In the words of one
manager's letter to employees:

A few days ago, one of my very good friends, a member
of a Union, said to me: "You know, something goes out
when a Union comes in--the sort of old "family feeling"
isn't there anymore."

It seems to me that my friend has put his finger on
something mighty important! Somehow, in spite of all
our normal gripes and grumbles, we are here because we
want to be associated with [company name]. None of us

Sections of this chapter were originally published as
"Resisting Unionization," in January/February 1982,
Business Horizons. Used with permission.

really want to lose that sort of inexplainable "homey" feeling that we have always had here. I know that I don't--that you folks who have grown up with us don't-- and that those who have come with us in recent years don't--want that lost feeling.

Believe me--and I honestly mean this--_you_ don't need a Union here!

The implication of this letter and one of the themes of the campaign was that the management and employees were involved in a sort of marriage that was in danger because of a third party who had no scruples when it came to the sanc- tity of that marriage.

The marriage analogy often is misleading in that one of the partners usually invites the attentions of outsiders through various forms of solicitation because they are dis- satisfied with the existing relationship. In nine organ- izing cases discussed in this Chapter, only one appears to have resulted from the union taking the initiative without first being invited by an employee.

In recent years, a trend is emerging that further threatens the marriage analogy. Increasingly the faithful partner, who was always assumed to be management, has begun to respond in kind. Managers now are inviting new partners into the relationship and the resulting situation, while very contemporary, rarely benefits the relationship and may do much harm. Management's invited partner increasingly is a consulting firm specializing in thwarting union organ- izing campaigns.

MANAGEMENT'S OUTSIDERS

The use of outsiders by management to resist unioniza- tion is not new. In the early days of the American labor movement, some managers resorted to outsiders in the form of Pinkerton agents and strikebreakers whose mission often was to "eliminate" the union outsider. More and more man- agers seem to be bringing a different type of outsider into the relationship. The management outsiders of today have cleaned up their act but still have the same basic objec- tives--to defeat the union.

Management's outsiders seem to operate on several fronts. Occasionally the outsider "volunteers" his ser- vices to management. A recent case that made the national news involved an organizing campaign against a southern textile manufacturing firm. A local motel manager informed the mayor of the town that organizers were staying at his motel. The mayor, in turn, summoned a number of industry officials to a meeting where he informed them of the situation and proposed to have the police record automobile license plate numbers of people attending union meetings and, after identifying the car owners, pass on the information to the industry officials. In April 1979 the union sued the mayor, chief of police, a detective, the motel manager, and several local industry officials. Most of the defendants settled out of court, but the original target of the organizing effort was being sued for $12 million. The company reportedly sued the union for $100,000 in damages and $15 million in punitive damages. At least one effect has been to lead the National Labor Relations Board to reopen a previously closed case involving the plant and, according to the Wall Street Journal, "the NLRB could end up declaring [the union] the workers bargaining agent even though there hadn't been a representation election."[1]

A second front is the "how to maintain nonunion status" seminar that typically is a two- or three-day program that may cost in excess of $500 per participant. Such programs usually stress ways to eliminate sources of employee complaints and techniques designed to counter a union campaign. According to one observer, much of the presentation "is surprisingly low key, with little pure anti-union rhetoric" and "would fit nicely into a lecture on worker motivation or personnel practices."[2]

A third front, and the one addressed in this chapter, is the paid consultant who will make many of management's decisions during a union organizing campaign, from what should be stressed in management letters to who should be discharged. The cost of such services can be as much as $800 a day. The total bill for one consulting firm's services to a large western manufacturing firm was reported to be in excess of $100,000, even though the firm's services were evenutally terminated and the election lost.

The paid consultant is of particular concern to the American labor movement. The late George Meany, in an address at a dinner marking the thirty-millionth vote cast in National Labor Relations Board representation elections, remarked that workers

> face the law of the jungle and the power of professional unionbusters and strikebreakers just as surely as their grandfathers did.
>
> Only the style has changed. Today's "labor-relations consultants" use different weapons and tactics. They carry briefcases instead of clubs and brass knuckles. They leave no visible marks on the victims.
>
> But their job is the same -- frustrate human hopes and nullify human rights.[3]

The AFL-CIO estimates that at least 300 consulting firms devote large portions of their effort to resisting union organizing afforts, and a recent estimate placed the annual take for such services at "up to $100 million a year."[4]

No doubt many managers turn to consultants out of fear. They may never have been through a union organizing effort and many may never have dealt with unions at all. Furthermore, they may have heard horror stories of situations where managers, through ignorance, committed sufficient unfair labor practices to have the election set aside and even have been ordered to bargain with the union as the agent for their employees, although the union may have lost the election. For example, in a campaign involving a New England grocery store, the union was invited in by an employee. During the course of the campaign, the store manager questioned individual employees about the organizing effort, threatened to reduce employees' hours, engaged in surveillance of employees, threatened to reduce some full-time employees to part-time status, announced improvements in benefits such as extending sick leave to part-time employees, offered a five percent employee discount on food purchases, reduced the hours for some employees, and changed job classifications for other employees. Although the union lost the election by more than a two-to-one margin, 25 unfair labor practice charges were filed by the union against management; the union also filed an objection to the election based on the unfair labor practice charges. Upon investigation and a subsequent hearing by the regional director of the NLRB, a cease-and-desist order was issued, as was an order for back pay for several thousand dollars. In addition, the election was set aside and, because it was felt that a fair election could not be held, the company was ordered to bargain with the union. The NLRB upheld unanimously the decision of the regional director.

Rather than run the risk of such results, more and more managers who want to remain nonunion are turning to outsiders. Where once employers looked to local attorneys for legal guidance, it appears that a substantial number of employers are now turning to specialized law firms and consulting firms who provide legal services and often manage the antiunion campaign as well. These outsiders have seen many more campaigns than the managers they service and can boast of very high success rates in defeating unions.

WHY NOT A MANAGEMENT OUTSIDER?

Before managers turn to outsiders (especially consultants) to help them in union organizing campaigns, they should seriously consider several factors that may offset some of the benefits they initially see.

The use of outsiders may signal to employees that unions are very powerful. If an employer turns to an outsider for help, it may say to the employees that this union that is seeking to represent them is indeed quite powerful. Otherwise, why would management need or want expert assistance to defeat the union? If the union is that powerful, it may be able to deliver on the benefits it has promised. Thus the management outsider may reinforce the view that the union can in fact redress some of their concerns.

Campaigns seem to change relatively few votes. In 1976, in one of the most thorough studies of the representation process, Julius Getman argued that once employees sign authorization cards, relatively little switching occurs.[5] If these conclusions are still accurate, one cannot help but question the benefits of bringing in outsiders to merely reinforce the views of some employees.

The election may be lost anyway. In some cases, the management–employee relationship is such that union success is virtually inevitable and to spend money on a desperation effort to remain nonunion seems very questionable. In one campaign, an attorney specializing in union campaigns was hired by management to orchestrate a campaign involving a unit of approximately 40 people. Even with his services the company lost by a vote of 30 to 5. In interviews after the election, employees described the company as "wonderful" and the president as "a nice guy," but they frequently reported that they could not present their problems to top management because of the plant superintendent. As one employee stated, "When you disagreed with the superintendent he would tell you that if you didn't behave he would give you a few days off; well, you wouldn't go over his head or you would be fired." The general reaction to any employee suggestion or request was reported as "you get out in the shop and work." Another employee stated the superintendent "would pick out the employees that he felt were good, or maybe he liked, and give them a raise. The poorest man should also be considered and receive something, but he never did." One of the original union organizers stated that on one occasion everyone in his work area except him received a $.10 an hour increase. When he questioned the superintendent about it he was told, "I forgot you, but I'll take care of it." Ninety days later, the employee received the increase. On another occasion, the employees suggested through a petition to the factory superintendent a $.50 per hour wage increase. No answer to this request was ever received, although they did get word "through the grapevine" that the request had been rejected. As most objective observers would see, there was little hope for a management victory unless the outsider had been able to get to the root of the problem. As the election results indicated, he did not.

Unions may begin to use outsiders. In recent years labor unions have been making more use of outsiders, not to conduct their campaigns but to assist them. In general, the response seems to be to use outsiders such as church groups to pressure employers. In one New England hospital, church groups were helpful in pursuading the hospital directors to drop a consulting firm.[6] In another case, church groups publicly endorsed the organizing effort that resulted in a union victory. Unions also have begun using the leverage that they have with their pension funds as a way of combating organizing resistance. For example, New York state's employee retirement system agreed to support the Textile Workers Union's organizing efforts against J. P. Stevens Company by voting its 393,000 shares against reelecting a Stevens executive to Sperry Corporation's board. Several unions have discussed excluding Winn-Dixie, Inc., from its pension portfolio because of its past resistance to union organizing campaigns.[7]

Outsiders can be very expensive. In one case mentioned earlier, the cost of consultants to run an ultimately unsuccessful antiunion organizing campaign was in excess of $100,000. In another case, the use of outsiders resulted in a lawsuit of $12 million charging illegal conspiracy to violate the rights to privacy, freedom of speech, and freedom of association. The use of special attorneys can also be expensive. One New England firm estimated that its mid-1970s organizing campaign involving 500 employees resulted in legal fees of approximately $55,000. At approximately the same time, another firm that employed only 30 hourly employees was quoted a charge of $50 per hour plus expenses by their labor attorney, with a total estimated cost to be in the neighborhood of $5,000 to $8,000.

Outsiders may reduce the effective themes available to management. As mentioned earlier, a common theme that managers use in organizing campaigns. is "we do not need an outsider telling us what to do." Yet some managers turn right around and bring in their own outsider. Such action shows an inconsistency in management's position. In the words of one manager, "How could we tell our employees not to bring in an outsider, the union, when we were going to bring in consultants?"

There is a public admission that management is unable to communicate effectively with its employees. When the consultants are brought in, management is publicly acknowledging that it is relatively ineffective in communicating with its employees. It cannot convince employees of its own policies. Consequently, a new mouthpiece has been hired to help management get its message through. Such

action seems to be an admission that the employees really
do need their own outsider to deal with management.

The outsider may become an issue in the campaign. In
some campaigns the outsider became an effective union issue
in the campaign. Some unions raise the question of the
outsiders' techniques as well as their cost. In one leaflet the union charged:

> Ever wonder where the supervisors disappear to . . .
> when they take off for a couple of hours . . . and
> why? WE'LL TELL YOU! The Company has HIRED and
> IMPORTED a group of GUYS . . . from Chicago . . .
> called Labor Relations Consultants. The firm name is,
> . . . . We understand that in some places . . . John
> is called "BIG BAD JOHN"! According to information he
> is required to file with the Federal Government, "BIG
> BAD JOHN" and his helpers charge around $250 to $300
> per day for their services.

> Here in [plant name] . . . their services consist of
> training supervisors and others on the techniques of
> convincing you that UNIONS ARE BAD . . . the company is
> good . . . and you should be willing to work for half
> price.

> In the meeting the supervisors are taught to repeat
> like a "Polly Parrot" . . . Scare Words and Catch
> Phrases deliberately designed to frighten you away from
> the union . . . and keep you willing to produce more
> . . . work harder . . . and earn less. Some super-
> visors are "Eager Beavers" . . . but some strongly
> resent being required . . . to "Stool" on those they
> supervise . . . who are fellow "[city name] citizens."

In the same election, when union officers learned that
the consulting firm had never declared its yearly income
from labor consulting with the Department of Labor, they
lodged an official protest with the DOL and asked for an
investigation. In another campaign, the union published
the monthly fee paid to a management's consulting firm and
compared it to the average employee's salary.

Even the use of certain lawyers can become an issue in
a campaign. In the early stages of one campaign, the union
continually stressed the kind of tactics that the company
lawyer would use as a way of alerting employees to likely
management actions. In addition, they stressed the cost of
the lawyer:

> When [company president] had you assembled at the meet-
> ing during working hours he forgot to tell you how much
> money [company name] is paying [laywer's name] to

TABLE 7.1

NLRB Historical Trends, 1936-1979

Fiscal Year	Percent of Union Victories	Number of Alleged Violations of NLRA Management	Union	Percent of Alleged Violations with Merit Total Management Union
1936	71.0	865		
1937	94.3	2,895		
1938	82.0	6,807		
1939	76.9	4,618		
1940	77.3	3,934		
1941	82.8	4,817		
1942	86.3	4,967		
1943	86.2	3,403		
1944	84.5	2,573		
1945	82.9	2,427		
1946	79.5	3,815		
1947	75.1	4,232		
1948	72.5	2,849	749	
1949	70.5	4,154	1,160	
1950	74.5	4,472	1,337	
1951	74.0	4,164	1,097	
1952	72.9	4,306	1,148	
1953	71.9	4,409	1,060	
1954	65.6	4,373	1,592	
1955	67.6	4,362	1,809	32.8

Year						
1956	65.3	3,522	1,743	32.4		
1957	62.2	3,655	1,851	N.A.		
1958	60.8	6,068	3,192	20.7		
1959	62.8	8,266	3,973	26.1		
1960	58.6	7,723	3,608	29.1		
1961	56.1	8,136	3,939	27.6		
1962	58.5	9,231	4,198	30.7		
1963	59.0	9,550	4,553	32.3		
1964	58.5	10,695	4,856	33.4		
1965	61.8	10,931	4,813	35.5		
1966	62.3	10,902	4,491	36.6	37.7	34.2
1967	60.7	11,259	5,747	36.2	38.0	32.8
1968	58.7	11,892	5,846	34.7	34.2	35.6
1969	56.0	12,022	6,577	32.3	31.9	33.0
1970	56.8	13,601	7,330	34.2	33.8	35.0
1971	55.1	15,467	8,250	31.2	31.2	31.3
1972	55.6	17,736	9,030	32.7	32.6	33.0
1973	52.8	17,361	9,022	31.9	32.6	30.7
1974	51.7	17,978	9,654	31.6	33.3	28.3
1975	50.4	20,311	10,822	30.2	32.3	26.4
1976	50.5	23,496	10,898	31.2	33.2	27.0
1977	48.8	26,105	11,601	32.8	36.0	26.1
1978	48.9	27,056	12,417	34.0	37.4	26.6
1979	47.9	29,026	12,105	34.5	38.0	27.0

N.A. = Not available.

Source: NLRB Annual Reports.

represent them in this mud sling operation. How about that [company president]? You would have been much better off if you would have taken the money you paid [laywer's name] and put it in the workers's pay evelope.

Unions lose more than one-half of all elections anyway. As Table 7.1 shows, even in the years before one heard much about consultants who would help managers resist unions, unions were winning fewer than 60 percent of all elections. For example, in the decades of the 1960s and 1970s, union success rates averaged 59 percent and 51.9 percent, respectively. Although in the last few years the percentage has dropped slightly to below 50 percent, the differential from the 1960s to the 1970s makes one at least question the cost benefit of consultants.

Use of consultants may lead to future legislative action. Since some consultants, it is alleged, encourage their clients to break the law in an effort to discourage employee unionization, the outsiders may result in the labor movement pushing for new legal restrictions on managers, or at least more severe penalties for violating the law. In the eyes of some legislators, it may be one thing for business executives to break the law in an organizing campaign and quite another for consultants to do so. After all, the executives may have done it out of ignorance; even if not, they at least serve a broader purpose in society in that they provide goods and services that are perceived as beneficial to the average citizen. The consultants, on the other hand, are the experts who are paid to know the law; furthermore, they produce no products or services that are directly beneficial to the public. In 1977 new labor legislation passed the House of Representatives, and in 1978 it almost passed the Senate. Among other things, this legislation would have restricted some practices of management in union organizing campaigns and provided stiffer penalties for certain unfair labor practices.[8] It is quite likely that similar legislation will surface again. In fact, in 1980 a House of Representatives labor subcommittee conducted extensive hearings into the activities of labor consultants.

THE DANGER OF ILLEGAL TACTICS

Even in cases where managers do not use an outsider, there is often the temptation to use illegal tactics to resist the organizing effort. Unfortunately such tactics as surveillance, interrogation, promises, threats, improved wages and benefits, special favors, reassignments, and even discharges are all too common in union organizing cases. As can be seen from Table 7.1, not only is the number of

unfair labor practice charges filed against managers continuing to increase, but the number of management charges
with merit has also increased in recent years. Although
thousands of unfair labor practice charges may lack merit,
they are often filed in large numbers as a way of penal-
izing an employer for unfair labor practices. In other
words, they become tactical weapons by the union organizer.
As one international representative claimed:

> It has become apparent to me that the use of . . . unfair
> labor practices charges, though they are mere window
> dressing, are vital to combating the many unlawful acts
> committed by most employers. . . . [N]othing should be
> overlooked. I am of the further opinion that upon losing
> of elections, unions should file objections and attempt
> to get bargaining orders and elections set aside.
> Nothing can be more frustrat- ing and costly to an
> employer than these tactics.

In nine organizing campaigns, chosen without any regard
for size, outcome, or industry, but merely because at least
one party would discuss the campaign in detail, the following conclusion emerges: illegal management tactics more
often than not result in union victories. This seems particularly true when large units of employees are involved.
As can be seen from Table 7.2, in both large units where
managements' campaigns are aboveboard, both resulted in
union defeats. In smaller units, illegal practices seemed
to result in union defeats. In at least one case, the
union defeat was reversed by the NLRB and the company was
ordered to bargain with the union because of extensive unfair labor practices. In another case, the union agreed to
drop its charges of unfair labor practices when management
agreed to reinstate a discharged union supporter. In the
third small unit case, the union did not pursue the unfair
labor practice charges, knowing that the odds of an order
to bargain were small. The union merely waited the mandatory 12 months before mounting another campaign, which was
successful.

In addition to not guaranteeing success, illegal practices in an organizing campaign also suffer from other
shortcomings. First, they can be financially costly to
management. Not only are there legal costs and management
time involved in fighting unfair labor practice charges,
but in cases where employees have been discharged, back pay
plus interest can be awarded. In some cases that has
amounted to millions of dollars. As indicated earlier,
once management commits unfair labor practices, some union
organizers respond with an abundance of charges that
further increases the cost to management and increases the
cost to the public by vitrue of the operating costs of the

TABLE 7.2

Common Management Campaign Tactics and Election Results

Unit Size	Union Victory	Management Victory
	Industrial Mfg.	Retail
	labor attorney	interrogation
	supervisory meetings	threatened employees
	bulletin boards	improved benefits
	letters	letters
	captive audience speech	bulletin boards
10-70	management committee	employee meetings
	reclassified employees	reclassified employees
	improved benefits and personnel practices	reduced employee hours
	Industrial Equipment Mfg.	Retail
	labor attorney	company lawyer
	letters	interrogation
	stalling of election	promise of improved wages
	employee meetings	improved benefits
		reclassified employees
		discharge surveillance
	Bank	Construction
	company attorney	labor attorney
	small group meetings	small group meetings
200-300	letters and leaflets	promise of improved wages and benefits
	stalling of election	surveillance
		leaflets (sample ballots)
		reclassified employees
		Plastics Mfg.
		company attorney
		supervisory meetings
500-600		management committee
		posters and leaflets
		information booklets
		small group meetings
		letters
		captive audience speech

Unit Size	Union Victory	Management Victory
	Electronics Mfg.	Cookie Mfg.
	consultants	company attorney
	supervisory meetings	letters
800-1000	employee benefits	supervisory meetings
	handbook	
	discharges	
	surveillance and	
	interrogation	
	small group meetings	
	letters and fact sheet	
	movie	
	buttons	
	stalling of election	
	reassigned employees	
	captive audience speech	

NLRB. A second management shortcoming is that if the unfair labor practices are severe enough, management may be
ordered to bargain with the union anyway. A third consideration is that unfair labor practices can become an issue
the union can effectively use against management in the
campaign. In one campaign a key issue became "you cannot
trust management." After several discharges one of the
union leaflets stressed "Are you next?"

> For "reasons" such as: "long hair," "talking too much,"
> "poor attitude," "couldn't get along with others," and
> "personality conflicts," many of your fellow workers
> have been discharged by the Company.

> Not one . . . we repeat, NOT ONE of the "missing . . ."
> ever had an opportunity to present their cases, prior
> to being discharged. Not one ever had a fair and
> impartial hearing. Not one, could ever do anything
> other than be marched out of the plant by a supervisor
> . . . much in the fashion as the "Viet Cong" parade
> American Prisoners through the streets of Hanoi.

Months later when several employees were ordered reinstated
with back pay, the union issued a new leaflet with pictures
of employees and a headline that read "Positive Proof The
Federal Government Protects Your Right to Organize."

188 / UNION ORGANIZING

A fourth and perhaps most important concern about the use of unfair labor practices is the effect of these practices in the management-employee relationship. Since many managers want to assure employees that they can be trusted and that employees do not need outside representation, illegal acts are inconsistent with a trusting relationship and may signal the need for union representation as a way for employees to protect themselves from an employer who will "stop at nothing" to keep employees from their legal rights.

Finally, even if a few managers continue to flagrantly violate the law in organizing campaigns, the ultimate result may be new, more restrictive, legislation that affects all employers. As mentioned earlier, in 1977, a labor reform bill very nearly passed the U.S. Congress that, among other things, would have strengthened the penalties that could be assessed against violators of the National Labor Relations Act. The effort was believed by many observers to be directly related to the persistent illegal actions of a few employers.

CONCLUSION

The intent here is not to tell managers whether they should oppose unions or not. This is a basic corporate decision that should be made at the very highest levels and only after considerable attention to long-term and short-term costs and benefits. Rather, the objective has been to raise questions in the minds of managers about the desirability of subcontracting to outsiders a significant element of their personnel function and the risks in violating the law in an organizing campaign.

This author believes in the use of outsiders to assist in the development of management and personnel practices that have as their objective the fostering of better management-employee relationships. In the marriage analogy, this would be similar to the use of a counselor who works with one or both parties to help them better understand themselves and thereby their relationship. When the counselor begins to give advice about how to thwart the other partner's goals and desires, it is either time for a new counselor or a lawyer who will help divide the property so that both parties can pursue their own interests with little regard for each other. On an industrial level, the latter situation can lead to little else but industrial instability--a situation that will further worsen our national productivity.

NOTES:

1   Urban C. Lehner, "As Union Organizers Get to Milledge-ville, Georgia, the Mayor Holds an Unusual Welcoming Party," Wall Street Journal, February 29, 1980.

2   James C. Hyatt, "Firms Learn Art of Keeping Unions Out, Figures Indicate They're Passing Course," Wall Street Journal, April 19, 1977.

3   George Meany, "The Case for Labor Law Reform," AFL-CIO American Federationist, April 1977, p. 2.

4   Ron Chernow, "The New Pinkertons," Mother Jones, May 1980, p. 51.

5   Julius G. Getman et al., Union Representation Election: Law and Reality (New York: Russell Sage Foundation, 1976), pp. 29-30 and 132-33.

6   Chernow, op. cit. p. 59.

7   Joann S. Lublin, "Unions Step Up Use of Pension Cash to Push 'Socially Desirable' Projects," Wall Street Journal, July 23, 1980.

8   D. Quinn Mills, "Flawed Victory in Labor Law Reform," Harvard Business Review, May-June 1979, p. 93.

8

DECERTIFICATION

To many managers, unions are large, monolithic, powerful organizations that are best left alone. If their company does not have a union, these managers assume they should avoid one at all cost; if they have a union, ignore it and hope for the best. The last thing a manager with a union should do, they say, is try to oust it.

A quick examination of statistics emanating from the National Labor Relations Board seems to suggest that managers are becoming less fearful of taking on unions. More and more attempts are being made to oust, or decertify, incumbent unions, and a growing number succeed.

In spite of the increasing frequency with which decertification petitions are filed and elections held, many participants are uninformed about the subject of decertification. In particular, managers frequently erroneously assume that there is nothing within the law that they can do once faced with such a situation. By examining a few facts about decertification and describing

Sections of this chapter were originally published as "When Employees Want to Oust Their Union," in March/April 1978, Harvard Business Review. Used with permission.
Sections also were originally published as "Decertification: Is the Current Trend . . . ," © 1981 by the Regents of the University of California. Reprinted from California Management Review, vol. XXIV, no. 1, pp. 14-22. Used with permission of the Regents.

some of the common reactions of both unions and management, this chapter will shed some light on what really happens in a decertification campaign.

DECERTIFICATION UNDER THE NATIONAL LABOR RELATIONS ACT

In 1935 the 75th Congress declared it to be

> the policy of the United States to eliminate the causes of certain substantial obstructions to the free flow of commerce and to mitigate and eliminate these obstructions when they have occurred by encouraging the practice and procedure of collective bargaining and by protecting the exercise by workers of full freedom of association, self-organization, and designation of representatives of their own choosing, for the purpose of negotiating the terms and conditions of their employment or other mutual aid or protection.[1]

Over the next 12 years the institution of collective bargaining was adopted by an ever increasing number of American workers. Whereas in 1935, 3,584,000 employees or 13.2 percent of the nonagricultural work force had joined the ranks of organized labor, by 1945 the number of union members was 14,322,000, which represented 35.5 percent of the work force.[2]

During most of this period of growing acceptance of collective bargaining, little attention was focused on the question of whether employees ever should be allowed to reject collective bargaining once it had been accepted. In fact, under the National Labor Relations Act of 1935, neither employers nor employees could decertify a duly chosen bargaining representative unless the employees wished to choose another union as their representative. Although the National Labor Relations Act of 1935 did not deal directly with the matter of challenging the representation status of an incumbent union, the NLRB quickly established a policy of refusing to accept employer election petitions of any kind for fear that they might "frustrate rather than effectuate true collective bargaining."[3] By 1939 the NLRB's policy had been modified to allow employers to petition for election when faced with claims of recognition by two or more unions.[4]

It could be inferred from a 1942 NLRB decision that the Board had no objection to employees wishing to shift representation from one labor union to another. In a case involving Rutland Court Owners, the Board ruled that "effectuation of the basic policies of the Act requires, as the life of the collective contract comes to a close, that the employees be able to advocate a change in their affiliation, without fear of discharge by an employer for doing so."[5]

It was not until 1943 that the NLRB was confronted with a request for decertification. Although a majority of the employees in the bargaining unit signed a petition asking the NLRB for "investigation and certification of the representation status" of the union, the Board ruled against decertification.[6] The NLRB rejection of the petition was primarily based on the employees' intention to return to nonunion status. It was argued that such an outcome would have gone against the national policy of encouraging collective bargaining. Thus employees could alter the form but not the fact of their collective representation under the Wagner Act. It was not surprising when, in 1945, confronted by three cases in which employers claimed that their employees no longer wanted to be represented by a union, the NLRB dismissed the petitions.[7]

During the first years of the NLRA, the only ways in which employees could reject a certified union were: to convince their employer to risk an unfair labor practice complaint by refusing to bargain at the end of a contract period, in the hopes that the union would petition for an election or file an unfair labor practice charge that would bring the representation issues before the Board; or to encourage another union to request recognition.

DECERTIFICATION UNDER THE TAFT-HARTLEY ACT

In 1947, as Congress began the process of amending the Wagner Act, one of the issues addressed was decertification. The chief argument among supporters of a decertification provision was "individual freedom." Opponents, including Paul Herzog, chairman of the NLRB, argued that employers would use such a provision to frustrate collective bargaining and would constantly be harassed by elections, and that unions would tend to make unreasonable demands in an effort to hold their members. In general, opponents argued that such a provision would result in industrial instability.

The intent of the proposed decertification section of the act was described by Senator Robert Taft:

Today if a union is once certified it is certified for-ever; there is no machinery by which there can be any decertification of that particular union. An election under this bill may be sought to decertify a union and go back to a nonunion status, if the men so desire.[8]

On June 23, 1947, the Taft-Hartley amendments, including an amended Section 9(c)1, which made it possible for employees to decertify an incumbent union, became law after having been vetoed by President Harry S Truman three days earlier. Section 9(c)1 now stated that

> whenever a petition shall have been filed, in accordance with such regulations as may be prescribed by the Board (A) by an employee or group of employees or any individual or labor organization acting in their behalf alleging that a substantial number of employees . . . (ii) assert that the individual or labor organization, which has been certified or is being currently recognized by their employer as the bargaining representative, is no longer a representative as defined in Section 9(a). . . . The Board shall investigate such a petition and if it has reasonable cause to believe that a question of representation affecting commerce exists shall provide for an appropriate hearing upon due notice. Such hearing may be conducted by an officer or employee of the regional office, who shall not make any recommendations with respect thereto. If the Board finds upon the record of such hearing that such a question of representation exists, it shall direct an election by secret ballot and certify the results thereof.

In 1948 the National Labor Relations Board acknowledged for the first time that it was now authorized by the 1947 amendments to entertain "that negative type of representation proceeding, known as a 'decertification' case."[9] In the same paragraph the Board defined this "negative type of representation proceeding" as the result of "petitions filed by employees seeking to escape representation by a labor organization or other representative previously designated."[10]

The negative tone of the 1948 announcement was in keeping with the position that the NLRB chairman had taken in hearings on amendments to the NLRA. Concerning decertification petitions he had argued:

> To give them [dissident groups in any bargaining unit] complete freedom to challenge the status of their bargaining representative at any time means that the employers will constantly be harassed by elections, that the certified union will never attain a secure position and will tend to make unreasonable demands to hold their adherents, and also that some employers will be given an inducement to stimulate anti-union activity among their employees. While there are arguments both ways, our conclusion is that the encouragement of collective bargaining and the maintenance of stable relationships already established, weigh in favor of advising against the proposal.[11]

In light of this pessimistic forecast and the current concerns by the labor movement over the increasing number of decertification efforts, this chapter will explore: first, the current situation regarding decertification, with particular attention on Chairman Herzog's concern for the impact of decertification on the "encouragement of collective bargaining"; and second, the decisions to be made in a decertification campaign.

HISTORICAL TRENDS

After years of fluctuating but gradual growth, the number of decertification cases coming before the NLRB in recent years has dramatically increased. Not only is the absolute number of decertification cases increasing over time, but decertification cases as a percent of all representation cases are increasing. As Table 8.1 reveals, between the years of 1948 and 1970 the number of decertification petitions filed each year grew from 458 to 766, or an average of 3.1 percent per year. In 1979 the number of petitions reached 1,793, an average growth rate of approximately 13.4 percent over the past ten years. In its first year of processing decertification cases, these cases represented 7.2 percent of all representation cases. During the next 22 years the percentage never rose above 6.6 percent. By 1979, however, the percentage had increased to 13.9 percent.

Not only has the number of representation cases increased, but the number of cases resulting in elections has increased from 97 in 1948 to 902 in 1980. Where once less than 30 percent of all decertification petitions resulted in election, by 1980 approximately 51 percent were reaching the election stage. Between 1948 and 1970 the number of decertification elections held per year increased from 97 to 301 or 9.6 percent per year, but between 1970 and 1979 the number increased to 777, for an average annual rate of 15.4 percent.

Also of concern to the labor movement is the declining percentage of union victories in decertification elections. Although unions have never won more than 38.6 percent, in recent years the percentage has dropped as low as 24 percent, and for the 1970s the figure was 27.3 percent.

An examination of NLRB annual reports since 1948 reveals that most of the decertification activity can be categorized rather easily. For example, as Table 8.2 shows, during the decade of the 1950s, 1960s, and 1970s, over 60 percent of decertification petitions were concentrated in three regions: East North Central, Pacific, and Middle Atlantic. In light of the large industrial centers in each of these areas, such concentration is not surprising. Due to industry

TABLE 8.1

Historical Trends in Decertification Petitions and Elections, 1948-1980

Year	All Representation Cases	All Decertification Cases	All Decertification Elections	Union Victories	
				Number	Percent
1948	6,395	458	97	35	36.1
1949	8,370	370	132	50	37.9
1950	9,279	374	112	37	33.0
1951	10,247	339	93	27	29.0
1952	10,447	402	101	27	26.7
1953	9,243	484	141	44	31.2
1954	8,076	480	150	48	32.0
1955	7,165	460	157	55	35.0
1956	8,036	360	129	40	31.0
1957	7,797	369	145	46	31.7
1958	7,399	489	153	59	38.6
1959	9,347	541	216	74	34.3
1960	10,130	607	237	74	31.2
1961	10,508	593	241	80	33.2
1962	11,286	698	285	99	34.7
1963	11,116	679	225	60	26.7
1964	11,685	679	220	67	30.5
1965	11,989	593	200	72	36.0
1966	12,620	651	221	64	29.0
1967	12,957	624	234	69	29.5
1968	12,307	767	239	83	34.7
1969	12,107	769	293	99	33.8
1970	12,077	766	301	91	30.2
1971	12,965	942	401	122	30.4
1972	13,711	1,080	451	134	29.7
1973	14,032	1,144	453	138	30.5
1974	14,082	1,177	490	152	31.0
1975	13,083	1,166	516	137	26.6
1976	14,189	1,457	611	166	27.2
1977	14,358	1,793	849	204	24.0
1978	12,902	1,754	807	213	26.4
1979	12,905	1,793	777	194	25.0
1980	12,400	1,778	902	246	27.3
		Summary			
1970-79	134,304	13,072	5,656	1,551	27.4
1960-69	116,705	6,660	2,395	767	32.0
1950-59	87,036	4,298	1,397	457	32.7

Source: NLRB Annual Reports.

TABLE 8.2

Regional Distribution of Decertification Petitions, 1948-1980

	East		Midwest		South			West		
Year	New England	Middle Atlantic	East North Central	West North Central	South Atlantic	East South Central	West South Central	Mountain	Pacific	Outlying
1948	30	98	90	34	42	27	39	14	73	11
1949	16	58	96	22	43	20	29	6	76	4
1950	25	63	110	23	41	21	24	11	49	7
1951	28	66	64	35	30	23	27	15	45	6
1952	29	62	120	34	32	19	31	23	46	6
1953	32	95	132	40	34	13	43	26	65	4
1954	30	99	83	40	53	25	45	17	82	6
1955	35	102	98	47	30	13	30	15	87	3
1956	25	63	98	37	32	16	28	16	40	5
1957	25	61	78	34	37	14	27	18	72	3
1958	22	114	104	43	35	25	39	16	84	7
1959	25	111	142	38	34	33	30	16	109	3
1960	25	127	134	48	51	17	59	26	115	5
1961	34	113	146	37	49	15	41	19	122	17
1962	33	118	200	61	42	19	52	42	122	9
1963	27	113	179	59	44	18	50	40	129	20
1964	33	103	188	50	61	21	45	32	141	5
1965	20	91	170	41	55	34	43	27	105	7
1966	30	117	147	56	58	25	53	39	120	6

1967	3	93	137	58	53	21	62	25	128	14
1968	34	120	193	71	54	22	68	60	139	6
1969	41	99	180	66	66	30	65	38	176	8
1970	28	99	191	62	55	27	58	33	201	12
1971	33	134	227	82	90	38	74	51	208	5
1972	43	134	290	97	83	43	90	40	246	14
1973	39	171	296	90	87	48	103	57	248	5
1974	40	170	273	102	87	45	93	63	298	6
1975	39	151	267	113	103	42	66	72	306	7
1976	40	187	370	124	92	56	93	83	392	20
1977	81	205	392	127	110	65	116	123	550	24
1978	95	266	375	136	114	57	108	100	487	16
1979	77	267	399	129	141	82	95	100	492	11
1980	69	241	382	153	123	72	109	93	526	10

Summary in Numbers

1970-79	515	1783	3080	1062	962	503	896	772	3428	120
1960-69	310	1094	1674	547	533	222	538	348	1297	97
1950-59	276	836	1029	371	358	202	324	173	679	50

Summary in Percent

1970-79	3.9	13.6	23.6	8.1	7.4	3.8	6.9	5.5	26.2	0.9
1960-69	4.7	16.4	25.1	8.2	8.0	3.3	8.1	5.2	19.5	1.5
1950-59	6.4	19.5	23.9	8.6	8.3	4.7	7.5	4.0	15.8	1.2

Source: NLRB Annual Reports

TABLE 8.3

Industry Concentration of Decertification Petitions, 1948-1980

Year	Manufac-turing	Mining	Construction	Wholesale Trade	Retail Trade	Transportation, Communication, and Other Utilities	Services	Other
1948	312	8	2	43	21	54	17	6
1949	258	7	1	28	23	40	10	3
1950	226	8	1	31	23	39	6	1
1951	216	6	0	28	38	28	14	9
1952	267	3	4	36	33	40	10	1
1953	325	8	2	42	51	42	12	2
1954	321	8	2	50	52	40	6	1
1955	335	4	0	41	29	32	17	3
1956	257	5	0	20	33	38	6	1
1957	264	3	1	34	22	30	12	3
1958	359	4	1	47	35	37	3	3
1959	380	11	4	45	45	38	16	2
1960	381	5	1	55	99	39	23	4
1961	362	4	3	58	73	70	23	0
1962	389	5	1	91	95	77	32	8
1963	291	9	3	71	108	64	30	3
1964	341	7	16	78	110	79	39	9
1965	355	9	4	66	59	66	31	3

Year								
1966	363	10	3	74	94	52	49	6
1967	320	9	14	78	85	69	46	3
1968	428	14	24	57	127	65	46	6
1969	397	8	13	87	125	78	50	11
1970	395	4	12	59	99	103	84	10
1971	505	12	20	72	150	96	73	14
1972	519	15	20	95	189	112	111	19
1973	521	9	20	104	211	129	134	16
1974	492	11	27	146	195	130	159	17
1975	479	12	21	92	227	150	167	18
1976	624	8	34	113	271	178	208	21
1977	714	20	38	151	368	201	274	27
1978	698	21	32	161	356	167	296	23
1979	687	13	41	178	318	250	283	23
1980	732	12	50	128	284	231	322	19

Summary in Numbers

1970-79	5634	125	265	1171	2384	1516	1789	188
1960-69	3627	80	82	715	975	659	369	53
1950-59	2950	60	15	374	361	364	96	26

Summary in Percent

1970-79	43.1	1.0	2.0	9.0	18.2	11.6	13.7	1.4
1960-69	54.5	1.2	1.2	10.7	14.6	9.9	5.5	0.8
1950-59	68.6	1.4	0.3	8.7	8.4	8.5	2.2	0.6

Source: NLRB Annual Reports.

199

migration to the Sunbelt, there has been a gradual shift of decertification activity from the northeastern states to the West Coast. As can be seen in Table 8.2, whereas in the 1950s the Pacific region accounted for 15.8 percent of decertification activity, in the 1970s the region accounted for over one-fourth of all petitions.

Not surprisingly, the heaviest concentration of decertification cases is in manufacturing. Table 8.3 shows that while absolute numbers in manufacturing industries have grown, as a percentage of all decertification petitions, manufacturing has declined from 68.6 percent in the 1950s to 43.1 percent in the 1970s. At the same time, retail and particularly service industries have become more prominent; the percentage of decertification activity in the service sector has more than doubled each decade.

It should be noted that within manufacturing industries, four industries consistently rank in the top five in terms of frequency of decertification petitions: machinery (except electrical), food and kindred products, fabricated metal products (except machinery and transportation equipment), and printing, publishing, and allied products.

In recent years, the companies and firms experiencing decertification efforts have varied so much in size and function as to include such diverse organizations as a West Coast dentist with seven dental assistants, Holiday Inns, Goodyear, Dow Chemical, Sears, American Airlines, and the Washington Post. On April 6, 1977, even the Wall Street district was affected when employees of the American Stock Exchange held a decertification election.

Although decertification elections are common among large companies, the size of the individual bargaining unit that is usually involved is quite small. In fact, in recent years approximately 90 percent of all elections involved bargaining units of less than 100 employees; 75 percent were in units of less than 50 people; and 25 percent were in units of under 10 employees.

In many cases it is impossible to tell whether the union or management was primarily responsible for the decertification effort. Nevertheless, based on interviews with labor officials and managers and the voting results in decertification elections, the perception of many observers is that neither the union nor the collective bargaining process has lived up to employee expectations. In light of the small size of most of the decertified units, it would not be surprising if many of the unions had, in fact, found the units too costly to service as the members thought they should be supported.

THE MANAGER'S PROBLEM

When confronted with rumblings of discontent in the work force, either in support of or opposition to a union, many managers frequently seem uncertain about what to do and what to expect. The actions of management in a large U.S. petroleum company illustrate the problem confronting managers facing decertification elections.

In the mid-1950s some of the technicians and office workers of a major laboratory in the corporation organized an independent association. When they later asked management to recognize them as the bargaining agent for all technicians and office workers at the lab, management refused. When the NLRB held a certification election at the laboratory, management, believing a majority of employees would vote against the association, chose to take a neutral position. To management's surprise, 52 percent of the participating employees voted for union representation.

During the next decade, management and the association maintained an amicable relationship. In the early 1960s when a group of employees that continued to oppose the association was able to hold a decertification election, the company again decided to play a neutral role. Explaining its decision, top management issued the following statement to supervisory employees:

> The company believes that its best position in this decertification case will be to remain strictly neutral, to let the employees decide the issue for themselves, in order to avoid any charges of "maneuvering" by the management.

This time, of those participating in the decertification election, 93 percent voted for the association. Although the association publicly thanked the company for allowing the employees "complete freedom in exercising this individual determination," the relationship did not remain cordial.

The leadership of the association became convinced that part of its problem resulted from the employees' view that it was a "company union" with little power to deliver for its members. To help remedy the situation, the association affiliated with a national union, and over the years the members became increasingly militant.

In the early 1970s when contract negotiations appeared to be getting nowhere, dissatisfied employees circulated a new decertification petition. Again management debated whether to become involved, but this time its decision was affirmative. In a statement to all managers, top management explained its decision:

With an attitude of aloofness, an unwillingness by
management to participate in the infighting, management
is the great loser. This fatal, fatuous posture is
promoted by the NLRB, and it is often adopted by the
employer who dreads the legal entanglements that
mistakes in a campaign can cause.
Aloofness may also be practiced in the belief that the
men will respect the management the more, and therefor
vote down the union. A more likely result is that this
attitude will be read by the men as disinterest, leaving
them free to maintain their allegiance to the company
and vote on the basis of a coexisting allegiance to the
union. A worker may thus be led to recognize no conflict in holding both a loyalty to the company and a
loyalty to the union. Management, by making its wishes
forcefully known, will bring a clear-cut test of
allegiance rather than a loss by default.
Finally, management aloofness may result from a belief
that neutrality during an election will bring
friendlier relations with a union if that union wins
the elections. Aside from the defeatist nature of this
view, there is no indication that a union would believe
other than that the employer is an easy touch, and hike
its contract demands accordingly when bargaining begins.
Unions (and employees) respect a hard-nosed, forthright,
and honest management, and there is usually a basic
dishonesty in a management pose that implies it really
does not care one way or the other about unions.

After a campaign during which top management held meetings with employees and all levels of management, issued
fact sheets for supervisors and bulletins for employees
comparing company policy with the association contract, and
taped telephone messages and letters and talks with the
president, "no union" received 74 percent of the votes cast.
Following the vote, the president called a top management
meeting to develop a plan of action that would "maintain
the nonunion status of formerly represented employees."
The petroleum company management campaign had many
features in common with other active management campaigns
leading to decertification. One of the major factors contributing to the reluctance of some managers to take a
position in a certification or decertification effort, however, is their uncertainty about what those common features
are and what they may entail.

THE CAMPAIGN ITSELF

Decertification campaigns do not differ substantially
from certification efforts. Perhaps the most significant

difference is that many managers seem to be more reluctant
to take an active role in a decertification than in a certification election. In fact, 40 percent of the managers
who participated in a 1976 survey indicated that they were
not active at all in the campaign, and another 40 percent
described themselves as being only "moderately" or "somewhat" active. Conversely, management described only 12
percent of the unions involved as not active at all, and 33
percent as only moderately or somewhat active.[12]

Managers seem to be inactive mainly because they assume
it is illegal to be involved. A few unions are inactive
because defeat is inevitable or because the leaders feel
the benefits of winning a campaign do not outweigh the
costs of waging it. According to one manager, "My company
being so small, the union didn't give the employees any
consideration." Another reported, "The union didn't even
know the campaign was going on, as far as I know." Usually
the unions do get involved, and their campaigns employ some
common tactics to persuade employees of the benefits the
union provides them.

Union Tactics

When asked what they considered to be the union's most
effective tactic during the campaign, managers repeatedly
mentioned (in order of the frequency of use) membership
meetings, house-to-house visits, and the mailing of literature to homes. On occasion, the union leadership used
membership meetings to expose the rank and file to an
international union official who had come to town to show
his interest in the unit.

Other tactics that managers occasionally mentioned were
informational picketing, telephone calls, telephone hot-
lines, pressure on the company or the initiator of the petition, parties, NLRB appeals, and concentrated attention
on one significant faction within the work force. There
seemed, however, to be no discernible correlation between
the tactics the union chose and the outcomes of the
elections.

Union Themes

It is possible to identify four major themes that
unions seem to stress during decertification camapigns.
"I've got an offer you can't refuse." A common theme
was intimidation. In some cases employers, employees, and
even customers were reportedly threatened, harassed, or
sabotaged by union representatives. According to one manager, who reported being pressured to tell the employees to

call off the decertification effort, "The union leaders said they would turn me over to the Health and Welfare Board for not paying health and welfare payments on all employees. They did. I face the possibility of paying a fine of up to $30 million because of it." When unions did use intimidation, however, in most cases the employees ultimately voted to decertify the union.

"I can get it for you wholesale." Almost as common, and seemingly more effective for unions than intimidation, were the unions' specific promises about what they would or could deliver to the members. According to several managers, when union leaders promised new benefits for specific groups of employees, they were particularly effective in winning support. This theme seems to indicate to the members that the union is indeed aware of their particular needs.

"Whom do you trust?" Another common message was that employees could possibly experience a loss of benefits once the union was not around to protect them. Managers frequently mentioned the stress that union representatives placed on job security issues such as seniority and layoffs. The implication was that without the union, such important matters would be completely in the hands of management.

"Count your many blessings." An apparently very ineffective but common union message was the general benefits of union membership. In every case in which it was reported that the union employed this theme, the union lost the election. One can infer that the rank and file are much more interested in specifics, particularly after they have been represented for some time by a union and have become disillusioned with its performance.

It should be noted that few managers reported being the object of a strong antimanagement campaign. As indicated previously, union representatives frequently raised questions in the minds of employees about the actions managers might take if there were no union around, but rarely did they make the campaign theme one of direct and open attack.

Management Tactics

Although many managers chose not to become involved in their employees' decertification campaigns, those who did generally relied on three major tactics: meetings, letters, and improved conditions.

The meetings, which managers cited frequently as the most effective campaign tactic, included one-on-one meetings, small group meetings, and meetings with entire units. Although the sample of employers using meetings was too small to allow for generalization, there does seem to be a tendency for the large captive audience meetings to precede union defeats more than other forms of meetings. One manager described his question-and-answer meeting, which included brief speeches by foremen, the plant manager, the director of corporate labor relations, a corporate vice president, and the company president, as occurring at the "twenty fifth hour." The smaller meetings seemed to result in relatively the same proportion of wins and losses.

Management Talent

Managers said they often used legal or expert assistance. Although some managers reported that they used experts to advise them in the campaign, they more frequently used them, according to one manager, to make "sure that the proper way to have a decertification election was known to the employees involved." Other managers reported using an attorney both to help the employees file the necessary papers with the NLRB and to offer legal assistance to employees as a way of "preventing union intimidation." Legal or expert assistance was often used when a union was decertified, but almost never when union representation was retained.

Management Themes

Although a few managers admitted to using emotional themes such as the dishonesty of the union by saying that the union was only interested in employees' money, or by claiming that the precarious economic position of the company was brought on in part by the union, most reported using some variation of three basic themes.

"Nonunion is better." The most common theme used implied how much better off the employees would be without a union. In such campaigns, management made frequent mention of how well the company's nonunion employees were treated and how costly union dues were for the members. One manager in a campaign message referred to a "past record of overscale pay and benefits—above the union agreement," and said as well that "without the union, you have no dues payments and no loss of benefits." Another manager reported stressing the benefits of "careers without two bosses."

In spite of the frequency with which managers stressed this theme, the results of using it were mixed. It seemed to work in some cases, but almost as frequently it was associated with recertification of the union.

"Don't let them push you around." The employer who wanted to signal his views to employees but did not want to run the risk of alienating the union too much commonly chose the "don't let them push you around" or "you have rights" campaign. Frequently preceding a vote to decertify the union, this tactic did not tell the employees how bad unions were or how good management was, but stressed the fact that the NLRB gives employees the right to decertify their union if they want to do so. Managers frequently accompanied this message with admonitions to employees to exercise their rights by voting, as well as with instructions on how to decertify--"if you choose to do so."

"You're in good hands." This theme stresses the employees' importance to management, the fairness with which employees will always be treated, and the management's desire to work together with its employees. According to one manager, "We had to let the employees know we would not let them down." Another said, "Management assured them that their status as employees would not be affected by the outcome of the election. We made the point that they were our employees first, union members second." The manager who recommended the "twenty fifth hour" meeting between employees and all levels of management reported:

> The basic theme of these talks was that this group of employees did not need to have union representation to be treated fairly by this company; that there would be no retaliation, regardless of the outcome of the election; that we could solve our problems without outside third party representation; and that the company would always pay the best wages and have the best benefits it could afford to pay and would make every effort to keep these as good as the average of the better companies in the area. In view of this policy, third party representation, as demonstrated in previous negotiations, was not likely to produce anything better.

Although this message was not as common as others, it seems to have been communicated often when employees ultimately voted for decertification.

IS WINNING WORTH IT?

Before deciding to campaign actively for union decertification, managers should realistically assess a broader question: What are the advantages and disadvantages of the current union-management relationship? Rather than reacting emotionally to a decertification possibility, managers would be wise to approach it as rationally as they would any other business decision. They should ask themselves what is gained and what is lost by actively campaigning for decertification.

A typical campaign may require the time and effort of legal experts, the personnel staff, and top management.

The conduct of a campaign can also be a disruptive influence on worker productivity. Although these costs are hard to quantify, they are real. By the same token, management may be confronted with a union-management relationship that is so bad that any chance for escape may be worth taking. Whatever the situation, managers need to undertake an analysis of the costs and benefits.

Managers should consider both the economic costs of a campaign and the implications of possible election outcomes. If management campaigns vigorously but the union wins, what is the labor-management relationship likely to be then? Will union leaders have to make major promises to the work force to win its support, and, if so, will they try to collect during the first round of negotiations? What will be the personal relationship between management and labor representatives after an unsuccessful management campaign? What will be the relationship between first-line supervisors and bargaining unit employees?

Alternatively, what are the implications of a union defeat? If the election is close, will work force factions create an unstable labor situation? Will a more militant union seek representation after one year? What new responsibilities will management have to assume when there is no union? Some managers who campaign to decertify unions after having dealt with them for many years find that the union has played a useful role as a communications link with the work force. With the union gone, management will have to establish its own link or run the risk of letting its relationship with the employees deteriorate.

Perhaps the most important point for both management and union officials to consider before deciding how to respond to an employee petition for decertification is what is in the best interest of the employees. It is very easy for both parties to let personal and organizational preferences blind them to the fact that the decision to certify or decertify a union is ultimately a decision that employees must make for themselves.

One factor that both unions and management should look at seriously before deciding to invest in a strong campaign is the percentage of the unit employees who sign the decertification petition. Although the NLRB will conduct an election in which as few as 30 percent of the employees sign the decertification petition, 30 percent will rarely signal a successful decertification vote. The author's data indicate that in those elections in which unions were decertified, an average of 75 percent of the employees in the bargaining unit had signed the petition. In those elections in which employees recertified union representation, the petition was signed on the average by only 48 percent of the employees.

It seems likely that the upward trend in the number of decertification petitions filed each year with the NLRB is likely to continue for the foreseeable future, but will have no dramatic increases over the next few years. In other words, the trend of the last decade seems likely to continue, with increases averaging around 10 percent (from a range of occasional slight declines to annual increases going from 20 percent to 25 percent).

Several factors lead to this projection. First, since many of the employees filing decertification petitions are in small units and the servicing costs of a small unit are likely to be greater on a per-member basis than those of larger units, unions may find it increasingly difficult to provide the kind of support that members in these small locals expect. Another contribution to the relative increase in decertification petitions among nonmanufacturing units may be the failure of some unions to adjust to the various needs and interests of newly organized employees. This case seems quite likely given the relatively heavy concentration of decertification petitions among a few large multi-industry, growth-oriented unions. A third factor is the tendency for more and more managers to develop various employee programs that they promote, either explicitly or implicitly, as alternatives to union representation.

CONCLUSIONS

If this chapter were to stop at this point, a logical conclusion might be that collective bargaining is in serious trouble. Not only is the number of decertification petitions and elections increasing and the percentage of union victories declining, but the decertification activity seems most pronounced in areas away from the American labor movement's traditional strongholds: manufacturing and the North. Thus one might conclude that American unions are losing ground in the areas where the economy is enjoying its greatest growth: the service sector and the Sunbelt.

Such a conclusion, while no doubt partially true, does not reflect as serious a threat to the institution of collective bargaining as might at first appear. As can be seen in Table 8.4, the size of the bargaining units experiencing decertification elections is decreasing over time. By 1979 almost one-third of all elections were occurring in units of less than 10 people, and almost two-thirds were in units of less than 30 people. Whereas in the 1950s 32.6 percent of all elections were in units of less than 20 people, in the most recent decade the figure was 50.7 percent. Thus most of the units affected are not the pacesetters of the American economy.

TABLE 8.4

Size of Bargaining Units Experiencing Decertification Petitions, 1951-1980

Year	Under 10		Under 20		Under 30	
	Number	Percent	Number	Percent	Number	Percent
1951	17	18.3	31	33.3	59	63.4
1952	11	10.9	31	30.7	45	44.6
1953	26	18.4	51	36.2	70	49.6
1954	30	20.0	61	40.7	77	51.3
1955	22	14.0	47	29.9	66	42.0
1956	25	19.4	53	41.1	64	49.6
1957	30	20.7	51	35.2	68	46.9
1958	20	13.1	44	28.8	73	47.7
1959	30	13.9	87	40.3	118	54.6
1960	34	14.3	87	36.7	115	48.5
1961	52	21.6	100	41.5	131	54.4
1962	55	19.3	121	42.5	160	56.1
1963	65	28.9	113	50.2	143	63.6
1964	59	26.8	112	50.9	139	63.2
1965	55	27.5	93	46.5	114	57.0
1966	46	20.8	101	45.7	135	61.1
1967	64	27.4	116	49.6	149	63.7
1968	61	25.5	113	47.3	143	59.8
1969	68	23.2	132	45.0	177	60.4
1970	76	25.2	135	44.9	174	57.8
1971	97	24.2	192	47.9	236	58.9
1972	120	26.6	222	49.2	278	61.6
1973	106	23.4	222	49.0	280	61.8
1974	118	24.1	218	44.5	301	61.4
1975	150	29.1	269	52.1	333	64.5
1976	171	28.0	314	51.4	393	64.3
1977	270	31.8	469	55.2	573	67.5
1978	232	28.7	432	53.5	523	64.8
1979	244	31.4	395	50.8	500	64.4
1980	267	29.6	450	49.9	565	62.7

Summary

1970-79	1584	28.0	2868	50.7	3591	63.4
1960-69	559	23.3	1088	45.4	1406	58.7
1951-59	211	15.1	456	32.6	640	45.8

Source: NLRB Annual Reports

A further consideration is the relationship between unit size and union success. Although there is no question that unions lose the majority of all decertification elections, their success rate is much better in larger units than in smaller units. For example, in 1979 unions won in units averaging 90 employees and lost in units averaging 38 employees. Even though unions won only 194 out of 777 elections in 1979, they retained the right to representation of 17,450 employees, while losing the right of 22,088 employees.[13] This situation is no doubt largely a reflection of the willingness of unions to more actively campaign against decertification in large units, since such units are more likely to contribute to the union's resources than drain them. In addition, it may reflect the closer physical and psychological relationship between management and employees in smaller units.

Perhaps the most significant argument that can be made against the current threat to collective bargaining is that decertification activity is very similar to certification activity both in terms of industry and geographical concentration. As Table 8.5 shows, the shift of decertification activity from manufacturing to service industries is very similar to the shift in certification activity. In fact, the service area, which has shown the most dramatic increase in decertification activity, shows an even greater increase in certification activity. Thus the unions organizing in the service industries may be involved in an increasing proportion of decertification elections because they are among the most active organizers. Only in retail trade is there a growing disproportionate concentration of decertification activity.

Table 8.6 reflects a somewhat similar conclusion when geographical concentration is compared. There is, however, a significant geographical exception. The Pacific region shows a substantially higher concentration of decertification petitions than certification. Even there, the ratio of decertification to certification has increased only slightly in the past two decades, from 1.4 (19.5 to 14.2) to 1.5 (26.2 to 17.8).

Although Chairman Herzog originally feared that decertification petitions might threaten collective bargaining, and more recent observers of the growth in decertification have expressed similar fears, it appears that the evidence suggests otherwise. The institution of collective bargaining appears to be quite healthy. Each year since 1963 more than 10,000 petitions have been filed for certification elections, while not once has the number of decertification petitions exceeded 1,800.

TABLE 8.5

Industry Comparison of Certification and Decertification
Petitions, 1950-79

	1950-59		1960-69		1970-79	
	RC[a]	RD[b]	RC	RD	RC	RD
Manufacturing	65.4	68.6	54.4	54.5	43.9	43.1
Mining	1.3	1.4	1.2	1.2	1.2	1.0
Construction	2.3	0.3	3.5	1.2	3.2	2.0
Wholesale trade	8.5	8.7	9.4	10.7	7.7	9.0
Retail trade	10.4	8.4	13.1	14.6	13.2	18.2
Transportation	8.7	8.5	10.2	9.9	12.2	11.6
Services	2.9	2.2	7.2	5.5	16.6	13.7
Other	0.6	0.6	1.0	0.8	2.0	1.4

Note: columns do not add to 100 percent because of
rounding.

[a]=RC Certification Petitions
[b]=RD: Decertification Petitions

Source: NLRB Annual Reports

TABLE 8.6

Regional Comparison of Certification and Decertification Petitions, 1950-79

	1950-59		1960-69		1970-79	
	RC[a]	RD[b]	RC	RD	RC	RD
New England	6.4	6.4	5.3	4.7	5.4	3.9
Middle Atlantic	20.7	19.5	18.9	16.4	18.6	13.6
East North Central	22.3	23.9	22.2	25.1	21.7	23.6
West North Central	9.9	8.6	8.5	8.2	8.1	8.1
South Atlantic	9.1	8.3	11.1	8.0	10.1	7.4
East South Central	4.9	4.7	5.3	3.3	5.4	3.8
West South Central	7.0	7.5	6.9	8.1	5.9	6.9
Mountain	4.6	4.0	4.3	5.2	4.8	5.5
Pacific	12.7	15.8	14.2	19.5	17.8	26.2
Outlying Areas	2.6	1.2	3.1	1.5	2.2	0.9

Note: columns do not add to 100 percent because of rounding.

[a]=RC Certification Petitions
[b]=RD: Decertification Petitions

Source: NLRB Annual Reports

If there is a threat to collective bargaining, it lies more with the relatively stable rate of certification petitions being filed each year and less with the decertification petitions. Over the last 20 years the numbers of certification petitions filed each year have ranged from a low of 9,177 in 1961 to a high of 11,897 in 1973, and by 1979 had dropped to 10,333. This would seem to suggest that those who have criticized the American labor movement in recent years for failing to emphasize organizing as it once did have a strong basis for their criticism.

Since the West Coast and the service industries represent relatively new areas of union organizing activity, the trends that have been identified in this Chapter might suggest that new ways of appealing to and servicing these employees are necessary if the labor movement is to reverse these trends.

In general, the increase in decertification does not yet signal a serious national threat to collective bargaining. Nevertheless, given the dramatic increase in decertification activity in the last few years, coupled with a stagnant level of certification activity, the phenomenon should be watched carefully in the future to determine if such a threat is arising. Furthermore, even if the numbers did signal a widespread rejection of collective bargaining, responsible managers should not only ask themselves if that is in the best interest of their companies, including their employees, but also if it is in the best interest of society.

APPENDIX

1. What are the general types of employer unfair labor practices that are forbidden by law?
    - Interference, restraint, or coercion.
    - Illegal assistance or domination of a labor organization.
    - Discrimination in employment for union activities.
    - Discrimination for participation in an NLRB proceeding.
    - Refusal to bargain in good faith.
    - Hot cargo agreement.

2. What are examples of interference, restraint, or coercion?
    - Threatening employees with loss of jobs or benefits if they should join a union.
    - Threatening to close down a plant if a union should be organized in it.
    - Questioning employees about their union activities or membership in such circumstances as will tend to restrain or coerce the employees.
    - Spying on union gatherings.
    - Granting wage increases deliberately timed to defeat self-organization among employees.

3. Can an employer give financial or other support to a labor union it favors?
    - No. Section 8(a)(2) of the NLRA states that it is unlawful for an employer "to dominate or interfere with the formation or administration of any labor organization or contribute financial or other support to it."

4. What are examples of illegal assistance or domination of a labor organization?
    - An employer taking an active part in organizing a union or a committee to represent employees.
    - An employer bringing pressure upon employees to join a union.
    - An employer playing favorites to one of two or more unions that are competing to represent employees.

214

5. When is a labor organization considered to be dominated by an employer?
   - When the labor organization is seen as the employer's creation instead of the true bargaining representative of the employees. This can happen if the employer interferes with the organization's formation and has assisted and supported its operation.

6. What does the NLRB do if it finds that a union is receiving illegal assistance and support from an employer?
   - The NLRB will order the employer to stop the support. Recognition of the union will be withheld until the NLRB has certified it as a legitimate representative of employees.

7. What does the NLRB do if it finds that a union is dominated by an employer?
   - The NLRB orders the organization to be disbanded as a representative of the employees.

8. What are examples of discrimination in employment for union activities?
   - Demoting or discharging employees because they urged other employees to join or organize a union.
   - Refusing to reinstate employees (when a job for which they can qualify is open) because they took part in a lawful strike.
   - Refusing to hire qualified applicants for a job because they belong to a union.
   - Refusing to hire qualified applicants for a job because they do not belong to a union or because they belong to one union rather than to another union.

9. What are examples of an employer refusing to bargain in good faith with an appropriate bargaining unit?
   - Making a wage increase without consulting the representative of employees when they have chosen such a representative.
   - Making a wage increase larger than that offered to the employees' representative in bargaining.
   - Refusing to put into writing an agreement reached with the employees' representative.
   - Refusing to deal with the representative of employees because the employees are out on a lawful strike.
   - Refusing to negotiate with the employees' agent concerning mandatory subjects of bargaining.

10. What are the general types of unfair labor practices that labor organizations are forbidden to engage in?
    - Restraint or coercion.
    - Attempt to cause discrimination for union activities.
    - Refusal to bargain in good faith.
    - Secondary boycotts and certain types of strikes and picketing.
    - Charging excessive or discriminatory initiation fees.
    - Featherbedding.
    - Recognitional and organizational picketing.
    - Hot cargo and subcontracting agreements.

11. What are examples of restraint or coercion?
    - Mass picketing in such numbers that nonstriking employees are physically barred from entering the plant.
    - Acts of force or violence on the picket line or in connection with strikes.
    - Threats to do bodily injury to nonstriking employees.
    - Threats to employees that they will lose their jobs unless they support the union's activities.

12. What are examples of union attempts to cause discrimination for union activities?
    - Causing an employer to discharge employees because they circulated a petition urging a change in the union's method of selecting shop stewards.
    - Making a contract that requires an employer to hire only members of the union or persons "satisfactory" to the union.

13. What are examples of a labor organization refusing to bargain in good faith with an employer?
    - Insistence upon the inclusion of illegal provisions in a contract, such as a closed shop or a discriminatory hiring hall.
    - An adamant refusal to make a written contract of reasonable duration.

14. What is an example of charging excessive or discriminatory initiation fees?
    - Charging old employees who failed to join the union before the union-shop · agreement took effect an initiation fee of $15.00, while charging employees hired after that date only $5.00.

15. What is featherbedding?
    - When a union forces or attempts to force an employer to pay money or something of value for services that are not performed or not to be performed.

16. What is a hot cargo agreement?
    - Where a company agrees to cease handling, using, selling, transporting, or otherwise dealing in the products of any other company.

17. What are examples of illegal secondary boycotts?
    - Picketing an employer to force it to stop doing business with another employer who has refused to recognize the union.
    - A union official calling union members at the place of their employment in a retail market to tell them that a wholesaler has been placed on the union's "unfair list."
    - Picketing directed at an entire construction project because one of the subcontractors doing part of the work on the project has nonunion employees.

18. What is a union-shop agreement?
    - When a union and an employer make an agreement that requires all employees to join the union in order to keep their jobs.

19. Does the National Labor Relations Act authorize union-shop agreements in all states?
    - No. Union-shop agreements are not allowed in states where they are forbidden by state law. Alabama, Arizona, Arkansas, Florida, Georgia, Iowa, Kansas, Louisiana, Mississippi, Nebraska, Nevada, North Carolina, North Dakota, South Carolina, South Dakota, Tennessee, Texas, Utah, Virginia, and Wyoming have passed right-to-work laws that prohibit union-shop agreements.

20. What are the requirements that must be met before a union-shop agreement is valid?
    - The union must not have been assisted or controlled by the employer.
    - The union must be the majority representative of the employees in the appropriate collective bargaining unit covered by such agreement when made.
    - The union's authority to make such an agreement must not have been revoked within the previous 12 months by the employees in a Board election.

The agreement must provide for the appropriate grace period of 30 days, except in the building and construction industry where it is seven days.

21. Can employees be punished if they participate in a strike that violates a no-strike provision of a contract?
    - Yes. Employees who participate may be fired and are not entitled to get the job back, unless the strike is called to protest unfair labor practices by the employer. Also, an employee who is subject to a no-strike contract can be fired for refusing to cross a picket line at the plant of another employer unless the contract specifically gives the employee the right not to cross a picket line.

22. What is an unfair labor practice strike?
    - When employees strike to protest an unfair labor practice committed by their employer. They cannot be fired or permanently replaced. When the strike is over, they are entitled to have their job back even if an employee hired to do their work has to be fired.

23. Is there ever a situation when unfair labor practice strikers might be refused reinstatement to their job?
    - Yes, if the strikers engage in "serious misconduct," which includes violence and threats of violence. Examples of serious misconduct are:
      1. Strikers physically blocking persons from entering or leaving a struck plant.
      2. Strikers threatening violence against nonstriking employees entering a plant.
      3. Strikers attacking management representatives.

24. What is an economic strike?
    - A strike that has the object of obtaining from the employer some economic concessions such as shorter hours, higher wages, or better working conditions. The strikers remain employees and cannot be fired, but they can be replaced by their employer. They are not entitled to reinstatement to their jobs when they come back to work if the employer hired bona fide permanent replacements. They are entitled to be recalled for jobs when openings occur.

25. What are examples of situations when recognitional and organizational picketing is illegal?
    - When another union already has been recognized by the employer as its employees' representative, and the NLRB would not conduct a representation election due to the existing contract with the other union.
    - Where the employees have voted in a valid NLRB representation election within the preceding 12 months.

- Where the union pickets for more than 30 days without filing a formal petition for an employee representation election.

26. Does the free-speech provision place any restrictions on what can be said in a campaign?
    - Any views, arguments, or opinions can be expressed as long as no threats or promises of benefits are made.

27. What are examples of statements not protected by the free-speech provision?
    - Implied threats by an employer that the organization of a union would result in the loss of benefits for employees.
    - Picket signs announcing to employees of one employer that another employer is "unfair," when the object is to induce the employees to engage in a secondary boycott.
    - A statement by a company official to employees, that they will lose their jobs if the union wins a majority in the plant.

28. What is an employer lockout?
    - When an employer keeps employees from working. A lockout may be legal or illegal.

29. When are lockouts legal?
    - When an employer does so to further its bargaining position and is engaged in good-faith bargaining. It is also lawful if intended to prevent unusual losses or safety hazards that could be caused by a sudden strike.

30. When are lockouts illegal?
    - If the employer continues operations by hiring replacements for those locked out.
    - If the employer is unlawfully refusing to bargain or is bargaining in bad faith.
    - If the purpose is to discourage employees in their union loyalties or activities.
    - If only the union employees are locked out.

31. What is collective bargaining?
    - Where the employer and the representative of its employees meet at reasonable times, confer in good faith about wages, hours, and other matters, and put into writing any agreements reached. The duty to bargain is required of both the employer and the union.

32. What is an appropriate bargaining unit?
    - A group of two or more who share mutual employment interests and conditions. The NLRB makes the final decision of what an appropriate unit is.

33. Does the bargaining representative have to be selected by any particular procedure, such as an election?
    - No, as long as the representative is the choice of the majority of the employees.

34. Can regular part-time employees be included in a bargaining unit?
    - Yes, as long as they have mutual interests with the full-time employees in wages, hours, and conditions of employment.

35. Can an employee or group of employees present a grievance to the employer and have it adjusted without going through the bargaining representative?
    - Yes, as long as the bargaining representative has the option to be present at the adjustment and the adjustment is consistent with the terms of the collective bargaining agreement in effect.

36. What employees are not covered by the National Labor Relations Act for the purpose of collective bargaining?
    - Employees in a business or industry where a labor dispute would not affect interstate commerce.
    - Employees of an employer subject to the Railway Labor Act (railroads and airlines).
    - Agricultural laborers.
    - Domestic servants.
    - Anyone employed by his or her parent or spouse.
    - Government employees.
    - Employees of hospitals operated on a nonprofit basis.
    - Independent contractors.
    - Supervisors (determined by authority rather than title).

37. What groups are not considered employers for the purpose of collective bargaining under the NLRA?
    - The U.S. or any wholly-owned government corporation.
    - Federal Reserve Banks.
    - States and political subdivisions.
    - A corporation or association operating a hospital, if no one benefits from net earnings.
    - Persons subject to the Railway Labor Act.
    - A labor union, except when it acts as an employer.

38. If a petition is filed requesting the NLRB to conduct
    an election, what items are investigated?
    - Whether the Board has jurisdiction to conduct an
      election.
    - Whether there is a sufficient showing of employee
      interest to justify an election.
    - Whether a question of representation exists.
    - Whether the election is sought by an appropriate
      unit of employees.
    - Whether the representative named in the petition is
      qualified.
    - Whether there are any barriers to an election in the
      form of existing contracts or prior elections.

39. Normally, the NLRB will not direct an election among
    employees who are covered by a valid collective
    bargaining agreement. What are some examples of
    contracts that would not bar an election?
    - The contract is not in writing, or it is not signed.
    - The contract can be terminated at any time by either
      party.
    - The contract contains a clearly illegal union-
      security clause.
    - The bargaining unit is not appropriate.
    - The employer's operations have changed substan-
      tially since the contract was signed.

40. What is a consent-election agreement?
    - Where an election is held by agreement between the
      employer and the organization claiming to represent
      the employees. The parties state the time and place
      agreed on, the choices to be included on the ballot,
      and a method to determine who is eligible to vote.
      They also authorize the NLRB regional director to
      conduct the election.

41. Who is entitled to vote in a representation election?
    - An employee who has worked in the unit during the
      eligibility period set by the Board and is employed
      by the unit on the day of the election.

42. How long is the eligibility period before an employee
    may vote in a representation election?
    - Usually, it is the employer's payroll period just
      before the date of the election. This does not
      apply to employees who are ill, on vacation, or
      temporarily laid off.

43. What is the difference in single-purpose and dual-purpose recognition cards?
    - Single-purpose cards are solely for authorization to recognize a union. Dual-purpose cards are for recognition and for calling for an election.

44. When are elections held?
    - Usually 30 days after they have been directed by the NLRB.

45. Who is in charge of the balloting during an election?
    - Ballots are furnished by the NLRB and nobody other than an NLRB agent and the voter may handle a ballot. Voting is by secret ballot and may be conducted by mail if the election involves voters who are widely scattered.

46. Where does the voting for an election take place?
    - In a location that is convenient for the voters. If possible, the election is usually held on company property.

47. Can an election for a bargaining representative be held on company time?
    - Yes, if the employer gives permission. If not, the election must be held on the employees' time.

48. What are some conditions that may make a ballot void?
    - If the ballot is unmarked, improperly marked, or if the identity of the voter can be determined, the ballot is considered void. A write-in vote is also void.

49. Are strikers allowed to vote?
    - Economic strikers may vote in any election that takes place within one year after the start of the strike.

50. If a person feels that NLRB election standards were not met, what action can be taken?
    - An objection to an election may be filed with the regional director, under whose supervision the election was held, within five days after the results have been made known.

BIBLIOGRAPHY

Anthony, Richard J. "When There's a Union at the Gate." Personnel (November-December 1976), 47-52

Brooks, Robert R. R. When Labor Organizes. New Haven: Yale University Press, 1937.

Building and Construction Trades Dept., AFL-CIO. From Brass Knuckles to Briefcases: The Changing Art of Union-Busting. Washington, D.C.: Center to Protect Worker's Rights, 1979.

Cangemi, Joseph P.; Clark, Lynn; and Harryman, M. Eugene. "Differences Between Pro-Union and Pro-Company Employees." Personnel Journal (September 1976), 451-53.

Chernow, Ron. "The New Pinkertons." Mother Jones (May 1980), 50-59.

Czarnecki, Edgar R. "Unions' Record in Repeat Elections." Labor Law Journal (November 1969), 703-15.

Foulkes, Fred K. Personnel Policies in Large Nonunion Companies. Englewood Cliffs, N.J.: Prentice-Hall, 1980.

Fulmer, William E. "Decertification: Is the Current Trend a Threat to Collective Bargaining?" California Management Review (Fall 1981), 14-22.

_____. Problems in Labor Relations. Homewood, Ill.: Richard D. Irwin, 1980.

_____. "Resisting Unionization: How Outsiders Working for You Can Work Against You." Business Horizons (January-February 1982), 19-22.

_____. "Step by Step Through a Union Campaign." Harvard Business Review (July-August 1981), 94-102.

_____. "When Employees Want to Oust Their Union." Harvard Business Review (March-April 1978), 163-70.

223

_____ and Gilman, Tamara A. "Why Do Workers Vote for Union Decertification?" Personnel (March-April 1981), 28-35.

Getman, Julius G.; Goldberg, Stephen B.; and Herman, Jeanne B. Union Representation Elections: Law and Reality. New York: Russell Sage Foundation, 1976.

Hunt, James W. Employer's Guide to Labor Relations. Washington, D.C.: Bureau of National Affairs, 1979.

Imberman, Woodruff. "How Expensive is an NLRB Election?" MSU Business Topics (Summer 1976), 13-18.

Kilgour, John G. "Responding to the Union Campaign." Personnel Journal (May 1978), 238-69.

Kistler, Alan and McDonald, Charles. "The Continuing Challenge of Organizing." AFL-CIO American Federationist (November 1976), 8-13.

Lewis, Robert. "The Law and Strategy of Dealing with Union Organizing Campaigns." Labor Law Review (January 1974), 42-48.

_____. Winning NLRB Elections: Management's Strategy and Preventive Programs. New York: Practicing Law Institute, 1979.

McDermott, Thomas J. What the Business Man Should Know About: The Taft-Hartley Act. Washington, D.C.: Public Affairs Press, 1959.

McDonald, Charles and Wilson, Dick. "Peddling the 'Union Free' Guarantee." AFL-CIO American Federationalist (April 1979), 13-15.

Morris, Charles J., ed. The Developing Labor Law. Washington, D.C.: Bureau of National Affairs, 1971.

Naffziger, Frederick J. "When Management Faces a Union Organizing Campaign." Management Review (August 1976), 24-29.

Payne, Phyllis. "The Consultants Who Coach the Violators." AFL-CIO American Federationalist (September 1977), 22-29.

Rohan, Thomas M. "Would a Union Look Good to Your Workers?" Management Review (June 1976), 52-55.

Schlossberg, Stephen I. Organizing and the Law. Washington, D.C.: Bureau of National Affairs, 1967.

U.S. National Labor Relations Board. A Layman's Guide to Basic Law under the National Labor Relations Act. Washington, D.C.: U.S. Government Printing Office, 1971.

_____. Summary of the National Labor Relations Act. Washington, D.C.: U.S. Government Printing Office, 1971.

Zimmy, Max. "Access of Union Organizers to Private Property." Labor Law Journal (October 1974), 618-24.

INDEX

ABOUT THE AUTHOR

WILLIAM E. FULMER currently is professor in the management and marketing area, and has served as director of the MBA program and director of graduate studies at the University of Alabama. He has taught courses in the human resources management area as well as the business policy and operations management areas. Most of his teaching has been at the graduate level. Prior to joining the faculty of the University of Alabama in 1978, he was on the faculty of Harvard University's Graduate School of Business Administration. He also served as an instructor at the Wharton School of the University of Pennsylvania.

Dr. Fulmer holds a Ph.D. and M.A. from the University of Pennsylvania. His major and minor fields of specialization were labor and industrial relations and business organization and operations, respectively. He also holds an M.B.A. from Florida State University and a B.A. from David Lipscomb College.

He is the author of Problems in Labor Relations and The Negro in the Furniture Industry, and is a joint author of The Objective Selection of Supervisors. In addition, he has published a variety of articles in such journals as the Harvard Business Review, California Management Review, Business Horizons, Personnel Journal, Personnel, and Industrial Management.